MIXED
EMOTIONS

MIXED EMOTIONS

Mountaineering Writings of

GREG CHILD

THE
MOUNTAINEERS

Published by
The Mountaineers
1011 SW Klickitat Way
Seattle, Washington 98134

Published simultaneously in Canada by Douglas & McIntyre, Ltd., 1615
Venables Street, Vancouver, B.C. V5L 2H1

Published simultaneously in Great Britain by Cordee, 3a DeMontfort Street,
Leicester, England, LE1 7HD

© 1993 by Greg Child

5 4
5 4 3 2

Manufactured in the United States of America

Edited by Linda Gunnarson
Cover photograph © Greg Child
Cover design by Watson Graphics
Book design and typesetting by The Mountaineers Books

Front cover photograph: Jeff Duenwald on the east ridge of Menlungtse, 1990.
    Mount Everest is at left on the horizon.
Back cover photograph: Greg Child leading the first ascent of Old Stealthbelly
    (5.13), Blue Mountains, Australia, 1990. (Photo by Michael Law)

Library of Congress Cataloging in Publication Data

Child, Greg.
    Mixed emotions : mountaineering writings of Greg Child.
        p.   cm.
    ISBN 0-89886-363-5
    1. Mountaineering.   2. Mountaineers.   3. Child, Greg.   I. Title.
    GV200.C45   1993
    796.5'22--dc20   93-28737
                                                           CIP

To Salley Oberlin

CONTENTS

MEETINGS WITH REMARKABLE MEN 153

MYSTERIUM TREMENDUMS 232

*There is no excellent beauty that
hath not some strangeness
in the proportion.*

—*Francis Bacon (1561–1626)*

FOREWORD

"SERIOUS CLIMBING," Greg Child has observed, "treads a thin line between recklessness and calculated risk, the path marked only by intuition, a capricious and often flawed instinct." But Child's own instinct in such matters appears to be anything but flawed; how else to explain the fact that this wry, compact Australian is still in the company of the living?

Face to face, Child comes across as humble, thoughtful, quick to tell a joke on himself. There is nothing in his unassuming bearing to suggest that you are in the presence of an exceedingly bold and accomplished climber. To immerse oneself in the pages of this book, though, is to gain a quick and sometimes disturbing appreciation of the seriousness of Child's deeds in high places—the razor-thin margin for error, the unrelenting intensity, the scarcely imaginable physical and mental demands.

Among the premier climbers of the late twentieth century, Child stands out for his unwillingness to specialize, for his refusal to limit his activities to any single facet of the vertical oeuvre. Child's virtuosity encompasses the full mountaineering spectrum—from short, tendon-ripping "sport climbs" in the modern idiom to ten-day A5 horror shows on the massive stone flanks of El Capitan to the most elusive summits of the high Himalaya. How many other alpinists can say they've been to the summit of K2 and red-pointed 5.13 routes at Arapiles and Smith Rock?

To climb brilliantly on ice, on rock, and at altitude is rare enough. But Child is a writer to boot—a damn good writer, as it happens, the real deal, the author of pieces esteemed as classics in the genre. A number of these classics—including "Lost in America," "On Broad Peak," and "Coast to Coast on the Granite Slasher" (which, astonishingly, was the first piece Child ever wrote for publication)—will be found between the covers of this collection.

"Never trust the written word," Child writes in the first line of Granite Slasher. "At best it's a second-rate account of reality. How can you duplicate the enormity of a personal moment? How can you truthfully record the feelings or events when the intricacies of each second of thought would fry the circuits of a computer?" How, indeed? I am at a loss to explain it, but Child has done nothing less in these pages, his opening disclaimer notwithstanding. This volume holds tragedy and great drama, troubling insights, gallows humor, flashes of beauty so intoxicating they take one's breath away. *Mixed Emotions* is an unforgettable book. Read it and marvel.

Jon Krakauer
Seattle, 1993

PREFACE

I'VE NEVER BEEN CERTAIN whether I'm a climber who writes or a writer who climbs. Torn between both, I have probably wasted a good deal of time writing when I could have been climbing, or climbing when I should have been writing. Still, I can't complain. Climbing has been good to me, giving me passion and purpose for more than twenty years, and giving me the raw material and the courage to write.

This collection of stories covers a lot of ground, from first ascents on the rock faces of El Capitan to summits of Himalayan massifs such as Gasherbrum IV, Trango Tower and K2, to treks in remote Nepal, to profiles of climbers I admire. For the most part, the setting for these tales is that strange world of high altitude. Some of these stories have appeared in magazines such as *Climbing, Rock + Ice, Outside, Backpacker, Summit, Mountain* in Great Britain, and *Rock* in Australia. Others have incubated in my journals before finding their place here.

I must admit, I've often felt mixed emotions about the life of climbing. Perhaps that's because so many friends have died in the mountains. Even so, throughout the last thirteen years and dozen expeditions, my wife, Salley Oberlin, has encouraged my climbing and my writing and has shared many climbing days with me. I thank her for letting me be what I am.

To most people, pursuing difficult and abstract goals like climbing mountains, and risking life and limb while doing it, is insanity, at best eccentricity. I tend to agree, in part, with that line of thinking. I will say, though, that the climbing experiences I've endured have made me feel my life acutely. The challenge of trying to capture those strange, quintessential moments when climbs were overwhelming me physically and emotionally was what prompted me to write in the first place. I don't pretend to fathom the reasons people climb, but by recounting the events, feelings and landscapes in which climbers immerse themselves we might find some clue to it all.

Greg Child
Seattle, 1993

EPIC!

Translated from the lingua franca of climbing to layperson's lingo, an epic is a bad day at the office on a cosmic scale. Many types of climbing experience qualify as epic: grand adventures, mind-bendingly terrifying ordeals, flirtations with disaster, character-building experiences. An uncomfortable bivouac on a ledge or getting benighted on a climb can qualify as epics too. So might a thorough soaking in a storm, or a long, tiring climb with hunger and thirst nibbling at your guts. Epics are a good reason to quit climbing, an awful time, and a heap of fun all rolled into one. Epics define us as climbers. Sometimes they destroy us. A climber having a proclivity for epics is termed an epic-monger. Such as myself, I suppose.

"Taking the Plunge," written in 1993, is an unreliable memoir about growing up in Australia, being bitten by a deadly snake and taking a hundred-foot nosedive onto the ground from a rock climb. "The Law of High Places," also written in 1993, examines the phenomenon of fear and the role it played in my more eventful climbs. On a more serious note is "The Obscure Object of Desire," which was written after a shivering bivouac near the summit of a 26,000-foot mountain called Gasherbrum IV. It appeared in 1986 in *Climbing* and the *American Alpine Journal*.

"On Broad Peak" describes another type of epic—a

tragedy. Until 1983 I didn't know much about storytelling, but then a trip to the Karakoram to a mountain called Broad Peak came along. The climb—a tragic and harrowing experience during which I lost a friend, and upon which I still often reflect, ten years later—was an important point in my life. The experience troubled me deeply, yet the world of high mountains exhilarated me too. I had feelings to purge and a need to examine myself. I picked up a pen and paper the day I returned home and quickly wrote the tale. "On Broad Peak" appeared in *Mountain* and in *Climbing*. It was the genesis of my book *Thin Air,* which was first published in 1988.

TAKING THE PLUNGE

By all accounts, I had strange hobbies as a youth in Australia. Rock climbing was just one of them. Herpetology—the study and collection of reptiles—was another.

I began collecting snakes and lizards at age twelve. At first, my parents viewed my pastime with circumspection, believing that snakes are poisonous, shifty and slimy. Said Dad in a stentorian voice, "If-you-think-you're-bringing-snakes-into-this-house-you've-got-another-think-coming, Sonny Jim." So I weaned my folks into it, first with a brace of lizards that I kept in cages in the yard of our Sydney home. These were harmless enough, my father consented. Perhaps even cute, my mother agreed. But my fascination with snakes, which eventually filled the cages, exceeded boyish fun. "You have dangerous tastes," Dad said of it.

He didn't see the beauty in the rhythmic movement of a snake, the way curve followed curve in a wave of muscle and glossy scales. He had never paused to watch the dignity of a snake as it hunted, its tongue flicking to detect the body heat of its prey, and then, when the snake's eyes had zeroed in on the kill, springing to bite and paralyze the meal. Snakes embodied professionalism, I thought. They were dedicated killing machines that existed only to hunt. When they missed a strike, their expressionless faces gave no hint of embarrassment, unlike the cries of derision heaped upon boys on the school green when the catch of a football was fumbled.

I didn't fathom Dad's interests, either. These consisted of killing fish with hook and line, tinkering with greasy car engines and constructing free-flying model planes from balsa wood and tissue paper. When pressed to accompany Dad to gatherings of his model-making cronies, I watched grown men joyously launch little motorized gliders to the heavens, as if they were giving birds freedom. They sighed as one whenever a plane fell Icarus-like and smashed into splinters. I enjoyed watching these disasters.

Despite all this, by the end of that first summer of roaming the bush with a gunny sack, my reptile menagerie swelled to such bountiful proportions that I had put Dad to work building spacious cages for their imprisonment and for housing the mice and frogs I bred to feed my snakes. Mum sometimes accompanied me on forays into the bush and even captured some sluggish specimens herself. If I whined enough, Dad allowed the non-venomous among my pets to be brought into the house in winter. At such times, fat foot-long skinks and a long python basked in front of an electric-coil heater like old cats, displacing our actual and mystified felines. Neighbors called us the Addams Family.

I was attracted to this pastime not only out of a fascination for reptiles, but for the attendant scene of tough, schoolboy bushmen who at pre-adolescent ages thought nothing of hitch-hiking a hundred miles from home to camp in a pup tent and then roam cross-country by map and compass to capture deadly snakes. They handled snakes confidently and spoke in cavalier tones about famed snake men of old who'd checked out of life after a deadly bite. In my first year of high school I earned a place among this cult of lads who assembled at lunch hour in a corner of the school quadrangle, swapping specimens and snake lore, and I rampaged with them through the bush on weekends in the pseudoscientific pursuit of the cold-blooded.

We could identify a hundred species at a glance. We traded in a currency of scaly beasts. On the high end, a lace monitor, which is a sharp-clawed, tree-climbing lizard, could be traded for a pair of green tree snakes; pythons of any kind were the blue-chip stock of choice; whip snakes, marsh snakes, geckoes and skinks were small change.

My father's ban on snakes in my collection gradually relaxed to a moratorium on the dangerously poisonous, which he forbade me to touch. Yet other boys had snakes that could kill lurking in their aquariums. Why couldn't I? I resented the ban. It was a rein on my freedom that I felt as keenly as a teenager commanded to have the car home by a certain hour.

Cunning and disinformation circumvented Dad's ban. I created fictitious names for deadly snakes and passed them off as harmless. The brown snake, which when aggravated bends its neck into an S and strikes like a coiled spring to pump a deadly toxin into the victim, and which when young is zebra-striped, I renamed the coastal banded snake. No such snake existed. I once found Dad staring at my coastal banded, which lay sunning itself in an aquarium. Dad was thumbing through a handbook of Australian reptiles, searching for a listing for the snake. "This book isn't much good," he said. "Your snake isn't in here at all." I diverted his attention to other matters, as expeditiously as possible.

At our all-boys school, our bazaar of reptile trading prospered. We who dealt in reptiles were revered by some lads, but we revolted others. One day, a lad produced a small, harmless snake from his pencil case in a math class. Holding it up by the tail, he offered to swap the snake for a gecko—a nocturnal lizard capable of walking across ceilings—that I had in a pillowcase in my briefcase. As we exchanged reptiles, the boy seated behind us became agitated. His phobia of snakes got the better of him. He took his steel-edged ruler, screamed and then broadsworded the snake into two equal lengths. The blow sent the half with the head toward the blackboard, where our teacher was scribbling an equation. Turning to address the commotion that now consumed the class, the teacher met a twitching half-snake that collided with his chest and bit into his tie as a parting gesture. For this, we suffered long detentions.

Harvesting the venom from snakes entertained us too. This was achieved by tightly covering a jar with the plastic wrap from our school lunches, then holding the snake's head in the manner we'd learned from a book by a famous old snake man named Eric Worral and forcing the snake to sink its fangs into the plastic. Venom would then dribble into the jar.

A communal jar we kept in a locker contained a cocktail of poisons from several species. The venom was a barely visible film, but, I'm certain, would have killed anyone who consumed it. We poked at the venom with our pencils. Making contact with it gave me a rush of excitement. One lad conducted an experiment to test the efficiency of the poison. He swabbed a microscopic pearl of the stuff onto a beetle. The insect shriveled instantly, as if electrocuted. It was some stuff, this potion. We fantasized about using it to silence a troublesome dog that chased us when we rode our bikes to school, and of spiking the teapot in the math teacher's dayroom.

One day a gangling youth named Stephen Lee was etching a tattoo on his arm with a pen and the point of a borrowed drafting compass. Unbeknown to Lee, the compass had been dipped into the venom jar. By the time he was warned it was too late. We watched while a change of color surged through his arm as the venom entered his body by subcutaneous pathways. "Oh, shit," he said before losing consciousness.

Our jar was confiscated and tossed into the school incinerator. Stephen spent two days in the hospital. He was probably the only person ever to survive the poisons of twelve different snakes in a single dose.

But the boy I admired most in that first year of high school was a veteran truant named Bruce King. He was a masterful shoplifter, had an enviable collection of knives and daggers mounted on his wall and owned the largest collection of things deadly I'd ever seen.

In his yard one day, with a lad named Peter Rumford, we were inspecting one of Bruce's specimens, a three-foot-long tiger snake. Only one Australian snake is deadlier than a tiger snake, and that is the taipan. A good bite from either can kill an adult in minutes, even seconds. Serum laboratories measure venom potency in terms of the number of lab rats a given dose of venom will wipe out. The number of rats a tiger snake can kill is on the order of tens of thousands.

Bruce seized the snake's tail and lifted it out of the aquarium. The snake flattened its head like a cobra, puffed up its throat with air and snorted through its nostrils. Bruce let its head rest on the ground. It squirmed to try to grip the grass with its ventral scales, the scales that propel snakes forward. Using a forked stick specially carved for the job—we called it a jigger—Bruce pinned its head to the ground.

"Pick it up," he told me.

"You do it."

He looked me in the eyes. The glance spoke challenge. He had a sort of snake-eyed charm himself. If I didn't grab the snake, Bruce would label me a wimp. So, I placed thumb and finger behind its head at the place where its ears would be, if snakes had ears. I gripped, but an instant before I tightened my squeeze, Bruce inadvertently relaxed the pressure on the jigger. The snake squirmed free. Its head turned. It bit my index finger.

Shock coursed through me. The moment stretched, long and lingering, and I still remember it. I stood up, with the snake fastened to my finger, watching it chew and pump venom. Then I flicked it off. It hurtled the length of the yard, like a piece of rope. Bruce tracked it down in an instant and reincarcerated it as his pet cockatoo screeched madly at the sight of the snake.

I thrust my finger into my mouth and began sucking, to reverse the entry of venom. I sucked, then spat, but panic dried my mouth. Bruce pulled a lace from his shoe and wrapped it above my elbow as a tourniquet. He produced a razor blade, held my finger, slashed an X into it and then pushed my finger back into my mouth.

"Suck!" he ordered.

Dizziness and nausea, headache and fatigue overwhelmed me. I vomited a dark, foul-tasting, blood-speckled bile. But ten minutes later I was still alive, though retching like a commode-hugging drunk. Bruce, whose judgments on these matters I held as gospel, assessed the situation: "If you're not dead yet, you're gonna live." I had, in fact, been lucky: one fang had deflected off the fingernail.

"Think I should go to the hospital?"

"I wouldn't, but maybe you should."

Rumford looked on, horrified. I'd forgotten he was there until he whined, "Man, is your dad gonna shit about this!"

The notion induced another wave of puking. My arm throbbed. The artery in the pit of my elbow turned blue. I felt as if I'd contracted all the flu viruses at once. Yet the thought of my father's wrath, its potential enhanced by this being Saturday, his special beer-drinking day at the local fishermen's club, filled me with greater fear.

Confessing to snakebite would cause my mother to panic. Dad would be enraged that I'd broken his law of never handling a deadly snake. He'd say I-told-you-so, cuff me about the ears and never let me forget what a klutz I'd been. I would be grounded for weeks. The local newspaper would get hold of the story, as it had the tales of other snakebitten friends. My name would be mud. Moreover, the knowledge that Bruce would tough it out solo rather than hole up in a hospital and let condescending nurses pump syringes full of antivenin into his rump, made me veto the hospital. Embarrassment was worse than death. At thirteen, I understood the former and knew nothing of the latter.

Rumford was agog at my intention to self-cure. He hedged about, nervous, certain that the two maniacs with him were implicating him as some kind of criminal accessory to manslaughter.

"Don't be crazy! Go to the hospital! Who knows what will happen?"

"Shut up!" ordered Bruce. "He's riding his bike home. You follow us. And don't say anything to his old man, understand?"

I mounted my bike and pedaled, zigzagging across the road in a sleepy stupor. A few blocks from where we began I blacked out and crashed.

When I came to moments later, my companions' faces hovered over me, as did a new face. It was the local Greek greengrocer, who'd seen me collapse while driving by.

"What drugs you been-a-take, boy?" he demanded.

I shook my head and vomited. The greengrocer loaded me into his car. Catholic medallions dangled from the rear-view mirror. As we sped off I saw Bruce and Rumford walking in the direction of my house, wheeling my bike between them.

When we arrived at home, Mum stood in the front yard watering our lawn, a miniature Gobi Desert that never produced a green thing in all the years I lived there. As I got out of the grocer's car, I vomited. Mum stared.

"What is wrong with you?" she exclaimed.

Fear of parents brought on an access to composure. I thought of excuses. Should I say I'd been drinking? I'd come home experimentally stonkered on a few nips of whiskey once before; Dad had patted me on the back and told me I'd get used to drinking as I got older, but that he'd belt me if I did it again. Still, a belting was nothing compared to the panic the truth would create, and anyway, booze was a poison my father comprehended and condoned.

Instead, I said, "It must have been that cheese and gherkin sandwich you made me for lunch, Mum."

"What?"

She visualized the sandwich, mentally checking each item she'd placed on it—cheese was fine, butter and bread were fresh, gherkins weren't off. The look on her face told me she knew I was lying. I scooted past her, fetched a bucket to retch into and hunkered down in my room in soothing darkness, behind a closed door.

Just when I was thinking how proud Bruce would be when he learned I had bluffed my folks, Rumford and Bruce arrived. Their voices shouted to cancel each other out.

"I've gotta tell you, Missus Child, he got bit by a snake," blurted Rumford.

"Oh, God! What kind of snake?"

"Harmless snake, no big deal. He'll be okay," interjected Bruce, lying loyally.

"It was a tiger snake!" exclaimed Rumford, foiling the charade.

Mum shrieked. There was a stampede of footsteps and a growling sound as my father was informed. A second later Dad appeared in my room. The veins in his forehead bulged with anger. First, by dabbling with a deadly snake I had disobeyed him. Second, I had got bitten, verifying his worst fears. For these infractions I was in deep shit.

The world swayed before my eyes. I performed my twentieth technicolor yawn into the bucket. I knew I'd weather this situation, but it would be ugly in the way only a kid can know. I managed to talk my way out of going to the hospital, but I never touched a deadly snake again.

Something, though, had to fill the excitement gap that snake-catching had occupied. It was a book that did the job.

I encountered it a year later, in the local library, while waiting for the bus home from school. The lads I loitered with made the normal beeline for the sports section, where they plucked from the shelves pictorial books on football, cricket, horse racing and cars. Such subjects, at age thirteen, were the locus of a Sydney boy's daydreams, though for me the maneuvers, jargon and heroes of the sporting life were anathema. Somehow I had missed the vital lesson that taught the mantra by which sports could be understood. I found football rules as incomprehensible as algebra. The sports stars we worshipped were large, violent and beer-swilling men. Whenever I was coerced into playing cricket, I drifted into the outfield, to a vanishing point where no boy could possibly smash the ball and

I could be forgotten. The lads called this position "right left out." From there I observed the nonevent of cricket until I could sneak away.

The book in question stood in a row of mountaineering volumes. It wasn't a best-seller, it wasn't even great literature. Unless you're a climber, you're unlikely to have heard of it. It was called *K2: The Savage Mountain.* I borrowed it.

It told the story of a handful of Americans traveling through Pakistan in 1953 to attempt a then-unclimbed, 28,250-foot mountain called K2. The only place higher was Everest, a place where the air was so thin that people carried oxygen bottles and masks for breathing. In Australia the highest point was a hill just over 7000 feet; in Sydney, I lived at sea level.

Photographs of climbers poised on vertiginous slopes and tongue-tying, multisyllabic names of Karakoram peaks mesmerized me. The mountain was a jagged black tooth. A cloud streamed from its summit, propelled by a hurricane wind. The image tattooed itself on my mind. I had, once before, climbed on a short sandstone outcrop with my Boy Scout troop. I enjoyed the feeling of moving up the rock face, but I had not reckoned, until absorbing this book, that such small steps were the building blocks of the ascent of great mountains.

I read on. The climbers became trapped in their tents at 25,000 feet during a week-long blizzard. They weakened. One of them—Art Gilkey—became immobilized by a blood clot in his leg. Some kind of infernal short circuit of his body chemistry due to altitude had caused it, and he was dying. Turning back, they fought their way through deep snow, lowering Gilkey in a makeshift stretcher. The dream of becoming the first to stand atop K2 turned into a nightmare. A diagram showed the seven climbers descending K2. Dotted lines and arrows marked paths down which five of the climbers fell. Another arrow showed where one man, Pete Schoening, had wrapped his rope around the shaft of his ice axe, saving his falling companions. Gilkey, though, had disappeared.

They must be supermen, I thought. Instead, they were Americans. To an Aussie schoolboy back then, anything was possible by Americans: American astronauts had walked on the moon; America had the atomic bomb, the fastest cars, the biggest planes, the best TV shows, the most exciting wars.

Images from the book filled my thoughts. While I defrosted the refrigerator I simulated the chink of ice axe and crampon into K2's frozen hide by jabbing the wall of the freezer with a fork until it bent. I held my hand against a pile of Dad's frozen mullet until my flesh turned white and lifeless. This sort of cold, I imagined, must have nagged the K2 climbers every day on the mountain. Cold, at that point in my life, was something I hadn't experienced. Heat is the climatic norm in Australia.

I showed my father the book. He dismissed mountaineers as reckless and ridiculous. I announced my intention to become a climber. "If you think you're gonna climb cliffs or mountains, think again, sport."

He swayed on his feet as he barked his decree, drunk again. The gulf between us grew wider. I could only watch, in those years, as he sank into a pit of sourness over how to support a family and his ailing mother with a business embezzled dry by a crooked employee.

He handed back the book. Minutes later he was asleep in front of the television. I returned my attention to K2. Climbing symbolized escape—an option unavailable to Dad—in which mortal troubles fell behind like discarded ballast. Climb high enough, I thought, and those troubles dropped so far below they were scarcely visible.

At school there existed no clique of climbers as there did with snake-catchers. The only other climber was an ex-snake man a year my senior—I was now fourteen—named Chris Peisker. He was pallid and skinny and had had a kidney removed not long before I met him. At the beach he told girls the crescent-shaped scar on his side was from a shark attack.

Together, we attended monthly meetings of the Sydney

Rockclimbers Club. Its elders looked disturbed that such inept-looking children were taking to the rocks. On the home front I disguised my climbing trips as camping jaunts, slowly easing my parents into the knowledge that I was a climber. My father judged that if my track record with snakes was an example, then only doom could result from my climbing, and he further divined there could be no living made from it. He would prove close to correct on both counts.

Peisker and I accumulated gear and made our own. In metalwork class we drilled holes in bits of hexagonal aluminum and threaded them with rope, to fashion homemade nuts for jamming into cracks. With our pocket money we bought pitons and carabiners and odd imported gadgets with names such as Clogs, Pecks and Moacs. We had fragile hemp ropes until I liberated Dad's salt-encrusted nylon cord from his boat. Later, my first girlfriend won my heart by buying me a real kernmantle climbing rope, imported from Switzerland. Armed with this hardware, we were ordered by the police to come down from ascents of telephone poles and the concrete cracks of nearby Cook's River Bridge.

But it was amidst the urban wilderness of the Blue Mountains, a tableland of sun-colored sandstone cliffs eighty miles west of Sydney, that roped climbing began and nearly ended for me. In those days, every Friday after school, I'd slip the knot from my school tie, toss it on top of an abandoned pile of homework, grab my rucksack and, with Peisker or some other schoolboy-climber compañero, escape Sydney—the Big Smoke, we called it—on a clattering train called the Fish.

The aqua haze that hangs in the valleys and gives the Blue Mountains their name is said to come from the leaves of the gum tree, which on warm days emit a vapor of eucalyptus oil that refracts blue when sunlight penetrates the air. These same leaves, when tinder dry, feed the bush fires that sweep the mountains every decade or two. The cliffs that border the towns of Katoomba, Blackheath and Mount Victoria are where Australian rock climbing began, back in the 1930s. At that same time, they provided work projects for depression-ridden Australia, when, for a while, the valleys echoed to pick axe and blasting powder as coal mines and tourist trails were etched into the cliff faces. The remnants of that era are overgrown trails and Inca-like steps winding down cliffsides and waterfalls. Beyond these byways, in deep canyons of rainforest, you can still get lost for a long, long time in a timeless, green world.

My first climb was up the first tower of the Three Sisters, a baroque-looking, triple-summited formation at Katoomba. Adjacent to a busy tourist lookout, it is also the most watched climb in the Southern Hemisphere. I was thirteen in 1970 when I sweated up that easy scramble. Sitting on the summit of the First Sister, gazing over the cliffs and forests of the Megalong Valley, I had a teen revelation: I would drop out of school, leave home and become a climbing bum the moment I turned sixteen, which in Australia is the legal age at which children are granted enough responsibility to wreck their lives.

By age sixteen I'd made the first moves toward independence. I'd quit school and saved $200 from a summer job, more or less left home (except for when the weather was bad or I needed a decent meal) and was inhabiting a cave above a Blue Mountains cliff that I shared on and off with other teenage climbers.

Three years of weekend cragging had taught us enough to be dangerous. One summer day as Peisker and I strolled beneath the cliffs of Mount Piddington to try a climb, we saw nothing portentous in the fact that this route was named Last Act.

I set off up the cliff and after a hundred feet reached a four-inch-wide ledge that provided me with a stance to edge my toes onto, and a small tree sprouting out of a crack, which I tied off with a sling and clipped myself to, with the rope. This was the belay anchor. It was shoddy and weak, barely enough to hold my weight, but I knew no better.

I began pulling in the rope as Peisker climbed to join me.

When he reached me he stood with toes poised on little flakes and legs stemmed across the corner, an arm's reach below me. Carefully, he passed me the gear I had placed in the cracks and that he had retrieved. He suggested that I lead again; something about the climb was psyching him out, he explained. Taking everything except one small nut—an aluminum wedge threaded with a loop of cord, for plugging into cracks—I mounted the tree to which I was secured to let Chris clip into the anchor.

Then something went wrong. The rush of air across my cheek told me I was falling, but, since I was the belayer, this was theoretically impossible. The sensation was of lightness, of weightlessness rather than acceleration. But when I cartwheeled over and saw Peisker clinging to the rock above me and receding into the distance fast, and saw a branch from the belay tree clipped to my waist harness, flapping angrily like a failed parachute, I took this as proof of falling. "This could be it," I thought, screamed, crashed into the limb of a tree, hit the ground 100 feet below and bounced down a steep hillside.

The rope was 150 feet long. Every bounce brought me closer to the point at which it would come against Peisker's waist and pull him off. I was hurtling headfirst through dirt and brush, thinking this, when my helmeted head rammed into something and I blacked out.

As I slowly regained consciousness from a deep quiet, I heard a cow mooing in the distance. The cow's call grew louder, closer; the stupid beast must have wandered up from the farm below and gotten lost beneath the cliffs, I thought. I decided to move, lest it trample me. I raised my head and lifted my knees to stand. My foot slumped at a crazy angle, like a dead fish. I looked around. Blood was everywhere. It was either mine or Peisker's. The cow started to cry pathetically, like a human. Then I realized there was no cow, that it was me wheezing through broken ribs at the pain of broken ankle, shoulder, nose, and concussion. I slumped back in resignation.

Then something moved beside me. I turned my head. A

yard-long black snake was wedging itself between twigs, shedding its skin. While it worked it kept its pupil-less eyes on me since, half in and half out of its skin, it was vulnerable. We stared eye to eye. Only the dry crackle of its old skin interrupted the sound of wind rustling eucalyptus leaves. It slithered onto the tree limb I'd brought down, jammed itself between the sharp, fresh splinters and slipped opportunistically out of its last fold of old scales. The snake emerged glossy and renewed. Watching it had a calming, opiate effect on me. The snake seemed oblivious to my presence now, as if I were invisible, like a ghost. And then I wondered: am I dead? No, I decided, I hurt too much.

I began to piece together the shocking puzzle of what had happened to us, and the possible consequences. No one had seen the accident; no one knew where we were. Peisker was probably lying somewhere nearby, as mangled as me, or worse. I watched an ant crawl onto my wrist. Yes, we'd be ant food by the time we were missed.

I'd stopped bouncing at 140 feet. Above, Peisker shook with fear. Between his legs the rope trailed down to a groaning dead weight on the ground. Above lay 100 feet of steep rock. The rope was clipped to nothing between him and me and oblivion. He had no way to climb up or down from his airy stance. His fingers were slowly peeling from the holds he held. He could conceive of only one thing to ease the horror he found himself in: jump.

Then he remembered the nut clipped with a carabiner to his harness—the only gear I hadn't taken from him. He wedged it into a pocket in the crack, tied the rope off and rappelled down the rope. Peisker looked at me lying there, like a blood-soaked rag, and ran to raise a rescue.

I spent the rest of the year in and out of the hospital. Dad was not impressed by the bills. Five operations installed two steel plates and thirteen screws in my ankle, most of which were later removed and became conversation pieces when I dropped back in to high school. And I read a lot of climbing books. Even if I had to limp there, I decided, I'd see those distant mountains. I'd taken the plunge into the climbing life, and there was no turning back.

ON BROAD PEAK

We were stepping over yak dung in the streets of Askole that summer of 1983, trying to act as inconspicuously as a pair of Westerners can in this village of mud-walled houses and warrens that treads a line someplace between now and the Stone Age. Neither Pete Thexton nor I were having much success in photographing the brightly dressed, goiter-ridden local ladies. Like startled cattle, they would run from us down alleyways or giggle and chatter behind shuttered windows. The few we did aim our lenses at screeched and threw themselves down in the grey dust, covering themselves with their many layers of ragged dress.

An open window invited us to peer into someone's home. Through the dust motes that eternally rise from these earthen floors we could see the straw bedding and blackened pots around a blacker fireplace. A goatskin sack hung on the wall, as did a few pictures. One was a charcoal drawing of a helicopter, that mysterious beast that sometimes hovers up the valley of the Braldu. The second was a poster of Bhutto, the ex-president of Pakistan, ousted and eventually executed by General Zia. In the corner of Bhutto's portrait a candle, freshly extinguished, symbolically wafted its last puff of smoke. Above both of these presided a photograph of the Ayatollah Khomeini, his cheerless countenance seeming to stare through the dim, dusty light and directly into our eyes.

In this almost lawless frontier of Pakistan it is odd to see a portrait of a past leader, but not surprising to see the face of

Islamic fundamentalism. While politics means little to the Balti, Islam is everything. Tied to the land as they are in this desolate place, perhaps a notion of God is all that they have. Of Bhutto, our liaison officer says evil genius. Of Khomeini, evil idiot.

We turned to the street again and soon confronted another cluster of women, threshing a heap of grain with green branches. Poised for purdah, they seemed ready to bolt, but Pete had another strategy. He emptied a bottle of bright red multivitamins onto the palm of his outstretched hand. The women inched closer and with doe-eyed temerity submitted to our cameras, gently taking the magic medicine from Pete's hand as if they were diamonds.

As doctor of the expedition, Pete's was the face that all the villagers knew. At each village along the approach he would no sooner arrive than the sick and ailing would mill around him, as if an identikit picture had preceded him. To these people medicine was more magic than anything else, and Pete was held in particular reverence. Each night he would spend a couple of hours doing what he could, even making house calls when asked. To us, nothing could have seemed more unlikely than hiking a long day in hundred-degree heat and finishing the day's consultations with a candle-lit gynecological examination of a Balti woman in her dusty home, with children, chickens and husband gathered around. But to Pete it was just another curious experience for a doctor in the Third World.

"If there is such a thing as reincarnation," I remarked, "and your past deeds are accountable, and you were to find yourself reborn into a place like this, then you could say with a fair degree of certainty that you had previously blown it."

"One could do worse," Pete replied.

I found it hard to imagine a station in life much more difficult than this, save for such hells as warfare or prison, which man contrives for his own kind for the sole purpose of misery. Pressed, Pete elaborated.

"Well, you could come back as an Askole chicken, for

instance," and he pointed to a brood of bedraggled and scrawny birds rooting about in the grey muck of a culvert.

That fate, we agreed, must be reserved for the really bad eggs of society.

A month later, after our twelve-member expedition had marched to the end of a buckling swell of ice called the Baltoro Glacier, we divided into smaller teams and set off to climb the west face of Broad Peak, a 26,400-foot mountain with a summit that rose 10,000 feet above our base camp. Just outside base camp, as we walked toward Broad Peak, Pete and I came to a zone of crevasses covered by a thin layer of snow. I poked my ice axe into a suspect snowpatch to test its strength. The very moment I assured Pete it was safe to cross it, the surface gave way and I dropped into a crevasse. I felt the foolish surprise one would feel standing on a glass-topped table that had suddenly shattered. More surprising was that the crevasse had a false floor and I had stopped just a few feet down.

"Crevasse," I stated in the quiet that follows smashed mirrors and glassware.

"Thought I'd lost you already," Pete said as I extricated myself. Then he added, "You'll be pleased to know you've got an audience." Some trekkers on this well-traveled tract of wilderness had seen the whole display from their camp a few hundred feet away.

"Don't worry," he said with a grin, "no one from our camp saw it."

The sun was setting on one of those rare Karakoram days when there is not a breath of wind from glacier to summit, nor any cloud or snow plume streaming from the giants. The rock on nearby K2 took on an orange glow.

By the time we were in the first couloirs of Broad Peak it was night. The snow was firm underfoot, and shortly the full moon rounded the south flank and doused the west face with bright light. We reached 19,000 feet, rested a while and then carried on in the moonlight.

Step after step, breath after breath, every hour the atmosphere became just a little thinner. Behind us the first hint of dawn was turning the horizon every shade of blue imaginable, while the moon sat great and white, refusing to evaporate. All the mountains glowed, every minute changing color like chameleons.

Daylight revealed relics of other expeditions: shredded tents, bits of fixed rope, an old oxygen cylinder. The path was already pitted with the tracks of four members of our group above. I briefly pretended to myself that I was following the tracks of Hermann Buhl back in 1957, the year of his first ascent of this, the twelfth-highest mountain on earth. Fifty-seven was also the year of my birth, and the year Buhl died while climbing on Chogolisa, a snowy pyramid that lay to my right.

At about 20,500 feet we met Alan Rouse, Andy Parkin, Roger Baxter-Jones and the Frenchman Jean Affanassieff, the four members of our expedition who'd set off up Broad Peak a day before Pete and I. Returning from their ascent of the previous day, they looked tired. Alan told of the damnably long ridge at the end of the climb and of the windless hour they'd sat on the summit.

We reached 21,000 feet an hour after passing our four friends and fell into a deep sleep inside the tiny tent we pitched on a small clearing in the snow. Doug Scott and Steve Sustad— two others of our group—caught up to us in the early afternoon and shared the same camp. Our tired minds were alive with fantastic dreams, and as we four set off together the next morning we compared the places these dreams had taken us.

At 22,800 feet we rested again. After rehydrating ourselves with cups of tea brewed over a small gas stove, we set out just as Don Whillans and the Pakistani climber Gohar Shar—the final members of our expedition—arrived. Those two bivied here while we climbed higher, gaining height for the next day's summit push.

Pete and I pitched a tent beneath a small ice cliff at about 24,500 feet, and Doug and Steve bivied 400 feet above it. It was late into the night before we finished melting snow to drink, and even then we felt we could have drunk a gallon more.

During the night the altitude crept into our heads and by morning it was bashing away from the inside. We'd chosen a very high spot to bivy—the highest I'd ever climbed. Waking was a long and difficult process. While brewing tea I heard Pete mumbling in his sleep.

"What about this rope then?" he asked.

"Rope? Our rope is in the pack," I answered.

"Noooo, not that rope," he chided.

"Then what rope?"

"This rope we are tied to."

"We're not tied in, Pete. We're in the tent, on Broad Peak."

"Noooo, you don't understand," he said, and I began to feel like a thick-headed schoolboy giving all the wrong answers. I plied him for more clues to his sleepy riddle and got this:

"It's the rope that all of us are tied to."

"Fixed rope?"

"Noooo," he whined.

"Umbilical cord?" Any wild guess now.

"Noooo!"

"Then you must be speaking of a metaphysical rope, eh, one that everyone is tied to but no one is tied to?"

But before I got an answer to this, the smell of sweet tea had woken him and we were trying to force breakfast down our throats. A few aspirin later and we were moving.

A short step of vertical ice to round a serac got our blood flowing. Doug and Steve were already close to the snowy notch that divided the rocky cappings of the central summit and main summit of Broad Peak when I caught sight of them. By the time we surmounted the steepish final chimney to the col, at just under 8000 meters, a strong wind was blowing. Suddenly we could see into China, where the wind was coming from. Rust-colored peaks and valleys contrasted sharply with the blinding white of the Godwin-Austen Glacier.

On the final ridge to the summit—a rise of 400 feet but a length of a quarter-mile—lay the hardest climbing yet: endless short steps of steep snow interspersed with rock. At perhaps 1:00 or 2:00 P.M. Doug and Steve passed us on their return from the summit. "It's even windier and colder up there, youth," Doug said, "and the top is two hours away at the rate you're moving."

Moving at this altitude was like wading through treacle. I became aware of a peculiar sense of disassociation with myself in which I felt as if part of me was external to my body and looking on. I felt this most acutely when setting up belays or making a difficult move; it felt like having someone peering over my shoulder keeping an eye on me, or as if I had a second, invisible head on my shoulders.

We went on for another hour to a dome of snow and cornices, where we rested. The sense of disassociation had begun to be punctuated by feelings of total absence, momentary blackouts, when neither I nor the guy over my shoulder seemed to be around. I would wake from these blackouts a few paces beyond where they had struck me, which led to a concern about stepping off the narrow ridge. "Like a dream," I murmured to Pete, but the wind snatched my words before he heard them.

Ahead, the ridge dipped down and curved left in a long, even slope to the summit, perhaps a half-hour trudge away, yet just twenty vertical feet higher. But here my fears about what was happening to me doubled. A vicious headache gripped me and a tingling in my arms grew so intense that my fingers curled tightly into a fist, making it hard to hold on to my ice axe. To articulate this to Pete was difficult, as speech and thought seemed to have no link in my mind; in short, I didn't know what was going on.

Exhaustion I can accept, and given that alone I might have

crawled to the summit; but something alien was going on within me, and I wasn't prepared to push my luck with it. I got it out that I wanted down. Pete knelt beside me, tried to talk me into going on, and his ever-present determination nearly got me going. There is a state of mind that sometimes infests climbers in which a particular goal achieves a significance beyond anything that the future may hold. For a few minutes or hours one casts aside all that has previously been held as worth living for, and one's focus falls on one risky move or stretch of ground, which becomes the only thing that matters. This state of mind is what is both fantastic and reckless about the game. Since everything is at stake in these moments, one had better be sure to recognize them and have no illusions about what lies on the other side of luck. This was one of those times. I had to weigh what was important and what was most important.

"It'd be nice to reach the top, you and I," Pete said. And so it would have, to stand up there with this man who had become such a strong friend in such a short time.

"Didn't you once say that summits are important?" Those were my words he was throwing back at me, shouting above the wind and his own breathlessness. Something I'd said a few weeks before on a granite spire called Lobsang Spire. I'd said it to encourage us when the rock turned blank and it looked like drilling bolts into the cliff—a tiresome process—was necessary to get up. I struggled to compose an intelligible sentence.

"Only important when you're in control.... Lost control.... Too high, too fast."

Pete nodded. I could see that he was feeling the strain too. We just got up and began the long path down. When I looked toward those red hills in China, I saw they were now covered in cotton wool clouds that lapped at Broad Peak's east face. We were so far above them. In two and a half days we had gone from 16,100 feet to 26,250 feet. It was the limit of what our bodies could do.

Three hundred feet below our high point I blacked out for

twenty minutes. I woke momentarily during this period, trying to force myself awake, and recall seeing Pete next to me, observing my state, as a good doctor should. When I regained control of myself, Pete put a brew of grape drink into my hands. I drank it down, then promptly threw it up.

"See…. Told you I was … sick." The purple stain I had made in the snow formed intricate arabesque designs that grew onto the snow crystals glinting in the afternoon light. Hallucinations.

Once we were moving I began to improve, when suddenly something else happened. Pete appeared over a crest, lagging on the end of the rope. He took short steps and looked stressed. Speaking in a slow whisper, he told me he suddenly couldn't breathe, as if his diaphragm had collapsed. His lips were blue, a sign of oxygen starvation. We had to get down, and fast, but a snail's pace was the best he could manage in this thin soup of air.

At perhaps seven in the evening we reached the col and rappelled sixty feet to the start of the snow. Wind had covered any sign of our tracks. Dragging the rope behind me, I began plunge-stepping down, making tracks for Pete. After 400 feet I turned and saw that he had barely moved. By the time I crawled back up to him through the soft snow, it was dark. He had his headlamp on, shining out into the windy night. When I turned to the glacier I could see a light shining back from base camp. It was Pete's girlfriend, Beth, giving the 8:00 P.M. signal, and Pete was returning it.

Conversation was superfluous. We knew that we were going to be on the go all night, very high, and the wind was rising. I tied the rope around Pete and began roping him down, length after length, till his strength began to ebb; then I began to talk him down, ordering and cajoling every step out of him. At about 10:00 P.M. he slumped in the snow and whispered that he could no longer see. So I guided him by direction, telling him to traverse forty-five degrees right, or straight down. With no tracks it was all instinct anyway, and the bastard moon shone everywhere but on the upper slopes of Broad Peak. And all the time, wind and spindrift blew.

Somewhere near was the band of sixty-foot ice cliffs we'd surmounted that morning. We had to find the low spot in them, but where that was was anybody's guess. Pete had gotten too weak to walk, so I was dragging and carrying him and both packs. The sensation of being outside myself was more prevalent than ever, my watcher checking every ice axe belay and every decision. He must have lent a hand in carrying Pete too.

At some point in this nightmare, I recalled reading about the first ascent of Broad Peak's central summit, made by a Polish team who were caught in a storm on the descent. The account, recorded in a climbing magazine, described what ensued as a "struggle for survival." Accompanying this story was a photo of Broad Peak, littered with crosses where four men had perished from falls and from the biting blizzard winds. Those crosses were now underfoot. I felt as if the ghosts of history watched in the shadows.

Around the lip of the seracs the angle steepened. Pete and I linked arms and shuffled along in the dark to what I hoped was the low spot. The wind howled. It became too steep to blunder about as we were, so I began making twenty-foot leads, shoving my axe into the soft snow and pulling Pete in to me. At the last belay he let go of everything and swung down to the lip of the serac. The shaft of my axe dropped alarmingly. I lost my cool and yelled a mouthful of curses at him as I hauled him back up.

"Sorry," he whispered calmly. Throughout this ordeal he had stayed composed, seemingly reserving his energy for matters of survival, rather than letting fear or emotion take hold. I clipped him to his axe and wrapped his arms around it.

"Just don't lose it now, brother. Please."

The wind seemed to attack with unprecedented malice, burning our faces with thick clouds of spindrift. Somewhere nearby in the black at the bottom of this serac was a tent, and if things had gone as planned, Don and Gohar were in it. I called till my throat was raw and shoved my axe into the snow as deep as it would go to lower Pete.

So much was confusion in the minute it took to lower him. Pete was so disoriented that he couldn't tell where he was, I was blinded by spindrift and the axe was again shifting and coming out of the snow. I wrapped the rope around my arm to distribute some of the weight while pushing the axe in with my knee. There was no way of telling if Pete was down, but he came to a stop anyway. I rappelled off my second, shorter tool, moving quickly before it slid out. Pete could barely move. We again linked arms to negotiate some broken ground and then reverted to piggybacking, when a light suddenly appeared.

"We've got a sick man here, Don," I called to the bobbing light. Pete crawled a few feet along a crest and then stopped totally. Gohar arrived, himself groggy, awakened from a deep sleep. While I sat Pete on my shoulders and slid us down the last fifty feet to the tent, Gohar belayed us with a rope. At the bottom, Don helped drag Pete into the tent, where we began warming and rehydrating him. It was 2:00 A.M. We'd been moving for twenty-two hours.

All of us lay crammed in together in the quiet of the tent. It took a long time for feeling to return to my hands and feet, and Pete's were ice cold, but remarkably not frostbitten. Warm liquid seemed to perk him up.

"How are you, Gregor?" he asked, his voice regaining its familiar, impish tone.

"Done in. Rest a couple hours till dawn; then we'll head on down." My eyelids closed under the weight of exhaustion and I dreamt of grassy places.

Those were the last words that we spoke together. At dawn Pete awoke to ask Gohar for water. A few minutes later Gohar pressed a cup of warm liquid to his lips, but Pete would not drink it. Don and Gohar looked at each other for a few seconds, then called me. "Dead," they were saying. But no one in my dreams was dead. We were making it.

Then sense prevailed like a sledgehammer. I tried to force life into my friend, through his mouth, with mine, breathing my own thin and tired air into him. His lungs gurgled loudly—pulmonary edema. And we pressed our palms against his chest to squeeze a beat out of his heart, but he would have none of it. He would only lay there with an expression of sublime rest on his face, as if dreaming the same dream I had.

We sat in silence for a while, our heads full of sad thoughts. Suddenly I hated the mountain. Over and over I muttered, "It's not worth it," till I couldn't talk for the tears. And what about the people below and at home who loved him, what about them? Outside the day was clear and calm, the Karakoram ablaze with light.

"Notice how the wind suddenly dropped?" asked Don. "Not a breath. It's always the same when death is about, always a lot of noise and wind, but as soon as it gets what it's after, it quiets down. I've seen it before and it's always the same."

I'm still thinking about that one, still wondering.

The wind rose up again a few minutes later, even stronger than before, and threatened to tear the tent apart with its claws, like some predator searching for us. I knelt beside Pete, incredulous and oblivious. Gohar took my arm and with a look of natural fear said, "Greg Sahib, we must go." We left everything as it was, zipped the door shut, said good-bye in our different ways and turned into the maelstrom. It was a long descent, every step full of a great sense of loss, and perhaps a foolish feeling of guilt at having to leave our friend as we did.

But the snow would soon settle over him and set him firm as earth. The snowfield would inch inexorably toward the ice cliffs and peel away in bursts of avalanche to the glacier, which would carry him within it to the fast-flowing Braldu River. His journey would outlive us, and no ashes could be scattered

more thoroughly nor a monument exist more lasting than
Broad Peak.

The terminus of the Baltoro is a huge, black tongue of
rubble and ice that lolls rudely across the breadth of the valley
and gives birth to the grey Braldu River. I had left the expedition
early with Don to get word to Pete's family. As we stepped off
the end of the glacier I began to feel like some harbinger of
terrible news, and my body felt wrought and knotted, like some
piece of gristle that the glacier had spat out, indigestible and
bitter.

Ahead lay the rotting villages of Askole, Chongo and Chokpo,
places lifted from the pages of some Graham Greene tale of
Third World purgatory. Behind, the others had chosen to stay
and attempt K2. All along our way were reminders of Pete:
places where he had sat and gazed at the mountains; boulders at
Urdokas that we had tiptoed upon and sheltered beneath.

Though I had only known Pete for the span of this expedition, we had become fast friends, seeing the same joke in this or
that, moving at the same speed in the hills, and talking, always
talking. Javid, our Pakistani liaison officer, between his sobs,
said that according to his religion every move that we make,
from beginning to end, is predestined by a higher force. But
others would talk about the randomness of death, its fickle
whims and unpredictable chaos. All that was sure to me at that
time was a nagging uneasiness in the pit of my stomach and a
certainty that it is just as poignant and terrible to lose a new
friend as to lose an old one.

Grey skies followed us for days, sweeping us out of the
mountains, disguising the fact that they were there at all. No last
glimpses of the Karakoram, no summits through the clouds,
nothing to tempt us. Good. We walked fast. There was no
reason to turn around. Nothing to look back on.

The Obscure Object of Desire

I saw it clearly.

A wall of snow, breaking up and rolling toward me, engulfing me in white chaos. Snow fills my mouth, my ears, my eyes, and the cold, relentless tide drags me down the mountain.

A dream.

I wake to the patter of rain on the window, the hiss of cars on slick roads, the wail of a distant burglar alarm. An April night in Seattle. In a few days I'll be on a 747 roaring toward a mountain in Pakistan called Gasherbrum IV.

"What is it?" asks Salley.

"A dream," I answer.

If we ever have children and they become climbers, I'll tell them, "Stay away from expeditions. They'll make you poor and neurotic."

There is a saying: "An unresolved idea is like a worm in the brain."

Each of us on the expedition had our reasons to go to that Karakoram peak. For me, it began in May 1983, with my first view of Gasherbrum IV. It stood twenty miles from where I sat with Doug Scott and Peter Thexton, on the summit of a granite tower called Lobsang Spire, on the lower reaches of the Baltoro

Glacier. A few days later, as we picked our way along the glacier toward our next objective, 26,400-foot Broad Peak, we again saw the symmetrical Gasherbrum IV standing in the after-mist of a storm. As the mist parted to reveal the broken tooth of the 26,000-foot summit, the worm—the idea—began to burrow into my mind.

Two weeks later, as Pete and I climbed at 26,380 feet along the summit ridge of Broad Peak, the dominant sight was Gasherbrum IV's unclimbed northwest ridge. Broad Peak seemed in the bag, and future climbs were already forming in our thoughts. I still recall Pete looking onto the summit of Gasherbrum IV below us, suggesting that someday we return to climb that alluring ridge.

But nothing is ever certain in the Himalaya. An hour later Pete developed pulmonary edema. We struggled through night and storm to shed altitude, but, at 25,000 feet, as dawn broke, Pete breathed his last.

I vowed never to return to the Himalaya. But the worm knew better.

The seven of us who planned to climb Gasherbrum IV's northwest ridge were still in diapers when, in 1958, Walter Bonatti and Carlo Mauri made the first ascent of the peak by a route on the opposite side of the mountain—the northeast ridge. By 1986, no one but the two Italians had reached the summit despite attempts by American, British, Japanese and Polish expeditions. The route most expeditions had tried—the northwest ridge—had been pushed to 24,000 feet by two American teams. Over on the west face, in 1985, Voytek Kurtyka and Robert Schauer had come within a few hours of the top, but had staggered away without the summit, exhausted by hunger and thirst after nine days on the wall.

But they'd almost done it, and furthermore, they'd descended the northwest ridge—the route we planned to climb.

When Voytek wrote me about this I paused long and hard, uncertain what it meant to our plans, then phoned Geoff Radford in Anchorage, Alaska. Geoff had contracted the worm—the notion—of climbing Gasherbrum IV as well and had already made an attempt to climb the northwest ridge in 1984.

"Geoff, Voytek just climbed the west face, missed the summit and descended the northwest ridge."

"Does that make any difference to you?" he asked.

"No."

"Me neither," he said.

If anything, it made the worm corkscrew about our heads more voraciously in those days before we left. The summit, untrodden for twenty-eight years, was the lure, the obscure object of desire.

Nineteen eighty-six was an uncertain time to visit an Islamic country. Rubble was still being cleared from the streets of Tripoli after Reagan's bombing lesson to show Libyan terrorists that Jihad was over. Consequently, it was open season on Americans. My friends in the British Embassy in Islamabad wrote me that, since Britain had been used as an aircraft carrier for U.S. F-111 strikes against Libya, walls were being erected around their embassy compound.

So, some of us took precautions. Randy armed himself with a gold crucifix on a chain around his neck, to wave off hijackers who might think his surname, Leavitt, sounded Israeli. As our flight streaked through the sky, the in-flight movie, *Rocky IV,* seemed an ironic counterpoint to the international situation seething beneath us.

Four other climbers made up the rest of our team: Tim Macartney-Snape, an Australian, who had climbed Everest without oxygen in 1984; Tom Hargis, a Vietnam veteran who worked as a mountain guide in the Pacific Northwest; Steve Risse, a psychiatrist and well-traveled climber; and Andy Tuthill, a geologist-cum-carpenter from New Hampshire.

Forty-six days later we have reached 23,000 feet on the northwest ridge, spent three stormbound days in a snowcave and retreated to base camp in a blizzard that consumed Gasherbrum IV for a week.

Our base camp on the West Gasherbrum Glacier has become a bleak, frozen place. Wind flaps the tents and rattles the contents of the kitchen, bringing gusts of Andy's banjo-playing with it. Amid tropical palm trees graffitied on the tent wall, Tim twiddles the radio dial. Leaking radiation from a near meltdown at a Russian nuclear plant in Chernobyl is the big news again on the BBC, but Radio Moscow keeps quiet about it.

"I wonder if we're sucking in fallout up here?" asks Tom.

"You'll probably know in about ten years, when you either have lung cancer or you don't," says Steve.

We've seen nothing but storm since reaching the mountain. The British team attempting the west face has abandoned their route. I wonder if our expedition will be yet another failure. The worm sits rotting in a quagmire of pessimism.

But Rosali, a Balti cook, gives us a shred of hope: "Good weather coming on June fifteenth," he says.

On June 16 the wind changes direction, from southwest to north, bringing clear skies. Three days later Geoff, Andy, Tim, Tom and I reoccupy the snowcave at 23,000 feet while Randy and Steve bivouac at Camp II, 1000 feet below. As the sun rises on June 20, the view through the entrance of the snowcave is of a cloudless Karakoram.

The five of us set out along the ridge, passing lengths of bleached rope, racks of pitons, and coils of rope, all fused to the mountain with ice—the relics of the 1984 attempt. At sunset we surmount a 600-foot rock band and hack out tent platforms. The altimeter reads 24,140 feet. Voytek and Robert's west face soaks the sun like a sponge. No wonder Voytek calls it the Shining Wall. Behind us the definitive forms of Chogolisa, Masherbrum, and Mustagh Tower glow in the dusk.

June 21. Cold, windy and clear. Between us we decide to carry the minimum—two stoves, two sleeping bags, two seven-millimeter ropes, a handful of pitons and slings—in the hope that traveling light will get us up the 1900 feet of ice and rock to the summit, and back, in one push.

Wumph! Acres of slope groan around us.

"Jesus!" somebody says. Our hearts explode.

"It's okay. The slope is settled now," says Tim.

We cling to the steeper ice and solo across firm ground for 900 feet. Geoff treads cautiously, cursing a snapped crampon. At 10:00 A.M. we regroup at 25,000 feet, at the 1000-foot marble headwall. We dump everything but climbing gear.

I take the first lead on the wall. The marble is glass-smooth. My crampons scrattle and I heave at the thin air. The only protection in 200 feet is a tied-off ice hammer swung into the frozen core of a crack. As Andy takes the next lead, Geoff calls up.

"I'm going down," he says.

I know what he's thinking—that we're too slow and we'll never make it before dark; that the weather has been good for five days and can't last much longer. He descends to bivouac at the foot of the wall.

Tim and Andy lead on to the crest of the wall, at 25,800 feet. It's 4:00 P.M. We can see the true summit to the south, barely higher than us, but 1500 feet horizontally away, across ice and rocks. Our bodies burn with fatigue. We stand there, watching dusk gather over the Karakoram. We've blown it. There is no chance of reaching the summit and returning to the bivouac before dark. If we descend, we'll never climb Gasherbrum IV. Everything seems about to turn to shit. Then the worm begins to twist in our minds. The crazy talk begins.

"I'm certain I can make it through the night without frost-bite," says Tim, the words ripped out of his mouth by wind. He'd been to the top of Everest without oxygen, had managed that without frostbite. It was possible....

"Bivouac out?" I ask.

"It's the only way."

We had nothing but the clothes on our backs. No water or stove. I'd read about Buhl enduring a solitary night without a sleeping bag on the summit ridge of Nanga Parbat, had heard Nazir Sabir's and Jim Wickwire's separate tales about bivying out near the summit of K2. Nazir suffered memory loss for months. Jim's bivouac had cost him a piece of lung. Now it was shaping up that we might sit one out on Gasherbrum IV. The worm twists.

"I'll risk it," I say.

Tom and Andy look about the clear horizon.

"Don't be talked into this by us. It could be a bad night. Maybe frostbite. Think hard," I say.

A hacking cough has hammered Tom's ribs all day. He is running on sheer determination. Andy had frozen his toes in years past. "I'm stayin,'" says Tom.

"It's not worth it to me. I'm going down," says Andy.

"Alone?" Descending the rock band unaccompanied seems dangerous.

"You're worried about me? I'm more worried about you! Anyway, tonight is the solstice, the shortest night of the year."

"Yeah? At least we've got that going for us."

Andy takes a rope, wishes us luck, and turns.

Now we are three. We continue on to look for a site to claw out a snowcave. At a suitable place on the ridge we begin to dig with our ice axes, scratching little handfuls of snow for five minutes each. The effort is almost more than we are capable of. As I take my turn at digging I think of the bridge we have burned, of what might happen and what might not. Framed in the entrance to the cave is Broad Peak, where Pete died and where he still lay. It is almost three years to the day since the struggle to drag him down from the summit ridge. As oxygen-starved as my thoughts are, my reasons for returning to the Karakoram fall clearly into place. Somehow, it seems that reaching the summit of Gasherbrum IV will resolve the past.

Tim calls to me to look at the sky.

Gasherbrums III, II and I poke up like huge tusks, their snows pearly white, their rocks shining amber. The sky is indigo blue, fading to a deeply pink upper atmosphere. Low on the horizon, a full moon blasts a surreal glow across the thin air, from the monsoon thunderheads over Indian Kashmir to Nanga Parbat in the west. A landscape from another planet. No, our own wild and beautiful Earth.

We stand looking, breathing. At that moment we all are quite certain we have chosen the right place to be. As we settle into our cave I feel like a stranded astronaut bedding down for the night on an alluring, yet hostile planet.

Cold.

"What's the time?" I ask.

"Don't ask," says Tim.

Time creeps.

"What's the worst bivy you've ever had?" he asks.

"This is," I reply without reservation.

Tom's teeth chatter like static. He coughs and spits up something awful from his lungs. He doesn't speak.

"My feet—they're going!" I say.

Tim unzips his down suit and I put my socked and lifeless feet against his chest. We squirm and shift positions in the tiny hole, looking like a ménage à trois in deep freeze. Tim produces an antique remnant of fruitcake from his pocket. It sits in our dry mouths like sawdust. We spit it out. Oh, for some water. A restless sleep, like an overdose of sedative, takes us into our own worlds. The night fills with strange mumblings.

June 22 dawns. The sun creeps into the snowcave and seeps into our bodies.

Between us and the south summit stretches a long ridge of wind-polished ice that drops over the west face. The wind from China slams into the mountain's east face and tumbles over the ridge like surf pounding a sea wall. At the end of the ridge a series of limestone towers, thrust up from primeval oceans, forms the summit. But to choose the right summit is a puzzle our altitude-addled minds can barely cope with.

My vision distorts as I lead over 5.8 rock. Halfway up I realize I'm heading to the wrong summit. The fever of being so close scrambles our judgment. Atop a teetering spire, I drape a sling over a spike and descend.

Tim takes over, skirts across verglas-covered slabs at the foot of the towers and leads up a snowfield to the final rocks. At ten o'clock in the morning we reach a small plateau of snow—the summit. The obscure object of desire is reached, the worm satisfied.

The catenulate shape of Broad Peak and the mighty pyramid of K2 loom beside us. We are too exhausted for profundities. I'd thought of leaving something for Pete on the summit. Instead I leave a fond thought. A few photographs later we jam a rock into a crack, sling it and rappel.

As I rappel I see Tim wandering on the summit rocks like a mad, lost thing. He turns after thirty feet and descends.

"I saw it—Bonatti's old rope, clipped to a carabiner and piton!" he says excitedly.

Tom solos the verglased traverse and shakes his head at its end.

"Rope up. It's bad," he calls, then heads for the north summit.

I lead across the traverse and sink a boot-axe belay into a shallow snowpatch.

As Tim hammers out a piton with his ice axe I look across. First I see his axe fly into the air and then him cartwheeling backward. He seems to fall in slow motion. I pull in a yard of rope. Still he's falling—forty, fifty feet. I look at the 10,000-foot drop beneath us and anticipate a grand tour of the west face. The belay seems a token gesture, a textbook theory incapable of holding a fall.

A jolt torpedoes boot and axe into the snow. Everything stops. I call Tim's name for five minutes. No answer, only the blasting wind. I look around. Nothing to tie the rope to. I tug on the rope. Can't haul him up. Then it occurs to me: if he is unconscious or dead, I'll be stuck here, holding him forever, as in situ as Bonatti's piton. If I untie and drop him, Tom and I will never get down the mountain. I feel the knife in my pocket and begin to think with the ruthless practicality of Clint Eastwood.

But the rope moves. I pull it in, and in, and in. Tim appears. Feathers fly out of his ripped down suit. He looks like he's been blasted with buckshot. He grips my shoulder with his hand.

"You just saved me from the biggest tumble of my life," he says.

"You just saved me from the longest wait of mine," I mutter to myself.

An hour later we are back at the snowcave. Tom is still ahead of us. As my legs begin to cramp from dehydration, I feel my self-control ebbing.

"Keep an eye on me, Tim. I'm on the verge of hallucinating."

Tim hands me his water bottle. Somehow, a teaspoon of snow has melted in it.

"Drink it," Tim says.

"We'll share it."

"No. Drink it all."

I swallow it.

We reach Tom, coughing wildly, above the headwall. We're in bad shape. Fatigue and dehydration detach our minds from our bodies. We begin rappelling, searching for Andy's anchors, but find only one. As we run out of pitons and slings we strip cord from jumars and ice tools and jam knots into cracks.

Late in the day. The base of the rock band. We find the stove Geoff and Andy have left. Our throats beg for water. We light the stove. Propane spurts from the valve, the stove erupts into a ball of flame and we kick it away.

"This is like a pub with no beer. Let's keep going," I say.

More rappels. Night falls. As we search for anchors we wander about the face unroped. I wonder if we know we are unroped. I pound the last blade into an amalgam of ice and rubble.

Hours later. Tim is calling from below. Tom and I have dropped off to sleep while standing at the belay, and Tim has fallen asleep while awaiting our descent. The difference between being awake and asleep has become barely distinguishable.

Moonglow lights our tents like a beacon. At 10:00 P.M. we crawl into them. As we drink our first water in thirty-six hours, our thirst is sated, just as the summit sated the worm.

A final dream, or hallucination, fills my head that night.

In that dream a man, a dear friend gone, wraps his arms around me, warming me.

The Law of
High Places

I felt ridiculous trying to outski an avalanche that had plunged, with an air-ripping crack, 5000 feet from the north side of Alaska's Mount Hunter and roared halfway across the Kahiltna Glacier in less time than it took to wipe the smile off my face. But a neat shot of adrenaline had my legs moving as if they belonged to a Nordic track champion. In my peripheral vision I watched a grey-white cloud steamroll toward me. It billowed and fumed, a demon unleashed from the stygian depths. "In trouble again," I thought to myself.

But where on this baby-bum-smooth snowfield did I think I would find protection? In the flimsy two-person tent that stood a hundred feet away? My partner, Michael Kennedy, stood at the tent's entrance. He wasn't smiling either.

"Oh Bubba, this one's coming our way!" he shouted to me as I poled the last few feet into camp. Michael held a camera to his face and shot a few frames, then his expression grew confused. "Am I a photojournalist or am I a pissing-pants-scared husband and father of a two-year-old?" the look seemed to say.

"Get in the tent. Weigh it down so the wind blast doesn't blow it away," I yelled.

"What are you gonna do?" Michael asked as he disappeared into the little shell of Gore-tex and aluminum poles.

"I'll get behind the tent."

Brilliant idea, I thought to myself. Like the Cold War tactic of sheltering from a nuclear explosion by digging a hole in the yard, hopping in it, then covering the ditch with the kitchen table. A mirage of protection. But with the grey morass now swallowing the grooves of my ski tracks, what else could I do? Lying behind the tent, I curled into a fetal ball, held my rucksack above my head, and peeked toward the rumbling cloud. I listened to my heart beat; it beat very fast. I heard Michael breathing inside the tent; he breathed very heavily.

The plume hung over us like a pall of smoke from a forest fire, or, more accurately, like photos I'd seen of the curtain of ash that descended from the eruption of Mount St. Helens. What I really thought about, though, was the time I inspected the remains of a Japanese expedition in China that had been smashed by an ice avalanche. A gargantuan serac had calved from the north wall of K2 and hurled down a tidal wave of wind and debris, uprooting the tents of the sleeping climbers and tossing them a hundred feet. Tents had ripped apart, emptying injured climbers and gear across the glacier. The mess resembled a highway pileup.

Cowering behind the tent, I felt my stomach muscles contract in anticipation of the coming cyclone. As the cold grey shadow descended and needle-shaped spicules of ice began landing on my clothing I hoped my will was in order, and I muttered subconsciously to Jesus, Mary and the Saints that I'd sell my ice axe and crampons if they let me off the hook just one more time. When the first shock wave rattled the tent I cringed like a kid flinching from a whupping. And then: the wind petered out, the greyness dissipated, and sunshine returned.

"Not so bad after all," I said, relieved.

"Nah, but you can never tell," Michael replied, his head emerging turtlelike from the tent.

Rising up from the lily-livered beastlike quadrupeds we had reverted to, we stood manlike again and dusted ourselves off. As my heart rate wound down to something approximating normal

I identified familiar chemicals of fear as they retreated from my bloodstream and returned to the glands of origin. We had, on that May day in 1993, reacquainted ourselves with a quintessential aspect of the mountaineering experience. In plain language, we had panicked. In the argot of climbing lingo, we had shat ourselves.

Twenty years of scaring myself and watching others get scared in the name of climbing has taught me that fear is a relative thing with degrees and boundaries that are different for all of us. We cope with little, childlike fears every day, like fear of spiders, the dark. Eek! A Mouse! Bigger fears, like phobias or psychological traumas, lurk deep in our psyches. When unleashed, these fears might turn a person into a gibbering maniac, or a frozen "'fraidy cat."

Just standing under the tottering potential energy of a mountain is enough to scare the average flatlander. But the difference between the fears encountered on a mountain climb and the momentary shock we experience when a snake drops out of a tree into our lap during a picnic is that climbers seek out and cultivate fear-filled circumstances, and they attempt to rein in this fear and master it like a wild mustang they've just lassoed.

In his memoir, the former Watergate burglar G. Gordon Liddy wrote about controlling his personal palette of fears. Rats were at the top of Liddy's list, so he went to an old pier, climbed down onto the rotting pilings, and sat in the shadows with dozens of sewer rats until they became no longer skin-crawling phobias, but simple fears. One could imagine that given enough time, Liddy might have found hanging out with rats to be pleasurable, in the same way that climbers learn to overcome the fear of heights and find a nervy sort of bliss when hanging by fingertips on a cliff, or when poised on an ice wall by the points of ice axe and crampons.

In my apprenticeship to mountaineering, I was too ignorant to realize just how scared I should have been when, in 1981, at age twenty-four, I found myself in India, high on an unclimbed spur of a 21,467-foot mountain called Shivling, a delta-shaped tusk sacred to the Hindu religion. It was an improbable place for me to be. I knew practically nothing about alpinism. I was a rock climber accustomed to sun-soaked cliffs below the snowline. My ice tools were undulled, and I was uneasy with tongue-tying alpine terms like bergschrund, cwm and couloir, which I consistently mispronounced. Common sense told me that a Himalayan climber is the product of a long apprenticeship on smaller peaks. But, at that point in my life, I lived by a seize-the-moment phrase from a novel by Kurt Vonnegut, which read "Strange suggestions to travel may be dancing lessons from God." Hence, when I was invited to Shivling for my first Himalayan expedition, I couldn't refuse the offer.

My partners on the first ascent of this mountain's sharply sculpted east pillars were Rick White, an Australian who had seen little more snow than I; Georges Bettembourg, a flamboyant Frenchman who earned a living hunting crystals and guiding in Chamonix; and Doug Scott, the iron-hard Englishman who had reached Himalayan summits such as Everest, Kangchenjunga and The Ogre. An unlikely foursome—two of the world's most accomplished alpinists teamed with two of the least accomplished (far from totally useless, Rick and I had been invited along for our rock-climbing skills)—we moved along the rocky ridge, from one tiny campsite to another.

Shivling presented Rick and me with daily, even hourly, opportunities to freak out. Being tiny dots on a 7000-foot climb that would require sixty difficult roped pitches was a sobering enough concept, but our surroundings and the exposed perches we slept on at night drove home the point that we were far from home and far beyond the warmth and help of humankind. As the winding Gangotri Glacier grew farther away each day, and the lifeless blue-white summits surrounding us grew nearer, an agoraphobic sense of loneliness and cold pervaded our thoughts.

The ridge, which seemed endless as a treadmill, took us

thirteen days to climb. When we ran out of food and went hungry for the last three days, I learned that hunger is a gnawing upset one never forgets. When we reached the point high up where we realized we didn't have enough equipment to descend the route in the event of injury or storm, and that we were committed to going over the top of the mountain and down the easier west side, I felt the lostness that a castaway adrift on a raft might feel. And another thing I learned to fear, which even today sets my heart thumping with trepidation, is the sight of black cloud banks sailing toward me across a gulf of warm blue sky to ram the mountain and unleash wind and storm and cold.

Oafish clumsiness nearly spelled disaster for Rick and me more than once. On the third day out we fumbled a stove gas canister and unwittingly let propane escape into the tent. When we lit the burner a second later the tent blew apart in a fiery explosion. Our shrieks echoed off Shivling's walls and woke Doug and Georges from their slumbers.

"What's wrong?" called Doug from out of the night.

"The tent! The tent!"

"What about the tent?"

"Is it insured?"

Patching the tent together and continuing on with scorched eyebrows, we reached the summit, pulling onto a wind-lashed dome of polished ice where we stood briefly, happily. From the summit, we climbed down tungsten-hard ice on the west face of Shivling, using blunt ice tools and balancing on weary, wobbly legs. Every step felt insecure. I was tense with the knowledge that my footing might skate from under me. Even when we stepped off the ice onto easier, snowier terrain, I felt gripped by the possibility that I might fall. It was an unshakable, negative cloud lodged in my thoughts. I paused to untie the rope linking Rick and me. If I did fall, why should I take a friend with me? But just as I began to unravel the knot I looked up to see Rick, a hundred feet above me, sliding down the slope, raking feverishly at a sugary patch of snow with his ice tool. The pick failed to arrest him. He gained speed.

"Here I come!" he yelled. It was the understatement of our lives.

The moment seemed to slow. A flood of possibilities entered my mind, and I examined my options: I could plunge the shaft of my ice tool into the slope and wrap the rope around it, but in the sun-softened snow it would rip right out; I could try to catch Rick as he slid by, but by the time I thought of that he had already zoomed past me; I could cut the rope, or untie it, but time had run out for that; or, I could jump off with him and ride the wild ride.

The coil of rope beside me whipped out as he fell, as if I had a harpooned whale on the end of it. Then, with a grand tug, the rope pulled against my waist, and I catapulted into the air.

We tumbled for 700 feet, legs and arms flailing like rag dolls, the wind beaten out of us as we bounced and bounced. Razor-sharp crystals of snow ground against my cheek as I slid face-first down the slope. A black blur, like a zebra stripe on the white field, signaled I had hurtled over a crevasse, then the white slide resumed. Slowly, we slid to a stop.

Only the hiss of sliding snow, running down the grooves etched by our falling bodies, broke the quiet windlessness of the next few moments. I stretched my limbs; nothing was broken. Rick lay face up, arms and legs akimbo, like a starfish, ten feet away. Georges and Doug arrived on the scene, expecting to find two corpses, but Rick, astoundingly uninjured, stood up and quipped to us all, "Well, it looks like we found the fast way down the mountain."

We had been out of our depth and out of control on Shivling, scared witless and shitless, but we still managed to function as climbers. My senses were reeling for days after we reached base camp. Strong images swirled through my head: of big mountains and outrageous circumstances, of thin air and of walking a tightrope between this world and the next, and of India, so exotic and strange. Near the foot of the mountain we visited a yogi who dwelled in a hollow tunneled beneath a boulder (yes, there are mystics who live like that). He pondered our notion of climbing Shivling and said, "First travel, then struggle, finally calm."

I wondered: Was our journey up Shivling just a climb? Or was there something to be learned from the fear and danger we had put ourselves through? Could there be more to climbing than just climbing?

I walked home through the crazy quilt of India wondering if there was some theorem—the law of high places, I eventually decided to call it—by which we could convert these magnificent and terrifying experiences on mountains into a measuring stick of the spirit. I imagined the law of high places as a Richter scale of fear. At the high end of the scale was a point beyond which the human organism could not function.

I had met a casualty of total fear meltdown once before, when I was fifteen years old. Oddly (or perhaps not) it was not on a mountain, but underground in a cave. The cave was one of hundreds riddled into a hillside in a place called Bungonia, a hundred miles south of Sydney, Australia. Four school friends and I were crawling on our hands and knees through a clay-floored passage that became progressively narrower the farther we probed. Periodically, the squeeze tunnel opened up into a dome-shaped chamber the size of a closet, and in these respites from the straitjacket-tight narrows we assembled to alternate the leader.

When it was my turn to lead, I slid into a hole the diameter of a heating duct. We achieved forward movement by an inver-tebratelike swimming motion, a sort of variation on the side stroke in which one arm was thrust forward and the shoulders and hips wriggled with contractions of the diaphragm. Earth-worms do it with more finesse.

The passage narrowed, forcing me to remove my helmet and push it along in front of me. Ten feet farther along it became tighter still, forcing me to twist my head sideways. My nose furrowed through moist ground. Smells of loam, bat guano and limestone were heady. As I inched along, the headlamp mounted on my helmet illuminated a gang of tiny eyes, crawling toward me. Several frogs appeared out of the dark. Washed into the tunnel by a recent heavy rain and now stranded and doomed in the pitch black, they flocked to the light. I collected them in my helmet with a mind to returning them to the surface, then I wriggled into another chamber, where I waited for my companions to emerge from the squeeze passage. When assembled again, we chose a new leader to spearhead our subterranean foray.

This kid crawled thirty feet into the passage, then stopped. We could see the soles of his boots, but when we asked why he wasn't moving he was as silent as a cork in a bottle. He lay still for ten minutes, until it occurred to us that he might have encountered a pocket of carbon dioxide and had lost consciousness. So we formed a human chain, and pulled on one another's ankles to drag him back to the chamber.

In the chamber he sat fully conscious but speechless. His face was white, and his eyes looked as glazed as yesterday's catch in a fish shop window. He breathed in rapid spasms, and he shivered even though the cave temperature was warm. He was not, we determined, cyanotic from CO_2, but he was stricken with an attack of claustrophobia so profound that he was in shock. We pushed, pulled and talked him back through the cave to the open air where, like the frogs I carried to the surface, he soaked up the daylight, breathed fresh air and returned to normal.

Claustrophobia was a fear this boy couldn't control, and I suspect he learned from this that caving wasn't in his future. But it showed me that in all of us there lurked a wavelength of fear so acute it could freeze the human system ice-solid. I supposed it lurked in me, too, but what would trigger it, and when, was something I had yet to learn.

In George Orwell's novel *1984,* the hapless character Winston is arrested for Thoughtcrime and incarcerated in the Ministry of Love. He watches as his fellow prisoners are reduced to hysteria whenever a guard fetches them from the cell and announces they are to be taken to Room 101. When Winston asks his torturer, O'Brien, what is in Room 101, he is told enigmatically, "You know what is in Room 101, Winston. Everyone knows what is in Room 101."

Winston learns the secret of the room when he faces O'Brien in it, toward the end of his interrogation. "The thing in Room 101," O'Brien informs him, "is the worst thing in the world."

"This varies from individual to individual," O'Brien explains. "It may be burial alive, or death by fire, or by drowning, or by impalement, or fifty other deaths. There are cases where it is some quite trivial thing, not even fatal."

Winston's worst fear in the world is (like G. Gordon Liddy's pet horror) rats, and O'Brien will duly terrorize him with a cage of them, but first O'Brien waxes lyrically on the subject of the limits of fear, saying, "… for everyone there is something unendurable—something that cannot be contemplated. Courage and cowardice are not involved. If you are falling from a height it is not cowardly to clutch at a rope. If you have come up from deep water it is not cowardly to fill your lungs with air. It is merely an instinct that cannot be disobeyed. It is the same with the rats. For you, they are unendurable. They are a form of pressure that you cannot withstand, even if you wish to.…"

I never thought circumstances would ever again get as out of hand as they had on Shivling, but, in 1989 on a granite spire in Pakistan, with a Coloradan named Mark Wilford, they got worse.

Trango Tower, sometimes called Nameless Tower, is a stiletto-sharp 20,463-foot rock turret of the Karakoram Range.

In its final 3000 feet it is encircled by smooth vertical cliffs that are seldom split by ledges. Mark and I planned to climb a new route on it, the northeast pillar. With enough food, fuel and equipment for a ten-day climb, we set off. To sleep on the vertical environment we toted a portable metal-framed hanging tent—a bunklike platform called a porta-ledge—which we suspended from pitons and nuts slotted into fractures in the cliff.

On a good day on Trango you can climb in a T-shirt. On a bad day it can kill you. For us, it snowed every day that first week on the mountain, at one point trapping us in the porta-ledge for three consecutive days. We emerged impatiently; claustrophobia and a diet of sardines and Power Bars made the atmosphere inside unbearable. It was like sleeping two in the trunk of a car—a Japanese compact, not a Cadillac.

A lull in the storm the tenth day conned us into striking our hanging camp and moving up. Almost as soon as we started climbing, high cirrus clouds, the harbingers of storm, blew in from the south. While Mark led around a formation shaped like a ship's prow, I hung below him, secured to an array of gadgets wedged into a crack. I watched the deteriorating weather. Premonitions that the mountain was going to turn ugly on us invaded my thoughts.

Mark inched carefully up a seamless stretch of wall on tiny steel claws called skyhooks, which he'd drape over pencil-thin flakes and hang on in etriers, or sling-ladders. Eighty feet into his lead, black clouds engulfed the tower. Snow began pouring out of them, then sleet. The temperature fluctuated like a fibrillating cardiogram, the wall became a fresco of ice. We were witnessing the phenomenon that ices the wings of jets and brings them down like plucked ducks. All the while, ice water gushed out of the crack I was secured to, pouring onto me.

"I'm freezing," I shouted, soaked after an hour. I noted the alien warble of hypothermia in my voice. It scared me. Dangling on that vast sheet of rock, I felt vulnerable and insignificant.

Mark, who was having no picnic either, did the only thing he could do: he kept climbing toward a good crack where he could secure the rope. Just as the temperature dropped another degree and the wall snap-froze into crystalline silence, Mark yelled "Come on up."

But ice had spread like a virus, freezing the rope into a snot-slick cable, clogging the cams of my rope ascenders and jamming the bearings of the pulley Mark would use to lift the bag containing our gear.

"Can't move," I called.

"Can't haul," Mark shouted back.

The situation was serious. We needed shelter now. A bivouac at my stance was unthinkable; it had become a waterfall. I had to reach Mark, and to do that, Mark had to drag up the haul bag and toss me a dry rope we'd stored inside it.

Shivering hours passed as we fussed with maneuvers to reunite us. I dropped a glove and my hand went numb. So I unlaced a boot, clipped it to myself and slipped off a sock to wear as a makeshift mitten. Even with the boot back on, my foot went numb. Plastered with ice, my Gore-tex suit creaked like rusty armor. Poisonous wet cold leached into my joints.

"Mark, if we don't get into the porta-ledge soon, we'll freeze," I called.

"I know," he said calmly, and slowly began to haul up the bag, hand over blistering hand.

Finally a dry rope snaked out of the fog. I clipped into it, swung across the wall, and ascended to Mark, who hung from a cluster of pitons hammered into a crack. By the time I reached him it was night. Waves of powder snow now cascaded over us, blasting our faces and coating everything with coral-like feathers. We fought with numb fingers to erect the porta-ledge, but ice clogged the snap-together frame and it refused to slot together. Just when we thought it was assembled and were able to sit in it, it collapsed, ejecting us into the night. Dangling from slings, we screamed insanely at the buckling contraption, the snow, the tower, each other.

"We're gonna die up here," I moaned in resignation.

"Shut up," retorted Mark.

I pulled myself together. By midnight we were inside the porta-ledge, massaging each other's cadaverous hands and feet.

For the next three days we lay like mummies in sarcophagi, listening to the static hiss of snow as it cascaded down the cliff and flowed over the pyramid-shaped nylon cover capping our shelter. Through the porta-ledge doorway, I gazed across at the ice-spattered 5000-foot northeast pillar of a neighboring mono-lith called Great Trango Tower. Shrouded in a thick white coat of mushy ice, the vertical wall was a mirror image of the cliff that trapped us. Five years before, four Norwegians had embarked on that wall's first ascent, a marathon climb lasting over twenty days. Only two had survived the ordeal.

The Norwegians' fate filled me with superstitious dread. There seemed to be a strange synchronicity between our adventure and theirs. Storms, altitude and too long on the wall had weakened the Norwegians until, during their descent, lax judgment caused them to place a bad anchor. It ripped out, and two of them plunged thousands of feet to the foot of the wall.

Trango Tower was sapping us, too. Our blood was thick and lazy in our veins. Our food and gas had dwindled. Outside, the air had warmed. Falling scabs of ice pounded the porta-ledge and our helmeted heads. To blot out this bedlam we concocted a nightly cocktail of a Halcion sleeping pill, codeine to numb our cramping limbs, and Ronikol to stimulate circulation in our perpetually cold feet. This didn't calm me, though. I felt we were living on borrowed time on Trango.

On the thirteenth day our pills ran out. Snow still streamed out of the sky. I asked Mark the big question: "How much more of this can you take?"

"As long as you can," he said stoically.

"Well, if we don't get out of here now, I have a feeling we'll never get down."

The words stuck in my craw. The hardest climbing was behind us; cracks above shot to the summit like an express lane on a freeway. Yet we'd run out of momentum. I chopped ice from the ropes and led off on the 2000-foot descent.

From outside, the porta-ledge looked like a car rammed into a Yukon snowdrift. We left it frozen in place, where it hangs to this day. Fifty feet down the first rappel my hands went numb. I thought of calling the retreat off, but the more I looked at the porta-ledge, framed in a halo of mist, the more it resembled a coffin, so I continued.

Manipulating carabiners and bits of climbing gear was a punishment. My mind felt befuddled. Cold wind bit into my face. I rappelled 150 feet, and hammered in a piton. It was now Mark's turn to rappel. When I looked up I saw the unthinkable: he was airborn, falling backwards in an arm-flapping reverse swan dive from his stance above me. A carabiner gate had twisted open, detaching him from the anchor when he had leaned on it. Squawking like a man having his throat cut, he lunged at a sling and clutched it at the last nanosecond.

"Jesus! Damn! My God!" he gasped along with a string of other expletives. He was shaken to the core.

Fifteen rappels and ten hours later, we flopped into base camp. Steam rose from our sodden, stinking clothes. "I don't believe we made it down alive," Mark wheezed in a dribbling slur. The gully beneath the wall had been chest-deep in snow. We'd waded down, trailing ropes from our waists, hoping that if one of us was avalanched, perhaps, just perhaps, the rope would lead the survivor to the victim.

Sleep took a long while to carry us away. Days of mayhem had filled our bodies with strange chemicals that kept us alert. Even when we did sleep it was a jumpy, paranoid slumber, filled with dreams of dodging falling iceblocks, of anchors ripping out, of smothering snowslides.

Our attempt to climb Trango Tower drained our minds and bodies for weeks afterward, yet after that stressful time we knew each other in a raw and honest way. We had lived, slept, eaten and crapped side by side for thirteen days. Our potential for conversation was spent. We had been close to the breaking point and had glimpsed the spiritual anarchy that lies beyond the threshold of the law of high places. Only by working together had we survived that Walpurgis Night of storm and the harrowing days around it. Still, I wondered: would I edge even closer to my breaking point?

The answer was yes. In 1990, on a river in the deserts of western China, a week after I had stood on top of K2, the law of high places exposed my Achilles heel and I found my own worst thing in the world.

The dozen members of our expedition were homeward bound. With three camel drivers and fifteen camels loaded with the material we had used to climb K2, we stood beside a minor tributary of the Shaksgam River, a little outflow of the North K2 Glacier. This ugly grey-brown torrent gushed with cyclotron velocity and chewed slices of dirt from its banks as if attempting to spill onto the land. We had to cross it.

The cameleers—Uigar men sporting natty flatcaps and dapper-looking, camel-smelling suitcoats—conferred with each other about the safest path across. They wore worried expressions. En route to the mountain in June, two months before, on this very crossing I had watched a camel tumble in front of me, and I had seen its Pakistani rider, my friend and expedition cook Ghulam Rasool, dragged away by the current. By an oversight of fate, man and beast were spat out 300 feet downstream, and though Rasool and his mount were beaten and bloodied, they were alive. Elsewhere, while we were climbing K2, an Italian expedition, which was crossing the nearby Suroquat River to reach the east face of Broad Peak—a river we, too, would have to cross—had watched a cameleer and three camels disappear in the current.

Our cameleers settled on a crossing and ordered us onto the backs of the animals. Atop boxes and duffel bags lashed to the stilt-legged creatures, we sat eight feet above the ground.

Ayub, the camel driver, glanced over his shoulder toward us, to check we were all mounted. His eye caught mine, and he studied my fear-contorted face. Something about the fast water made the corners of my lips twitch. My whole body trembled. Maybe, after the near disaster on this stream with Rasool in June, it was a case of once bitten, twice shy. Or maybe those days on K2 had left me a nervous, febrile wreck.

Ayub cast me a canny yet puzzled smile. "How can it be," he no doubt mused to himself, "that this foreigner who a few days ago stood on the summit of the Great Mountain trembles like a scared rabbit when faced with a little river crossing?" Then he prodded his beast forward and the caravan entered the water.

Clutching yak-hair ropes securing 200 pounds of equipment to the back of my camel, I lurched about as the animal loped through the stream with tentative steps. In midstream the roar of water was earsplitting. Melon-sized rocks clattered in the current like billiard balls in a busy pool hall. A rushing wind paralleled the current.

Near the far shore the water suddenly deepened, rising to the camels' bellies. The current forced the animals downstream. Breaking formation, they snapped the string nose-tethers that connected one beast to another. Weighed down by their loads and floundering in a deep hole, our ships-of-the-desert buckled at the forelegs and began to sink. Waves splashed my legs and chest. We clambered atop the loads.

The camels' long sea-serpentine necks poked out of the foaming water, and they screeched eerie, prehistoric-sounding cries of distress. A mental headline flashed in my mind: AUSTRALIAN-AMERICAN EXPEDITION CLIMBS WORLD'S SECOND-HIGHEST PEAK BUT PERISHES IN RIVER DISASTER.

I remember the feelings of the next seconds as a cavalcade

of hide-saving responses. I wanted out. I wanted home. I wanted to vomit. It was time to take up golf or gardening. But I felt frozen, immobile.

Until adrenaline took the helm. Following in the footsteps of my companions Greg Mortimer and Lyle Closs, I bounded from camel to camel, stepping in the crooks of the camels' necks and on their heads, then threw myself across the water onto the stony bank. Our movements were exact, our strength explosive, our timing perfect. We dragged the camels from the river, as well as a wide-eyed Ghulam Rasool who, on terra firma, checked the date on his watch and announced that this day—August 31—was, for him, another "lucky number day."

With the excitement over, I found myself walking in circles, hyperventilating, shaking and stuttering when I attempted to speak. My stomach muscles were painfully cramped, my arms and lips tingled electrically. I was petrified by fear and overdosed with adrenaline. I shuffled behind a mound of river stones, out of sight of my friends—they didn't need to see this, and anyway, it would be too hard to explain—then I dropped to my knees and let the emotions drain out of me in gasps verging on sobs.

Like the schoolboy in the cave, like Winston in Room 101, I had plumbed the depths of the law of high places and found a hellish and incapacitating fear, not on a mountain, but while perched atop a stinking, sinking camel on a frigid torrent in China. An elegantly humbling discovery for someone who considered himself to be unflappable after twenty years of climbing.

K2

THE WORLD'S SECOND-HIGHEST PEAK, K2, drew me three times before I climbed its north ridge in China in 1990. While my teammates and I took our chances on Gasherbrum IV in 1986, a tragedy was playing itself out on K2, a few miles from us. "The Dangerous Summer" describes that season, in which thirteen of the world's best climbers perished in a succession of accidents. Written in collaboration with Jon Krakauer, the story appeared in *Outside* in 1986. At the time we wrote it, little was known about the ordeal, as most participants were dead or hospitalized, so many hours were spent on long-distance lines hunting down facts. The story meditated on the element of risk inherent in climbing big peaks. Since that season on K2, the odds have caught up with several of the top alpinists who figure in the story: Michel Parmentier froze to death on Everest, Jerzy Kukuczka fell from near the top of Lhotse, Petr Bozik perished near Everest's summit and Wanda Rutkiewicz disappeared high on Kangchenjunga.

While hiking home from an unsuccessful attempt on K2 in 1987 I penned "In Another Tongue." Though ostensibly a piece of fiction, the impressions in it are based on my talks with Balti porters, whose paths I've crossed many times over the years. Ever since my first trip up the Baltoro Glacier, I'd wondered what the Balti thought about us foreigners pitting ourselves against their mountains. The story is a look at mountaineering through their eyes. It appeared in *Climbing* in 1988 and in the Diadem/ Sierra Club Books omnibus of climbing fiction, *One Step in the Clouds*.

Our successful ascent of K2 in 1990 was a complex venture that carried thirteen people across China by airplane, truck and camel. I'd never felt so fired up to climb a mountain as with K2, and when *Climbing* asked me to write about the climb I focused on the drama of our last day to the summit, on August 20, 1990. "A Margin of Luck" struck me as an apt title, as we pulled off the ascent in the last days of the season and with the last of our energy.

THE DANGEROUS SUMMER

In the northernmost corner of Pakistan, in the heart of the Karakoram Range, is a thirty-five-mile tongue of rubble-strewn ice called the Baltoro Glacier. Six of the seventeen highest mountains on the planet loom above the Baltoro, and last June, at its head, were pitched 150 tents sheltering expeditions from ten nations. Most of the people in those tents, whose ranks included some of the world's most highly regarded and ambitious climbers, had their sights set on a single summit, K2.

At 28,250 feet, K2 is almost 800 feet lower than Mount Everest, but its sharper, more graceful architecture makes it a more striking mountain—and a much harder one to climb. Indeed, of the fourteen mountains in the world over 8000 meters, K2 has the highest failure rate. By 1985 only nine of the twenty-six expeditions that had attempted it had succeeded, putting a total of thirty-nine people on the summit—at a cost of twelve lives. Last year the government of Pakistan granted an unprecedented number of climbing permits for K2, and by the end of the summer, an additional twenty-seven climbers had made it to the top. But for every two who summited, one would die—thirteen deaths in all, more than doubling the number of fatalities in the preceding eighty-four years. The toll would raise some thorny questions about the recent course of Himalayan climbing, a course some believe is growing increasingly reckless.

The present direction was set, it's generally agreed, in the summer of 1975, when Reinhold Messner and Peter Habeler pioneered a new route up 26,470-foot Hidden Peak without bottled oxygen, a support team, fixed ropes, a chain of pre-established camps or any of the other siege tactics that had traditionally been de rigueur in the Himalaya. In a single stroke, they significantly upped the ante in a game that never lacked for high stakes and tough odds to begin with. When Messner first announced he would climb an 8000-meter Himalayan peak in the same manner that climbers tackled routes in the Tetons and the Alps, many of the world's foremost climbers called the attempt impossible and suicidal. But after he and Habeler succeeded, anyone with designs on staying at the top of the heap had no choice but to attack the highest mountains in the world by what Messner has pointedly termed "climbing by fair means."

The most coveted prize on K2 last summer was its unclimbed south pillar, a "last great problem" that Messner had nicknamed the Magic Line. Soaring two miles to the summit, it demanded more steep, technical climbing at high altitude than anything previously done in the Himalaya.

There were four teams attempting the Magic Line last summer, including an American one under the leadership of a thirty-five-year-old Oregonian named John Smolich. On June 21, Smolich and partner Alan Pennington were climbing an easy approach gully at the base of the route when, far above them, the sun loosened a truck-size rock from the ice, sending it careening down the mountainside. As soon as it struck the top of the gully, a fifteen-foot-deep fracture line shot across the low-angle slope, triggering a massive avalanche that engulfed both men in seconds. Climbers who witnessed the slide quickly located and dug out Pennington, but not in time to save his life. Smolich's body, buried under tons of avalanche debris, was never found.

The surviving members of the American team called off their climb and went home, but the other expeditions on the mountain regarded the tragedy as a freak accident, simply a matter of being at the wrong place at the wrong time.

Indeed, on June 23, two Basques—Mari Abrego and Josema Casimaro—and four members of a French-Polish expedition—Maurice and Liliane Barrard, Wanda Rutkiewicz and Michel Parmentier—reached the summit of K2 via the easiest route, the Abruzzi Spur. Rutkiewicz and Liliane Barrard thereby became the first women to stand on top of K2, and they did so without using bottled oxygen.

All six climbers, however, were forced by darkness to bivouac high on the precipitous flanks of the summit pyramid. They survived the night, but by morning the clear, cold skies that had prevailed the previous week had given way to a bad storm. During the ensuing descent, the Barrards—both very experienced Himalayan climbers with other 8000-meter summits under their belts—dropped behind and never reappeared. Parmentier guessed that they had fallen or been swept away by an avalanche, but he nonetheless stopped to wait for them in a high camp, while Rutkiewicz and the Basques, whose noses and fingertips had begun to turn black from frostbite, continued down.

That night, June 24, the storm worsened. Awakening to a complete whiteout and vicious winds, Parmentier radioed base camp by walkie-talkie that he was descending; but with the fixed ropes and all traces of his companions' footprints buried by fresh snow, he soon became lost on the broad, featureless south shoulder of K2. He staggered around in the blizzard at 26,000 feet with no idea of where to go, muttering "grande vide, grande vide" (big emptiness), as climbers in base camp tried to guide him down over the radio by their recollections of the route.

"I could hear the desperation and fatigue in his voice as he went back and forth in the storm, looking for some clue," said Alan Burgess, a member of a British expedition attempting the northwest ridge. "Finally, Parmentier found a dome of ice with a urine stain on it, and we remembered it. By this insignificant landmark we could guide him down the rest of the route by voice. He was very lucky."

On July 5, four Italians, a Czech, two Swiss and a Frenchman, Benoit Chamoux, reached the summit via the Abruzzi route. Chamoux's ascent, a single twenty-four-hour push from base camp, was a mind-boggling athletic feat, especially considering that just two weeks before he had sprinted up the neighboring slopes of 26,400-foot Broad Peak in seventeen hours.

The real action, though, was on K2's south face: a two-mile-high expanse of ice-plastered vertical rock, avalanche gullies and hanging glaciers delineated on one side by the Abruzzi Spur and on the other by the Magic Line. On July 4, Polish climbers Jerzy Kukuczka, thirty-eight, and Tadeusz Piotrowski, forty-six, started up the center of this unclimbed wall in light, impeccably pure style, hell-bent on pushing the limits of Himalayan climbing to a new plane.

Kukuczka was the heir apparent to Messner's unofficial world high-altitude climbing title. When he arrived at K2, he was hot on Messner's tail in the race to knock off all fourteen of the world's 8000-meter peaks. He had already bagged ten of them, an especially impressive accomplishment considering the expense of mounting Himalayan expeditions and the absurdly low exchange rate of Polish zlotys. To fund their expeditions, Kukuczka and his Polish comrades had been routinely forced to smuggle vodka, rugs, running shoes and other unlikely commodities that could be bartered for hard currency.

Just before sunset on July 8, after a lot of extreme technical climbing and four rough bivouacs (the last two of which were without tent, sleeping bags, food or water), Kukuczka and Piotrowski struggled to the summit in a howling storm. They immediately began to descend the Abruzzi Spur. Two days later, totally strung out and still battling their way down through the blizzard unroped, Piotrowski—who, because of numb fingers, had been unable to properly secure his crampons that morning—stepped on a patch of steel-hard ice and lost a crampon.

He stumbled, righted himself, then lost the other crampon. An attempt to self-arrest wrenched his ice axe out of his hands, and he was soon hurtling down the steepening slope, out of control. Kukuczka could do nothing but watch helplessly as his partner bounced off some rocks and disappeared into the clouds.

By then the summer's death toll was beginning to give pause to most of the climbers still on the mountain, but for many the lure of the summit proved stronger. Kukuczka himself departed immediately for Nepal to attempt his twelfth 8000-meter peak and gain ground on Messner in the race to knock off all fourteen. (The effort would prove to be in vain after Messner reached the summits of Makalu and Lhotse later in the fall, claiming the fourteen-summit title.)

Shortly after Kukuczka returned to base camp to tell his grim tale, the renowned Italian solo climber Renato Casarotto, thirty-eight, embarked on his third attempt that summer to climb the Magic Line. This would be, he had promised his wife, Goretta, "the last time." Although Casarotto had achieved acclaim through solo ascents of difficult new routes on FitzRoy, Mount McKinley and other major peaks in South America and the Alps, he was, paradoxically, a very cautious, calculating climber. On July 16, a thousand feet below the summit and not liking the look of the weather, he prudently abandoned his attempt and descended the entire south pillar to the glacier at its base.

As Casarotto made his way across the final stretch of glacier before base camp, climbers watching through binoculars from camp saw him pause in front of a narrow crevasse and prepare to hop across it. To their horror, the soft snow at the edge of the crevasse gave way and he suddenly disappeared, plunging 120 feet into the bowels of the glacier. Alive but badly injured at the bottom of the ice-blue hole, he raised his wife on his walkie-talkie and she summoned a rescue party. They hauled him out after an all-night struggle, but back on the surface of the ice, Casarotto stood up, took a few steps, and then lay down on his rucksack and died.

The only expedition on K2 to make no effort to conform to Messnerian ethics was a mammoth, nationally sponsored team from South Korea. Indeed, the Koreans cared little how they got to the top, as long as they got someone there and back in one piece. To that end, they employed 450 porters to haul a small mountain of gear and supplies to base camp and then methodically proceeded to string miles of fixed rope and a chain of well-stocked camps up the Abruzzi Spur.

Late in the day on August 3, in perfect weather, three Koreans reached the summit using bottled oxygen. After starting their descent, they were overtaken by two exhausted Poles and a Czech, who, using conventional siege tactics but no oxygen, had just succeeded in making the first ascent of the coveted Magic Line. As both parties descended together into the night, the famous Polish alpinist Wojciech Wroz, his attention dulled by hypoxia and fatigue, inadvertently rappelled off the end of a fixed rope in the dark—the seventh casualty of the season. The next day, Muhammed Ali, a Pakistani porter ferrying loads near the base of the mountain, became victim number eight after he was hit by a falling rock.

Most of the Europeans and Americans on the Baltoro last summer had initially disparaged the ponderous, dated methods by which the Koreans made their way up the Abruzzi Spur. But as the season wore on and the mountain prevailed, several weren't above using the ladder or ropes and tents the Koreans had erected.

Seven men and women from Poland, Austria and Great Britain succumbed to this temptation after their expeditions had packed it in, and decided to loosely join forces on the Abruzzi. As the Koreans got ready for their final assault, the ad hoc, polyglot group made its way up the lower flanks of the mountain, and, in fact, all five men and two women joined the Koreans at Camp IV at 26,250 feet—the highest camp—the day before the Koreans mounted their successful summit bid.

While the Koreans made their way to the top in flawless

weather, the Austro-Anglo-Polish team remained in the tents, having decided to wait a day to make their own push for the summit. The reasons for this decision are complex. That anyone could contemplate "resting" at nearly 8000 meters is hard to imagine, but the nights of August 2 and 3 were sleepless due to the overcrowding of tents when the Korean and Magic Line teams had appeared, on their ways up and down, looking for shelter.

Incredibly, there were only three tents at Camp IV for a dozen climbers. Though Diemberger and Tullis, and Rouse and Wolf brought two tents up, the Austrians Bauer, Imitzer and Weiser were using a tent belonging to the Koreans. They'd carried it up from a lower camp when they'd found their own camp had been avalanched. Kurt Diemberger, in fact, had warned them of this, when he'd found debris on the glacier he recognized as having been swept down from the Austrian camp, but the Austrians hadn't heeded the warning.

When the Austrians found themselves without a tent, they struck a deal with the Koreans to pitch their tent at the high camp, sleep in it on August 1 and make a summit bid on August 2, but they agreed to vacate the tent and descend that afternoon to let the Korean summit team use their tent. As it turned out, the Austrians climbed only part way through the deep snow toward the summit on August 2 and were back at Camp IV that night, begging and arguing with the newly arrived Koreans for shelter. No one slept, and August 3 was even more crowded when the Magic Line team appeared at Camp IV.

By the time the European team finally started up the summit tower on the morning of August 4, the weather was about to change. "There were great plumes of clouds blowing in from the south, and it became obvious that major bad weather was on the way," says Jim Curran, a British climber and filmmaker on the unsuccessful British northwest ridge expedition who was down at base camp at the time. "Everyone must have been aware that they were taking a great risk by pressing on," he adds, "but

I think when the summit of K2 is within reach, you might be inclined to take a few more chances."

Thirty-four-year-old Alan Rouse, one of England's most accomplished climbers, and Dobroslawa Wolf, a thirty-year-old Polish woman, were the first to start up the summit pyramid, but Wolf quickly tired and dropped back. Rouse continued, however, taking on the exhausting work of breaking trail for most of the day until, at 3:30 in the afternoon, just below the top, he was finally joined by Austrians Willi Bauer, forty-four, and Alfred Imitzer, forty. About 4:00 P.M. the three men reached the summit, and Rouse, the first Englishman to reach the top of K2, commemorated the event by hanging a Union Jack from two oxygen cylinders the Koreans had left. During the threesome's descent, 500 feet below the summit, they saw Wolf asleep in the snow, and after a heated discussion, Rouse persuaded her that she should turn around and go down with him.

Soon Rouse met two other members of the team on their way up, Austrian Kurt Diemberger and Englishwoman Julie Tullis. The fifty-four-year-old Diemberger was a celebrity in Western Europe, a legendary Bergsteiger—mountain leader—whose career spanned two generations. He had been a partner of the heroic Hermann Buhl and had climbed five 8000-meter peaks. Tullis, forty-seven, was both a protégé and close friend of Diemberger's, and though she wasn't as experienced as many of the others on K2 that year, she was very determined and very strong and had been to the top of Broad Peak with Diemberger in 1984. Climbing K2 together was a dream that had consumed the two of them for years.

Because of the late hour and the rapidly deteriorating weather, Rouse, Bauer and Imitzer all tried to persuade Diemberger and Tullis to forgo the summit and head down. They mulled over this advice, but, as Diemberger later told a British newspaper, "I was convinced it was better to try it finally after all these years. And Julie, too, said, 'Yes, I think we should go on.' There was risk, but climbing is about justifiable risks." At 7:00 P.M., when

Diemberger and Tullis got to the summit, that risk appeared to be justified. They hugged each other, and Tullis gushed, "Kurt, our dream is finally fulfilled: K2 is now ours!" They stayed on top about ten minutes, snapped a few pictures and then, in the evening's gathering gloom, turned to go down, joined by fifty feet of rope.

Almost immediately after leaving the summit, Tullis, who was above Diemberger, slipped. "For a fraction of a second," says Diemberger, "I thought I could hold us, but then we both started sliding down the steep slope, which led to a huge ice cliff. I thought, 'My God, this is it. This is the end.'" At the foot of the mountain during the ascent from base camp, they had come across the body of Liliane Barrard, where it had been deposited after her 10,000-foot fall from the upper slopes three weeks earlier, and the image of Barrard's broken form now flashed into Diemberger's mind. "The same thing," he thought, "is happening to us."

But somehow, miraculously, they managed to stop before shooting over the edge of the ice cliff. Then, fearing another fall in the dark, instead of continuing down they simply hacked out a shallow hollow in the snow and spent the remainder of the night there, above 27,000 feet, shivering together in the open. In the morning the storm was upon them in earnest, Tullis had developed frostbite on her nose and fingers and she was having problems with her eyesight—possibly indicating cerebral edema—but they had survived the night. By noon, when they reached the tents of Camp IV and the company of their five fellow climbers, they thought the worst was behind them.

As the day progressed, the storm worsened, generating prodigious amounts of snow, winds in excess of 100 miles per hour, and subzero temperatures. The tent Diemberger and Tullis were in collapsed under the brunt of the storm, so he crowded into Rouse and Wolf's tent, and she moved in with Bauer, Imitzer and Hannes Weiser, an Austrian who hadn't gone to the summit.

Sometime during the night of August 6, while the storm

continued to build, the combined effects of the cold, the altitude and the ordeal of Tullis's fall and forced bivouac caught up to her, and she died. In the morning, when Diemberger learned of her death, he was devastated. Later that day, the six survivors used up the last of both their food and fuel, without which they couldn't melt snow for water.

Over the next three days, as their blood thickened and their strength drained away, Diemberger says they "reached the stage where it is hard to tell dreams from reality." Diemberger, drifting in and out of bizarre hallucinations, watched Rouse go downhill much faster than the rest of them and sink into a state of constant delirium, apparently paying the price for the energy and fluid he had expended breaking trail on the summit day. Rouse, recalls Diemberger, "could speak only of water. But there wasn't any, not even a drop. And the snow we were trying to eat was so cold and dry it barely melted in our mouths."

On the morning of August 10, after five days of unabated storm, the temperature dropped to –20° F and the wind continued to blow as hard as ever, but the snow stopped falling and the sky cleared. Those who were still able to think clearly realized that if they didn't make their move right then, they weren't going to have enough strength left to make a move at all.

Diemberger, Wolf, Imitzer, Bauer and Weiser immediately started down. They believed they didn't stand a chance of getting Rouse down in his semicomatose condition, so they made him as comfortable as they could and left him in his tent. No one harbored any illusions that they would see him again. The five conscious survivors, in fact, were in such bad shape themselves that the descent quickly became a case of everyone for himself.

Within a few hundred feet of leaving camp, Weiser and Imitzer collapsed from the effort of struggling through the waist-deep snow. "We tried in vain to stir them," says Diemberger. "Only Alfred reacted at all, weakly. He murmured that he couldn't see anything." Weiser and Imitzer were left where they lay, and with Bauer breaking trail, the other three kept fighting their way down. A few hours later Wolf dropped behind and did not reappear. Diemberger and Bauer waited awhile and then decided she must have fallen after inadvertently becoming unclipped from one of the fixed ropes. In fact, she'd expired on the ropes, and her body—brittle as a piece of driftwood—was found and buried by climbers the following year.

Bauer and Diemberger made it to Camp III at 24,000 feet, only to find that it had been destroyed by an avalanche. They pressed on toward Camp II, at 21,000 feet, where, after dark, they arrived to find food, fuel and shelter. Late the next night, August 11, Bauer—horribly frostbitten and barely alive—finally staggered into base camp "looking like an apparition," in Jim Curran's words.

Unable to speak properly, he nonetheless managed to communicate that Diemberger, too, was still alive somewhere above, and Curran and two Polish climbers immediately set out to look for him. They found him, in the middle of the night, moving at a crawl down the fixed ropes between Camp II and advanced base camp. They spent all of the next day getting him to base camp, from where, on August 16, he and Bauer were evacuated by helicopter to face months in hospitals and multiple amputations of their fingers and toes.

When garbled word of this final disaster reached Europe, it became headline news. Initially, particularly in England, the once-popular Diemberger was vilified by the media for leaving Rouse to die at Camp IV after Rouse, instead of beating a safe and hasty retreat from high camp on August 5, had waited to make sure that Diemberger and Tullis would return from their overnight ordeal on the summit pyramid.

Curran insists that such criticism is unjustified. Rouse and the others, he believes, stayed at Camp IV on August 5 not just to wait for Diemberger and Tullis, but because they "must have been incredibly tired from the day before, and the storm would have made it extremely difficult to find the route. Everyone was aware that Michel Parmentier had nearly gotten lost trying to find his way down there in similar conditions."

And when the descent was finally begun from Camp IV, says Curran, "there was absolutely no way that either Diemberger or Willi Bauer could have gotten Rouse off the mountain alive. They were both nearly dead themselves. It was an unimaginably desperate situation; I don't think it's possible to pass judgment about it from afar."

Still, it's difficult not to compare that turn of events with a strikingly similar predicament eight K2 climbers found themselves in thirty-three years earlier—at very nearly the same place on the mountain. The climbers, led by Dr. Charles Houston, were camped at 25,000 feet on the then unclimbed Abruzzi Spur, preparing to make a push for the summit, when hit by a blizzard that pinned them down for nine days. Toward the end of the storm, a young climber named Art Gilkey came down with a deadly ailment called thrombophlebitis, a clotting of the veins brought on by altitude and dehydration.

Gilkey's seven companions, in no great shape themselves, though considerably better off than Diemberger and company, realized that he stood almost no chance of surviving and that trying to save him would endanger them all. But, says Houston, "so strong had become the bonds between them that none thought of leaving him and saving themselves—it was not to be dreamed of, even though he would probably die of his illness." In the course of being hauled down the mountain, Gilkey was swept to his death by an avalanche.

It can be argued that the decision not to abandon Gilkey in 1953 was the height of heroism, or that it was foolishly emotional—that had an avalanche not taken Gilkey off his teammates' hands, their chivalrous gesture would have resulted in eight deaths instead of one. Viewed in that light, the decision by those who survived K2 in 1986 seems not cold-hearted or cowardly, but eminently sensible.

But if the actions of Diemberger and Bauer appear to be

justified, larger, more troubling questions remain. If it is natural in any sport to seek ever greater challenges, what is to be made of a sport in which doing this means taking ever greater risks?

For as long as people have been climbing in the Himalaya, a significant percentage of them have died there as well. But the carnage on K2 in 1986 was something else again. A recent and comprehensive analysis of the data shows that, from the beginning of Himalayan climbing through 1985, approximately one of every thirty people who has attempted an 8000-meter peak has not come back from it; on K2 last summer that figure was, unbelievably, almost one of five.

It is hard not to attribute that grim statistic at least in part to Reinhold Messner's astounding string of mountaineering feats over the past decade and a half. Messner's brilliance has, perhaps, distorted the judgment of some of those who would compete with him, giving unwarranted confidence to climbers who lack the uncanny "mountain sense" that has kept Messner alive all these years. A handful may have what it takes to stay at the table in the high roller's game, but some seem to have lost sight of the fact that the losers in such games tend to lose very big.

Jim Curran, who spent the entire summer on the Baltoro, cautions that you can't really make generalizations about why so many people died in the Karakoram last summer. He points out that "people got killed climbing with fixed ropes and without fixed ropes; people got killed at the top of the mountain and the bottom; old people got killed and young people got killed."

Curran does say, however, that "if anything was common to most of the deaths, it was that a lot of people were very ambitious and had a lot to gain by climbing K2—and a lot to lose as well. Casarotto, the Austrians, Al Rouse, the Barrards were all—the word that comes to mind is overambitious. If you're going to try alpine-style ascents of 8000-meter peaks, you've got to leave yourself room to fail."

Too many people on K2 last summer, it would appear, did not.

IN ANOTHER TONGUE

The Balti porters had returned to the base camps at the foot of the mountain that foreigners call K2. For the climbers the season of 1987 was over. Winter was in the air. The last expedition was packing up to trek back down the Baltoro Glacier.

Young Karim and his uncle, Hussein, stood on the glacier, beneath the big pile of stones, crosses and inscribed plates where foreigners commemorated their dead. Both porters came from the village of Ste Ste, a little green patch on a hillside above the Braldu River. This was Karim's first season portering on the Baltoro. It was Hussein's twelfth and, he promised, his last. K2—the Balti call it Keetu—stood upvalley. Although the sky was clear, a strong wind blew a long stream of cloud westward from the mountain's summit. Hussein was just finishing telling Karim about the many tragedies on K2 the summer before, in 1986.

"Success, then death; success, then death. That was the way it was last year. They would reach the summit but never get back down. Some of them are buried here," Hussein said, indicating the stone memorial.

"And the others?" asked Karim.

Hussein pointed to K2.

"There," he said.

"They must become very rich and famous, to risk their lives

like that, *cha cha*," Karim said, addressing his uncle with the affectionate title given to elders.

"They will tell you otherwise. They will tell you they are poor men, every one of them."

"But look at all they have! Look at what they leave behind. Enough food to feed a village! Enough boxes to build a village!" exclaimed Karim.

Karim and Hussein looked toward the narrow strip of moraine on which expeditions camped. Tents were coming down, bags were being packed, bonfires of unwanted things were melting black pits in the ice. Around the base camp porters sat huddled in groups, wrapped in their ragged blankets, while *poroks,* the fat ravens that roost in the cliffs at the foot of K2, perched on boulders waiting, like the porters, for unwanted things to be tossed to them.

"If they do not become rich by climbing Keetu, and they are not already rich when they come here, why do they do it, *cha cha?*"

"They answer that question in many ways. But I'll tell you that the truth is one of three things: either they are liars and all of them are rich, or they tell the truth and all of them are mad, or they have good hearts and are hunters."

"Hunters?" Karim asked, a little confused.

"Yes. They stalk the summit the way we stalk ibex, the way your grandfather once stalked snow leopard and bear. Perhaps for them, each of these mountains is a different animal. Some are easy to hunt. Others, like Keetu, are very dangerous."

Karim considered his uncle's analogy while looking from the mountain to the memorial.

"I think the mountain is the one that is stalking the sahibs," he concluded.

"Yes. But that is all part of the hunt," said Hussein.

Hussein did not know his age, but he knew that he was too old to carry many more heavy loads into the mountains. He would not have left Ste Ste that year except for the pledge he had made to Karim's father—Hussein's older brother—to look after the boy on his first carry up the Baltoro. Karim's father, Muhammet, had died the year before while rebuilding a rope bridge that spanned the turbulent Braldu River. Hussein had been with Muhammet, his elder brother and the village bridge-maker, securing strands of twined willow twigs. Some day, they hoped, a strong cable bridge would replace this rickety affair, but till then they repaired the rope bridge each spring. "Hussein, I must ask you to look after the boy if he works as a porter next year," Muhammet had said. "He is of age and the family needs the money. I'd go, but you know that the aqueducts to the upper pastures must be rebuilt and the village can't spare me."

Hussein complained to his brother that his knees and ankles crackled from too many carries up and down the Baltoro. He wanted to stop portering. He had saved enough money now to make his pilgrimage to Mecca, and he wanted to go the next year.

"We'll discuss it later. I must go to the other side of the bridge and finish some things there," Muhammet had said.

But when he was in the middle of the swaying rope bridge an errant gust of wind had rushed down the valley. The bridge vibrated and bounced like a piece of string. The violent jolt took Muhammet by surprise. He lost his footing and fell into the surging river and was never seen again. So, like a blood debt, Hussein had accompanied Karim into the mountains, to teach him all he knew about finding the way in and out of that frozen wasteland and to educate him in the strange ways of the foreigners.

"If it's money you want, then it's money I'll teach you about. To get rich, you don't carry just for one expedition, you carry in and out for them all," Hussein told the boy. So, together, they went with Spanish, Japanese, French and Americans, in and out, to and from the Gasherbrums, Chogolisa and K2. Karim watched his pockets swell with rupees. In one summer he earned as much money as his family's land could produce in a whole year.

Karim was young, about twenty, yet already he had a wife and child, and now, with his father gone, the responsibility of supporting his mother and grandparents fell onto him. Being a young Balti, he looked beyond the boundaries of his village for a dream of the future. He did not want to be a landlocked farmer all his life. In Karim's short lifetime much had changed in the Braldu Valley. Foreigners were pouring in to climb and to trek. The border war with India had brought the army with its helicopters. If you worked as a porter for the army, the pay was double what you would make as an expedition porter. But you were paid to be shot at as well. The border strife was also pushing the road from Dassu toward the town of Askole, across the river from Ste Ste. It would be only a matter of time before a jeep could drive up the valley in a day, whereas now the foot journey from Dassu to Askole took three days.

It was to the road that Karim looked for his future. He had been to Skardu, where the streets teemed with jeeps and Toyotas and tourists. He'd seen how rich the jeep drivers and jeep owners could become by transporting expeditions and trekkers up the road to the start of the foot trail. To own a jeep and take the wealthy foreigners up the Braldu Gorge was Karim's dream.

Old Hussein's dreams were less ambitious. Experience had taught him that all he could count on from life was hard work, and more hard work. With the money earned from the season of portering he would buy another yak to pull his plough and a few sacks of flour to tide the family over through the winter. Like last year, spring had been late again, promising a lean wheat harvest. When the snows came in winter and travel along the valley became impossible, neither dreams of roads and jeeps, nor fat piles of rupees, would feed hungry bellies. These things Hussein knew.

With his dreams of the future, Karim absorbed all the knowledge he could from his uncle, until by summer's end he could sniff his way along the glacier like an ant following a scented trail, sensing the best path through the stones and fissures in the ice. It was as if those instincts of mountain travel had always been within him and he'd only needed Hussein's coaching to draw them out.

Hussein had been along the glacier so many times that he recognized almost every rock and rise. He showed the boy how to secure a load to his back without rubbing his shoulders raw, the best places to sleep in every camp, hiding spots on the glacier in which he could store rations, the paths along the river in high water and low water and which wild plants could be eaten along the way. He taught him which village men to trust and which ones to be wary of, and introduced him to groups of his old friends so that Karim would always know someone on the trail and be able to spend a night singing around a fire in a cave or in a stone circle with good people. He taught Karim the peculiarities of the peculiar, like the porter Ibrahim, who often woke at night screaming of approaching mountain demons, and who could be sobered only with a bash on the head. He showed Karim how to move through snow and probe for crevasses, where there was danger on the glacier and where there was not, the pace at which to move with a heavy load and how to use a wooden stave for balance on slick ice.

Karim learned these things quickly and learned other things too. He saw that a sirdar—the manager of a porter caravan—earned a better wage than a porter, didn't carry a load and gave orders to everyone. He saw that a guide hired by trekkers earned even more and was provided with fine clothes and good shoes. As was an expedition cook, who earned more than them all. There was money here, and in time he would do these things.

As they walked back to camp they chanced across the rubbish pit of a past expedition and Karim poked at something protruding from a snowpatch. Hussein bent down and extracted an unopened packet of foreign food. The two Baltis opened the packet, sniffed it, but could make nothing of the contents.

"What do you suppose it is, *cha cha*?"

"Who knows? It is a mystery to me how these people eat such things. You know, boy, I've seen them eat pig! Pig!"

The foreigners were strange, thought Karim. They looked, lived, acted and talked differently. When they came to the mountains they brought a homeful of belongings with them, but they brought so much that they left half of it behind. And not content with their own things, they bought up the wares from the villages. Old hats, old shoes, bowls, rocks, anything. Karim remembered that when he was a boy his father had taught him to catch grasshoppers and sell them for a rupee to expeditions. Sometimes the sahibs, usually the ones from Japan, would buy the insects and then release them. Karim's father and his friends always collapsed in laughter when the sahibs bought a grasshopper. "See? They'll buy anything!" his father used to say, laughing.

The sirdar of the expedition for which Karim and Hussein were carrying shouted that it was time to gather up the loads and depart for Concordia. Old Hussein looked at K2 one last time. If all went as he hoped, he would never see it again.

"*Cha cha,* is it true that no sahibs climbed to the top this year?" Karim asked, suddenly aware that all the labor of the foreigners had amounted to nothing.

"Yes. The weather has been very bad, just as I prayed for it to be."

"What do you mean?"

"After I learned that so many of the sahibs for whom I carried last year had died after climbing K2, I prayed to Allah for storms to rage all summer so that none of them would have a chance to climb to the top. That way they would live a little longer. And see? Allah does answer a just prayer."

"Do you really think that Allah has answered your prayer, uncle?" Karim asked with a skeptical grin.

"Of course, boy! The weather has been bad all summer and no one has reached the summit. Ask the sahibs yourself."

"But one man died."

"True, Karim. That just means I'll have to pray harder next year."

A Margin of Luck

I hate the cold. I hate the way it seeps into my bones like an invading army, leaving my toes and fingers narcotically numbed and cadaverous in the wake of total corpuscular retreat. So what am I doing here, at 8000 meters on the north ridge of K2, swinging my hands back and forth to force blood into them?

It's a question I cannot answer. Maybe Himalayan climbing is just a bad habit, like smoking, of which one says with cavalier abandon, "Must give this up someday, before it kills me."

Last night was a lousy, cramped bivouac. Four sets of lungs sucking at the walls of the tiny tent, coughing and hacking up bits of trachea, mumbling in a half-sleep as if possessed by spirits.

The stove putters pathetically against the morning cold. It's as if the flame has rigor mortis. It takes two hours to melt enough ice for a cup of water each. I peel the wrapping off a Power Bar, take a bite and then put it in my pocket. We eat like sparrows up here. Bites constitute meals. I watch my companions waste away day by day, a sort of physical evaporation into the ether.

As I crawl from the tent at 11:40 A.M. the vapor in my nostrils freezes into two plugs. Shadowed by the finlike walls defining the great couloir at the top of K2's north face, the air is cold. It has a taste: blue.

A line of tracks rise from the tent. Swenson is in the lead, then Mortimer, then Ershler. Every few steps they slouch over their ice axes to rest. Their torsos heave. I enter the tracks and begin the journey toward the summit, 2000 feet above. It's going to be a long day.

If you get to the point in your climbing career that you seriously start to consider trying K2, then you are in for a nasty piece of work. Statistics on K2 don't paint a pretty picture: in 1986 it killed thirteen climbers; between then and 1990, despite the efforts of eleven expeditions, not a soul stood on K2's summit.

Lower than Everest by a half-dozen rope lengths, K2 is intolerant of human presence. It's been called the savage mountain, the mountain of mountains, the hardest mountain in the world. The atmosphere near its summit contains one-third the oxygen of sea level. Arctic cold and hurricane winds batter the mountain year-round. Vertiginous walls of rock and ice ring the mountain. Those are lousy odds to bet against, but something about K2 brings out the gambler in people. The chips you play with in this game are your fingers and toes; bets are made on life and death. The totality of climbing K2 is more than just a tally of pitches and camps leading to a summit. In fact, the fascination the mountain holds really has nothing to do with climbing. K2 represents an ordeal. To climb it is to confront your own mortal fears, for K2 is the geologic personification of angst.

Steve Swenson, Phil Ershler and I knew how unwelcoming K2 could be. Swenson had reached 26,000 feet on K2's north ridge in 1986; the next year, he, Ershler and I were blasted off K2's south face three times from 23,000 feet. Even before we'd broken base camp in 1987, we were making plans to return to the steep, bladelike Chinese north ridge in 1990. We'd spent one expedition together and could still stand the sight of one another, so we figured we could endure one more stint.

Rarely are expeditions meetings of the minds. Often, the only common ground a team will have is the desire for the summit. We three, and the Australian Greg Mortimer, were in many ways a mix of personalities rather than a blend, even, at times, a cacophony rather than a chorus. But we each gave something to the enterprise of climbing K2 that made us stronger together rather than weaker.

Swenson, who in the real world is a civil engineer, had the patience to deal with the frustrating paper trail that led to K2; Ershler, a mountain guide who'd climbed Everest and Kangchenjunga, the world's highest and third-highest peaks, had a sixth sense about the mountains; and Mortimer, a geologist from Sydney whose personality combined equal portions of reticence and optimism, had climbed Everest without oxygen in 1984 and possessed two legs that never tired of plugging steps up K2. As for me, if there is a quality that I brought to the party, it was, after nine Himalayan expeditions, a gluttony for punishment.

As we traverse into the great couloir, Swenson's steps broadcast shock waves across a five-acre avalanche slope. The snow across the gully is vibrato tight, like the skin of a drum. Ershler turns toward me with a sick look on his face and says, "This shit is bad. Really bad." Swenson, 300 feet ahead, is cannon fodder. If the slope cuts loose, he's a goner. We wait till he reaches safe snow; then we follow, one by one, treading gently.

It's about 4:00 P.M. when I pass Ershler at 27,000 feet. A lattice of clouds races over the summit. Valleys 12,000 feet below are filled with mist. Grey lenticulars creep in from the south. The clear skies we need for the summit are being replaced by the signs of storm.

We leave the fixed ropes at 27,500 feet. A hundred feet above me, Swenson and Mortimer frontpoint up a fifty-degree slope. We pause as a cloud of haze engulfs us all. A rainbow rings the stilted sun. The sky is flecked with glinting ice crystals drifting about the couloir.

Swenson looks down: "Should we go for it?" A long pause follows. Nothing could be more uncertain.

"Yes!" Mortimer finally shouts, prodding us into action and out of the inertia of doubt.

"This is crazy," I think to myself. "A storm is moving in and we're going for the summit, without oxygen, without bivouac gear." But, I rationalize, this is our last shot at the mountain. If we go down now, we'll never climb K2. A little more luck is all we need.

I set my ice tools and crampons into the gully and begin kicking up. Breaths come in short, rapid spasms. I manage bursts of three upward steps, fueled by multiple gasps. Light and shadow play on the snow in front of me as clouds roll by. When I look at the horizon, I see peaks that had towered above us for weeks while we were low on the mountain, now far beneath us, their summits like tiny islands in the clouds.

At 27,700 feet an empty yellow oxygen cylinder pokes out of the snow. The relic makes me wonder: How long can I keep up this pace without oxygen before my lungs give out? Will I be too wasted, too addled, to reverse this steep gully when it comes time to solo down? Six years ago Mortimer's Everest climb had left him like a zombie for weeks. Medical journals made no bones about the deleterious effects on the brain of oxygen starvation. So, why did people like Mortimer, like me, return to such high, frozen places? I knew that long-distance runners become addicted to marathoning because they crave the release of natural opiatelike chemicals—endorphins—that their bodies produce under stress. Could high altitude trigger a similar release of chemicals and create a similar addiction that draws us back to the Himalaya for higher and higher doses?

I look between my legs at Ershler outlined against the North K2 Glacier below, frontpointing slowly toward me. He keeps pausing to scan the skies, as if torn between his desire for the summit and the inner voice of self-preservation warning that we are getting ourselves into a borderline situation. At any minute the storm could erupt with explosive force. As I veer left off the main couloir into a diagonal gully, Ershler stops and clips himself into his ice axes to wrestle out his decision. Two weeks before we left for China, his father, a retired navy carrier pilot, had passed away. Today flight commander Ershler's wings are in his son's pocket, as a measure of luck. As the clouds close in around us, it looks very much like our luck is running out.

At 6:15 P.M. we hit the summit ridge at 28,000 feet. The angle relents. Mortimer seats himself in the snow to video the disappearing panorama of the Aghil Peaks in China and the Pakistani Karakoram. The sky is turning white as milk. My thoughts become dreamlike. Icicles hanging over cliffs transmute into fixed ropes; the squeaks of my axes and crampons in the snow become sentences spoken by persons I've never met.

"Where is Phil?" Mortimer asks me.

"I think he turned back."

It's ironic, but up here, where we need one another's help the most, it's every man for himself. The decision to go up or down rests entirely with the individual. But the fact that Ershler has descended makes me doubt the sanity of our choice to press on. Has he seen or felt some sign of catastrophe we have missed?

I break trail across a knee-deep crust of snow. Every step is a battle of willpower. Swenson passes me and gets us to the crest of the ridge. From my position thirty feet below him it looks as if he is on the summit.

"Are we there?"

He looks down with a face drained of expression: "Another hour." The news comes as a blow. I want to stop. I want to sleep.

At 28,100 feet we see the profile of the Abruzzi Ridge rising from Pakistan and our last 150 feet to the summit. Every ounce we carry drags us down, so we dump our fanny packs, harnesses and second ice tools on a flat knoll. The time is 7:20 P.M. In three hours it will be dark.

"This is killing me. I don't know if I'll make it," I tell Swenson.

"I'm going for it," he says, turning toward the undulating ridge and marching off. Swenson is hungry for this summit. He seems to convert pure determination into calories to burn.

I muster and follow him. Diaphanous outlines of the Baltoro Glacier and Broad Peak appear, then fade in a swirl of cloud. Perfect snowflakes float onto my Gore-tex suit. I pause to stare at these fellow travelers to nowhere. They magnify before my eyes, occupying my entire field of vision, each a little perfection of geometry. Time slips away. When I look up from my museum of snowflakes Swenson is gone, hidden by a curl of the ridge. I look behind me. Mortimer and Ershler are nowhere in sight. The sudden lack of human contact frightens me. I feel the same eerie solitude I knew as a kid, when my mother would put me to bed and turn out the light. In the darkness, the room would grow infinitely huge, too big and empty and unknown to comprehend, and I'd pull the covers over my head.

Tracking Swenson's crampon prints in the perfect snow, I plod out the last few feet. I concentrate on moving slowly, anaerobically. Voices keep whispering to me. When I turn to hear them, the landscape is empty. At about 8:00 P.M. Swenson reappears, descending.

"How far?"

"Just above. I'm heading down."

"I'll wait for Mortimer."

"It's late."

"I know. Listen, if Mort and I don't make it down tonight, don't write us off. We might have to bivouac at the foot of the summit ridge."

"Bivouac?" The lunacy of the idea astonishes him. It astonishes me, too, but the odds are we won't get down in the dark.

"I'll wait at the tent," Swenson says, then turns and leaves, virtually running down. He's spent three minutes on top. In distant Seattle, his second child is still in its mother's womb. He doesn't want to become a statistic of K2. I watch him descend and wonder if we'll see each other again.

When Swenson reaches the top of the couloir he stops, remembering a deed unfinished, and reaches into his pocket for two tiny palm crosses. Back in America, before we left, a friend had given him these crosses to leave on the summit in memory of Dave Cheesemond and Catherine Freer. Four years earlier Steve had climbed high on the north ridge with them, and news of their deaths on Mount Logan reached us while we were at K2 base camp in 1987. Holding the crosses in the palms of his gloves, Steve watches as the wind lifts them up and blows them across the ridge toward Pakistan.

In the months before I left for the mountain, doubts began to creep into my mind. In the middle of the night I'd find myself lying awake, thinking, "No way. There's no way I can climb K2." Never having been so high before, I could only guess I could function at such a height. We would, after all, be climbing close to the cruising altitude of a jet.

But more unsettling than my physical doubts, I'd begun to view Himalayan climbing as a crapshoot where pure, dumb chance dictated whether you made it home. Almost every time I picked up a mountaineering magazine an obituary would confront me of someone whose life I'd brushed past in my travels around the Himalaya and Karakoram. My own run of bad luck in the Himalaya in recent years made me feel that I was beating my head against a brick wall: stormed off K2 in 1987; misjudged the weather and lost Makalu's summit in 1988; coated with ice, hypothermic and retreating down Trango Tower in 1989; baffled by impassable cornices on Menlungtse in spring 1990. Why would my luck be better in a second round on K2?

Before the expedition left for China, I dreamed I was discussing K2 with Alan Rouse, with whom I climbed on an expedition to the Baltoro Glacier in 1983, and who, in 1986, became the first Briton to climb K2. Alan warned me of the long, arduous slopes leading to K2's summit and of the punishing work I'd be in for.

"Get down from the summit as fast and as far as you can," he'd warned in my dream, "because the longer you linger the more your strength will be sapped by the altitude." I listened to Alan's advice intently. He knew what he was talking about. Trapped in a tent at 8000 meters by a multiday blizzard that struck after he'd summited, Alan had died on the Abruzzi Ridge of K2. He's still up there.

At 8:05 P.M. I break onto the summit, an icy windswept dome split by a narrow crevasse, fringed by rocks on the Chinese side and dropping off steeply on the Pakistani side. A pinnacle rising from the west face absorbs the twilight and throbs with alpenglow.

I wander in circles around the summit, stunned to have arrived at a place I'd dreamed of for half a lifetime, a place I never really thought I'd reach. Finally, I sit on the snow, lean on my ice axe and wait for Mortimer.

It's windless, soundless and surprisingly warm under the blanket of cloud. As I stare down the ridge the line between mountain and heavens begins to blur. "If it turns to whiteout up here, we'll never get down," I think. I check my watch. Somehow, fifteen minutes have lapsed since my arrival. It seems like fifteen seconds. I wipe my nose and knock a long icicle of condensation dangling from it; a drift of snow has formed around my backside. I've been staring statuelike into the void, spacing out the whole time. I recall reading a theory of Reinhold Messner's about climbers falling into trances on the high summits and never coming down.

So I get up and occupy my time by taking self-timer shots

of myself. Mortimer and I are the first Australians to climb K2, so I scratch the Aussie flag into the snow with the spike of my ice axe. I keep looking at my watch, nervously making reality checks. Where are you, Mortimer?

An empty oxygen cylinder among some rocks sixty feet below me catches my eye. The rocks form a little circle. They look inviting. I start cramponing toward them. I'm seeing an image in my mind of me hunkered among the rocks, warming my hands over a campfire. "That's right," I think, "I'll build a fire down there. When Mortimer arrives we'll get nice and warm." I've got it all worked out.

A second later the fantasy dissolves and I backtrack to the summit. My actions at 28,250 feet are alarming me. If Mortimer doesn't arrive in five minutes, I'm out of here. At 8:30 P.M. his red suit appears out of the whiteness.

"Welcome to the summit."

"Pity about the view."

"We can't expect everything."

We hug each other. The feel of him and the sound of our voices makes the moment real. Until his arrival I'd been so outside myself I'd begun to doubt I was really on the summit. I'd even begun to doubt my own existence. These seem ludicrous thoughts at sea level, but up here in la-la land, where brain cells are shorting out by the bucketload, anything is possible.

We shoot some video footage and at 9:00 P.M. begin down the summit ridge, staggering, falling in the snow. Storm clouds have drifted all around us, but we are still above the cloud ceiling. At the top of the great couloir I stare down the huge funnel. It drops for hundreds of feet, terminating in a line of ice cliffs that overhang the north face. While I watch Mortimer climb down, I gather myself together by taking steady breaths. Darkness is nearly upon us. The air is chilling rapidly.

I face in and begin climbing down, kicking my crampons and slicing my ice axes into the crunchy snow. With each move I think of poor Yukihiro Yanagisawa, one of the Japanese climbers who made the first ascent of the north ridge in 1982, but whose luck ran out on the descent. Weakened after a forced bivouac near the summit, Yanagisawa slipped down the great couloir and hurtled over the ice cliffs, never to be seen again. I take my headlamp from my fanny pack, which I'd retrieved as I passed the knoll. Ershler's advice from the preclimb packing session returns: "I'd rather take a headlamp than a bivy sack." No, I'd never make it through a night in the open. I must keep moving. Pausing to rest, I look one last time to the cloud-covered horizon. The blazing red sun is sinking into western China. I've watched many sunsets before, but this one is unlike any I'd seen: the sun is far below me.

By 10:45 P.M. it is pitch black. Little sloughs of powder snow hiss by me like quicksilver. I keep frontpointing straight down till I locate the fixed ropes at midnight. As I rappel I see three lights below me. One is Swenson crawling to the tent. The other is Ershler, inside the tent, wondering if we'll ever appear out of the night. And on the glacier far below, our friends in base camp, who've watched our progress by telescope, are dancing around a bonfire of boxes and crates to celebrate our success.

At 26,800 feet my headlamp flashes on a figure lying face down in the snow. I think to myself, "It's Mortimer. Poor bastard has dropped dead from it all." As I reach him he pops up from the snow like a mushroom, very much alive.

"Waiting for you to get here with a headlamp. Looks like a vertical bit ahead."

We rappel over a bergschrund and begin the long traverse across the avalanche slope to the tent. Swenson's tracks have filled with fresh snow. At 12:30 A.M. I falter. My hands lose their feeling, and I become obsessed with rubbing the circulation back into them. Minutes pass as I wring my hands like the mad Lady Macbeth. "Keep moving. They'll never get warm here," Mortimer commands. We march another half-hour, then 300 feet from the tent I become completely apathetic and collapse.

"I can't make it."

"Of course you can."

Every fiber in my body aches. An overpowering urge to curl up and sleep wells up in me. "Take the headlamp and go," I tell him.

Something like a laugh escapes from Mortimer. He is a man who doesn't suffer fools. He's making fun of me. "Get up. We can do it." We crawl the last leg to the tent.

Swenson and Ershler are dozing in their sleeping bags, with the stove chuffing between them, when we burst into the tent at 1:00 A.M. Judging by their expressions, we are a frightful sight. Medusa-like tendrils of frost ornament our faces. Our lips are cyanotic blue.

"Man, I never thought I'd see you again," says Swenson. "I thought you'd be stuck up there bivouacking and never get down."

Seeing the pot of hot water on the stove, I plunge my hands into it. Searing pain assails me as blood floods back into blanched flesh. Ershler thrusts my hands under his armpits, and Mortimer squeezes in beside me. We tear off our double boots and check for frostbite. Our feet are not frozen. We'll be taking home as many fingers and toes as we came with.

We gasp, cough, moan, wheeze, splutter and bitch our way through the dark hours. Powder avalanches rumble down the great couloir all night. We still have a long way to go before we are out of harm's way, but lying there in that tent, shoulder to shoulder with my companions, the fear drains out of me. I'm feeling lucky again.

BIG WALLS

Before I ventured into the Himalaya, Yosemite's huge sweeps of granite and the life of literally hanging out for days on a big-wall climb served as my training ground for the mountains. In the late 1970s and early 1980s I made several ascents on El Capitan, that 3000-foot monolith coveted by climbers all over the world. Among the walls I climbed were two new routes on El Cap: Aurora, and Lost in America. The latter climb engendered the story "Lost in America," which appeared in 1985 in *Climbing* and the *American Alpine Journal.* "Coast to Coast on the Granite Slasher" describes earlier big-wall climbs. Written in 1980 and published in *Rock* in Australia, I cringe at its naivete and out-of-fashion 1970s lexicon and sentiments. Yet the story captures events and a spirit of climbing that I felt strongly about. In 1983 it was published in the Diadem Books anthology *Mirror in the Cliffs* as one of a pair of introductory stories.

LOST IN AMERICA

Night had fallen. Randy Leavitt and I were high on the over-hanging east face of El Capitan, at the end of a new route, setting up our last hanging bivouac. Behind us lay nine days of difficult climbing and 2700 feet of granite. As I sat on my porta-ledge I chanced to look over my shoulder.

"Christ! Look!"

Leavitt turned toward an exploding sky. In the west, two white-hot pinpoints of light traversed the heavens, heading east. In their wake a silver tail trailed off for dozens of miles before dissipating to a lingering evanescent blue against the mauve dusk. The dots climbed into the upper atmosphere, then vanished, leaving ghostly contrails. It was an eerie conclusion to our climb.

"What the hell was that?" Leavitt asks.

Speculations: comet, UFO, ICBM, WWIII, L.A. and San Francisco up in smoke. We scanned the skies for mushroom clouds.

"What a pity to be vaporized now," I think to myself, "just as we're about to finish. Maybe we'd be the only survivors. We'd reach the top on scorched ropes and stumble out of the valley onto the plains. Cars melted to roads, roads glazed to earth. Nowhere to go, nothing to do, no one to give a damn about our climb. We'd be lost in America."

Later we would learn that this was a test of a Tomahawk

missile, self-destructing in a ball of flame, but on that last night of our climb it fired our imaginations.

The beginning of this idea to climb a new route on El Cap began in the fall of 1984 when I met Leavitt in Yosemite.

Grasping the fin of his Cadillac like a handrail, Randy limped across the parking lot toward me. His dislocated knee crackled like a bowl of Rice Krispies as it dragged a weary foot through thick drifts of pine needles piled against flat tires of long-dead vans. He looked thinner for eight solitary days on Aurora, a route on El Cap created by Peter Mayfield and me back in 1981, unrepeated till Randy's solo ascent. We shook hands. I asked about his knee. He had taken a short fall, caught his foot in a sling and hung upside-down, like a cowboy fallen from a horse with his boot caught in the stirrup.

"Too bad about your route," he said.

I agreed. I'd driven to California to complete an El Cap route I'd attempted twice before, to find that someone had gotten the jump on me. Not only had I lost a route, but a name as well. Heart of Darkness, a fine Conradian piece of nomenclature heavy with intimations of soul-searching in a sinister realm, as well as geologic applicability to boot—namely, an arrow-straight line bisecting the jet black diorite of the North American Wall—was now named Sheep Ranch of Wyoming, a gauche slap-in-the-face nightmare of bestial images.

Sheep Ranch's main protagonist, parachutist/climber Rob Slater, had snatched the route as his swan song before embarking on a high-powered career as aspirant Wall Street broker. His sole regret in leaving Yosemite to seal this Faustian pact with money was forfeiting the chance to climb the sisterline to the Sheep Ranch, prenamed Iowa Pig Farm. I recalled a long-silent outcry by sage Royal Robbins against names like Tangerine Trip, Mescalito and Magic Mushroom due to their druggy connotations. What would he say about atrocities such as these?

After talk of climbs past we spoke of climbs future. Leavitt suggested a jaunt to the Arctic Circle, to Baffin Island, to climb some alpine monstrosity.

"Climb it and…?" I asked warily.

"Jump."

This is the problem with Leavitt. Not content to climb a steep wall, he must parachute it as well. It's all part of the up-down fixation among these hybrids of climbing and BASE jumping—BASE jumpers being those who jump from Buildings, Antennae, Spans (bridges) and Earth (cliffs).

"You'd leave me on the summit, all alone?"

"You could jump too."

"Thanks, but I don't jump."

He offered to teach me. I repeated that I don't jump. He suggested I toss the haul bags off and descend the back side solo. I countered that he'd be an airdrop for a polar bear and I'd get lonely. Impasse reached, I proposed an alternative: El Cap, via the second-last good new route.

"Where?" asked Leavitt, skeptically.

We spoke in the arcane tongues of climbing and unfolded our mental road maps of El Capitan. Flakes and chunks of rock were our landmarks on these blue highways.

"Between Tangerine Trip and Zenyatta Mondatta."

"When?"

"Next spring."

Our correspondence that year concurred that this route would rewrite the book on big-wall climbing. With the combined experience of thirty walls, we knew precisely what luxuries were needed. This hedonistic desire to attain unsurpassed levels of comfort on an overhanging environment accounted for the overkill wattage of our ghetto-blaster, pillows for porta-ledges, changes of underwear, shaving kit and premoistened towelettes, books, newspapers, gourmet food and other excesses totaling 400 pounds. If we were going to live on a rock for ten days we were going to do it in style.

Arriving at a Yosemite of thundering waterfalls and overcrowded, heavily policed campgrounds, we head directly to the base of El Cap to fix the first pitch, mindfully avoiding the greatest single danger to the route, the Mountain Room Bar. Greater climbers than we have been sucked into this intellectual vacuum, to spend all their money on drink and talk nonsense for nights on end, only to see their ambitions and brains turn to mush. On those too-comfy stools, surrounded by empty bottles of overpriced beer and sneaky-strong cocktails, the timelessness of the valley stretches like plastic wrap over the season, so that by the time the victim finally escapes this climate-controlled vortex, winter has set in and he kicks himself, wondering where the dream went.

Leavitt wins the toss for first lead. He joys to the therapeutic chime of hammered steel and dull thwack of copperheads; I can see it in his eyes. At a perfect ledge we fix a rope, haul our bags (we call them pigs) and rappel to the rattlesnake-crawling scree, gazing at a daunting sheet of rock above a swaying nylon strand hanging fifteen feet free of the wall. Every pitch as steep or steeper, each fifteen feet of leaning rock will join the next to total 250 feet of tilt from ground to summit, making retreat an unlikely possibility.

At dawn the next day, we cut all ties with the ground, beginning our ten-day ascent. Only three days in the valley and we are on the wall. We haven't even seen the bar: an unheard-of achievement.

My lead begins with a hand crack that fades to blank after sixty feet. A silver, bulging wall surrounds me, interrupted by occasional thin overlaps. Only 200 feet off the ground and already exposure consumes us. A few rivets reach overlapping onion-skin flakes. They expand as I hammer knifeblades underneath them. Too much hammering and the natural elasticity in the rock is lost, not enough and the piton won't grip. Chouinard steel rings like a tuning fork as it slides between leaves of granite. Wait for the right note, stop hammering, clip in, step up. At rope's end, in the middle of the featureless wall, I drill a bolt belay. All day for one pitch, a mere 150 feet, but that's the pace. We name the pitch the Big Country, gateway to the vertical prairie.

To haul the pigs through a pulley demands our combined weight and sweat. By nightfall we are spent, prostrate on porta-ledges. Leavitt slips a tape into the machine and constructs tuna sandwiches. The wind drops. Perfect acoustics.

The climbing rack for this route: a jangling juggernaut of scrap metal bristling with hooks, pitons, cabled devices, even masking tape to stick hooks to flakes as runners and to pad sharp edges from gnawing the rope.

Now, when it comes to the hardware of climbing, Leavitt combines a propensity for invention with the acquisitiveness of a bowerbird, while on rock the compact, thoughtful Californian is a bantam-weight with yardbird reflexes. Incipient flakes on the third pitch give him a chance to use his "stars," tiny, pointed hatchet-pitons, a tenth the size of RURPs, with the fall-holding power of a paperclip.

Then he spies something totally out of place on our virgin climb: a fixed nut twenty blank feet above us. Nausea over-whelms me. Has someone been here before? But no, relief, it's part of the unfinished girdle traverse of El Cap. The only thing more abstract than climbing up a wall is to traverse it from one side to the other.

Leavitt snags the nut with his cheat stick, a sectioned tent pole with a hook on the end and a ladder of cabled loops attached to the hook. He clips up the cable and avoids an hour of drilling. We dub the pitch the Astral Lassoo.

Our bivouac that night hangs level with the great arch of the Tangerine Trip. Bats drop from its dark interior, and we recall tales of tragedy, bad taste and black humor born beneath that arch. Shadowy and oppressive, it has the look of a bad place, where "things happen." A severed rope, a death; a climber becomes unclipped from her jumars, another death. Death cloaks a route with a sinister shroud, until fools eager to shatter the aura rush in where angels fear to tread and cross the tainted arch clad in Ghostbuster T-shirts and devil masks procured from a Fresno magic store.

The next day we enter the brittle quartz of the Badlands. Hanging from hooks perched on crumbling flakes, I reach an enormous detached scimitar of rock. To beat pitons into it would pry it from the face, slicing Leavitt and me from the wall like stalks of wheat felled by a scythe, so I slip nuts behind it, moving as cautiously, slowly and silently as a man crossing a frozen lake.

Climbing up the vibrating flake mesmerizes me. Serious climbing treads a thin line between recklessness and calculated risk, the path marked only by intuition, a capricious and often flawed instinct. As with a house of cards, every placement must be exact. The mind computes the right move, finds the way out, but only by pushing you deeper into it, until, in the end, the construct of cards is so delicately stacked that there is no choice but to trust your intuition. This bridge-burning paradox of willingly climbing into a hazardous situation that you are then forced to climb out of stinks of adrenaline. But intuition, or luck, holds out and puts me at a hanging belay.

On the fourth day Leavitt drops a nut behind a distant flake with the cheat stick, swings onto it and proceeds to meld copperheads into an arch. At its end the wall tilts back, abruptly turning from orange to moody black. Finding no crack, Leavitt begins to hook upward. Dead-ended, he gingerly hooks back down. Bits of grit pop under the weight of his hooks and strike him in the eye. Treading his own patch of thin ice, he tries a hook traverse out right, but it too goes nowhere, so he makes a belay.

"Too hard to hook. Maybe it has to be free-climbed."

He's right. The sixth pitch runs it out thirty feet on a 5.10 face, relents to fist crack, then hits a ledge.

Hauling the pigs to this place is a cursed ordeal. The five

bags have developed separate personalities and dangle entangled like a family of suckling hogs crowding the belly of an enormous central sow. The hog mother and her cluster are herded onto the ledge, which we name the Bay of Pigs.

Leavitt throws his hip into an off-width, levitates past a huge, loose block and nails a sweeping arch. Belay. With daylight left, I put some time into the eighth pitch, an A4+ hook traverse to a blade crack that splits the blank wall. Now in the mode of doing 1.4 pitches a day, we see the ground fall behind, the pines become pencils and the peregrine falcons, nesting far below, accept us as fact.

Hunting to feed their newly hatched young, the peregrines rip the air in dives aimed at swallows and pigeons, smashing them in explosions of feathers and then catching their stunned prey in midair. High-pitched shrieks from the male signal a successful catch. The female rises on an updraft, collects the swallow from her mate's talons and then accelerates with folded wings, pulling out of a 3000-foot dive to land as lightly as a tuft of down on the rim of her eyrie to feed the catch to squawking offspring.

The eighth evening sees us on a foot ledge beneath the headwall, a looming bulge that surpasses all else on El Cap for steepness. Leavitt peers down glassy-eyed. I would have restrained him were he not clipped to the belay.

"What a place to jump!"

"But we're only two-thirds of the way up. Don't you need more height?"

He who had jumped off antennae as low as 500 feet eyed me—a poor uninitiate who had never known the rush of free-falling—with pity.

"It isn't quantity, it's quality. There are parts of El Cap worth jumping from that are nowhere near the top. I've considered doing certain climbs just to reach those spots." He meant grand ledges, such as El Cap Tower or the Continental Shelf, to name but two. The usual place to jump was atop the Dawn

Wall, a sloping prow of rock that beckons one to the edge. And right at that hour was the best time to jump, when the evening stillness had set in and El Cap was saturated in soft light.

"Nothing beats seeing the landmarks of El Cap that you know as a climber rush past at thirty-two feet per second squared. You dive, spread your limbs and feel the acceleration build. Reaching terminal velocity is like hitting a pillow. You don't go any faster. The illusion is to float, to fly, but you're moving fast and have to snap out of the trance to open your chute. There's a crack as silk hits air, a pull upward, and a slow ride to the ground. Free fall. That's where it's at."

It. Quintessential. Definitive, yet undefined.

I felt the suction of the space below begin to pull like a current.

"It's addictive. You get hooked. You forget fear. You feel immortal. That's why I retired. I was getting too blasé. Yeah, it gets under your skin, like a terrible itch that just has to be scratched. Slater calls it Bad Craziness."

Then Leavitt told about the time he jumped into the Black Canyon of the Gunnison, the worst craziness I'd ever heard.

"Rob Slater and I planned to jump in and then climb out. While we were waiting for the wind to drop he mentioned that the buzz was wearing thin with jumping, so I suggested we try something different and jump hand in hand. Whenever you jump tandem you preplan to release, to veer off in different directions and for one person to open his chute before the other. To avoid collision.

"So Rob is flying in front and to my left, looking over his shoulder for my open chute while trying to track the right path, because it's a narrow gorge with only one place to land. But he doesn't see me. He just keeps looking over his shoulder, falling, falling. Split seconds pass. I open my chute, but he's still falling, still trying to spot me. At 300 feet above the ground he finally opens. The last thing I see before I land is Rob flying toward the cliffs. On the landing zone I look around, certain he's dead, but there he is, landing safely, but on the wrong side of the Gunnison River. The river was a torrent. He nearly drowned getting over. All that happened in seconds. The story takes longer than the jump. We never did climb out...."

In all Leavitt's hundreds of jumps he'd accumulated just a few minutes of free fall. It was a very dangerous drug.

"If it wasn't illegal to jump El Cap I'd still do it."

His third jump from the Dawn Wall marked the end of his career. Arrested by park rangers for this victimless noncrime and crucified by the internal justice system of Yosemite, he languished in a valley cell like some political prisoner of a regime against fun and escaped a lengthy prison term only because a lawyer detected violations of his constitutional rights. But bureaucracy had won. No one was jumping anymore.

He stares at me. "Someday you gotta jump. You gotta."

The next day Leavitt climbs to beneath the headwall and traverses right, jamming everything from Friends to blades into the crack until it blanks out before reaching the summit corners. As he drills through the headwall bulge toward these corners I hear a strangled shriek, feel a tug on the rope and look up to see him dangling. A snapped rivet hanger floats to the ground. Back up again, he inches up the bottomless corner on RURPs, blade tips and copperheads.

"If this pops..." he says shaky-voiced, "it's fly or die...."

Darkness. Leavitt belays; I jumar. Sparks shower the face like flint asizzle as I clean the pitch. I pluck out the final RURP with my fingers. In the last eighty feet of his lead every placement is barely capable of supporting body weight. If one had popped he would have ripped the entire string and fallen 160 feet.

Another morning breaks and grows blustery as sunlight swamps the wall. Anticipating the summit, we break out the shaving cream, mount our sunglasses in front of us as mirrors and mow down a week's stubble. Leavitt even changes his underwear. But the pitch is long and slow and consumes every one of our thirty-five bent and beaten blades. Beneath me the antenna of the radio glints in the sun while Leavitt thumbs through a week-old *Wall Street Journal.* The wind carries a San Jose traffic report up the wall. Rush hour and the freeway is jammed.

The corner stops twenty feet from another route, called Zenyatta Mondatta. I sink four bolts into the wall; belay. Our line has ended, like a place of dead roads. Tomorrow we'll swing into the last 300 feet of Zenyatta, and be off by night.

Leavitt reaches me as alpenglow saturates the High Sierra so close it seems we can touch it. The shapes of Yosemite's skyline stand like black cutouts on the horizon. One of the peregrines makes a last dive back to its nest, while below us headlights map the valley loop. And far away, a military mind presses a button and launches a Tomahawk missile that paves the sky with fire, annihilating the alpenglow and, in our blackest dreams, human-kind itself.

COAST TO COAST ON THE GRANITE SLASHER

Never trust the written word. At best it's a second-rate account of reality. How can you duplicate the enormity of a personal moment? How can you truthfully record the feelings or events when the intricacies of each second of thought would fry the circuits of a computer? And how can you honestly describe awe in the face of the event? No—it's like rendering color memories into muddy monochrome negatives. It's vernacular butchery. It's slashing at reality.

As with subtitled movies, something vital is lost in the translation. This missing link between the original thought or event and the recorded outcome has led me to believe that the finest moments, thoughts and images fail in print. How could they not?

Talking to a friend once, I launched into an animated rave about a previous personal experience, faltered on my inadequate words, shrugged and concluded, "Well, you really had to be there." Of course! So obvious, yet so true. It is by involvement, and not through this armchair account, that an understanding of climbing and its attendant escapism will be found. All you will find here is another razor murder of the experience.

A surfer planing down a wave or a biker leaning into a fast corner isn't thinking of board dimensions or mechanics. He's in there for the ride. Our intellect has given us technology, which has given us a specific variety of devices suited to escapism, which in turn stimulates our emotions. A full circle in which humans have used their intellect to stimulate that intellect. Technology is the conveyance to put one in these distant situations. On arrival, the metaphysical becomes as apparent as the physical, and ideas, feelings, surroundings and events merge into a total experience that leaves one slashing for words.

The notion of mountains or big walls as a medium for enlightenment is nothing new. Climbing literature brims with it. These high places are magnets to the escapist, allowing one to wrest one's mind from the humdrum of everyday reality and focus on things otherwise inaccessible. Realities nonetheless, but so separate from the norm as to be unique in our lives.

Strangely juxtaposed in an ex-wilderness setting is a monolith that epitomizes the big-wall image, indeed gave birth to the term. Vast sweeps of scalpel-sliced granite, huge bays and inlets formed of glinting sheets of surreal patterns and tones, dwarf tall pines in size and age. Humans today call this formation El Capitan, and it stands at the head of Yosemite Valley.

Gazing from the meadows at its base, I felt like a pinpoint against it; it seemed so huge, so unattainable. Yet in the spring of 1977 I found myself manteling over the grey headwall of a route named Mescalito, a line near the fabled Dawn Wall. As I waited for my partner, Eric Weinstein, to jumar up and join me, I noticed how my metabolism was still vibrant with the energy that had accompanied us for six days. A surging and anticipatory energy that we felt could have kept us going for another week. As dusk filled the high country we found a clearing amid twisted hemlocks and slabs and dropped into a deep sleep. By morning that energy was gone. Waking slowly, stretching stiff limbs and swollen fingers stained black with oxides from the ever-clutched 'biners, I realized that the energy was controlled by the subconscious. Now, on top, our minds told our bodies that the journey was over, so the flow of vital chemicals had diminished. Above all, our minds were exhausted, taxed by the continual concentration on each move.

We jettisoned the haul bag laden with iron down the steep east face. With a hammock clipped to the top as a parachute, it sailed to Earth like a returned space probe, landing with a distant thud on the talus below.

As we descended to the fleshpots of the valley, hearing the bustle of civilization, it seemed that the energized clarity our minds had known was being smothered by our reentry. That night, back in the campground, with heads full of wine, that energy was briefly rediscovered. We talked all our friends to sleep, then talked for hours to each other. Yet on the wall we hardly spoke; it just didn't seem the place for small talk. Suddenly the origin of that sureness and clarity became apparent. Up there, isolated from society and its trappings, the mind had no use for the babble and clutter, the ever-racing mental chatter that usually fills it. Our "internal dialogue" had switched off, letting us focus on the task at hand, revealing a crystal-clear confidence and relationship with the wall that heightened each day. The night slurred on, and we spoke of the afternoon breezes that lifted our ropes in aerial dance and of the kamikaze swallows that strafed us and made us cringe, as from the buzz of falling rock, such was their sound.

It wasn't long before the postwall high left and the horizontal world of Yosemite became old. In the central section of the east face, where a vast black diorite intrusion has mapped a likeness of the North American continent, is a sea of calms and swells along the West Coast. By midsummer I was part of a team of four sailing across what was then the epitome of the epitome: the Pacific Ocean Wall.

Our number bolstered our confidence against the aura of the route. The night before we embarked, Darryl Hatten, our mad-dog Canadian, downed a fifth of vodka and demolished a building with a broomstick in a bicycle joust. Eric, Kim Carrigan and I agreed that the pact was sealed with madness.

For a week we tapped slowly upward, hauling our life-support units—our haul bags—behind us. We were modern Michelangelos and worked gently and carefully, regarding each placement like a crucial work of art, of copper and steel on granite. The wall swept drastically away beneath us. While jumaring a slowly spinning thread of nylon fifty feet out from the rock, I felt so frail and dependent on technology—helpless without it, yet at the same time suspicious of its hold over us. Perhaps there is a harmony, a delicate interplay of humanity, technology and the environment, but as I hung there with the valley revolving giddily around me, a healthy distrust of my immediate dependency rocketed me to the belay.

The last hours were chaos: Kim screaming at a crack, Eric singing reggae tunes, while beneath them Darryl and I beat hammers to a Neolithic chant, our water gone and the sun baking our brains. Then suddenly it was all over. The top again. As we commended the bags to the deep it all seemed so ephemeral, like a dream, or an opiate euphoria. That timeless yet fleeting state of mind found only on the vertical.

The summer baked on. From my patch in the meadows I was just one of many drawn to the walls. I wondered what it was like when those first adventurous climbers lay here and stared at these then-virgin walls until their gaze fell on the obvious striking line that slices through the center of El Cap. Perfectly hewn cracks and corners, as if the rock had been designed to climb. I wondered if, in 1958 when the Nose route was first climbed, the team ever imagined the changes that El Cap would witness— the lacework of routes weaving across it and the changes to Yosemite Valley itself, from the valley that John Muir wrote of to the wilderness Disneyland of today. Traveling back further in my mind, I wondered what the Native Americans, who must have revered this monolith as something sacred, would think of all this. The roads and cars, the phony shops such as the Pohono

Indian Gallery, where knobby-kneed tourists in garish check-ered shorts can buy vinyl table mats with a stylized Geronimo face beaming forth, and where the nearby Native American village is a sanitized version of the past. What ever happened to the Valley's original inhabitants anyway? Then I remembered that the very meadow in which I was camping had once been forest, cleared by settlers in the 1800s. For a while I felt guilty and in some way implicated in this web.

So I escaped to the anonymity of the Nose with a tall, glib Englishman named Tom Whittaker and a young local, Charlie Row. By climbing in the early fall we avoided the hordes that usually swarm up the route, though we had to contend with the usual dry heat.

Three days later, bivying on Camp VI with tongues like dry leather, I gave the larger Tom the larger half of an orange, and for this gift of moisture he pledged eternal gratitude. Camp VI was an exfoliated flake with a wide crack behind it full of a mixture of tins, empty water jugs, gear and shit. With a skyhook we fished out a few relics. Jamming up long hand cracks we passed mutilated iron and nuts. Man's passage was evident everywhere.

Another half-day and we stood atop the shimmering bul-wark, weak and parched. The view of the sparkling Merced River meandering below taunted our thirst as we hiked down.

"Christ, youth, I'd give anything for a swig o' water," rasped Tom as we passed by a boulder at the edge of the Tangerine Trip.

"The hand is quicker than the eye," I retorted, plucking from behind a boulder a gallon jug that I'd stashed from Mescalito three months before.

"That's twice I owe you, youth," replied an astounded Tom, guzzling the green, scummy water.

Two years passed before I returned to Yosemite, during which time I spent a season roaming around the base of FitzRoy in Patagonia, a place that eats men forever. All that time I dreamt of the friendly walls of El Cap, so gentle compared to the icy, windswept towers of the Torre Valley.

Jetting out of the poverty of South America, I headed straight for Yosemite and a northern spring. When the spring deluge ceased I joined up with a fellow wanderer and doctor of rockaneering, Matt Taylor, on the soaring Magic Mushroom route—a nail-up in the classic sense that penetrates the Shield headwall via continuous groove systems.

The route was a celebration of spring. Green shoots sprouted from cracks and hummingbirds hovered by our bags, searching for flowers. In the morning sun, chunks of ice fell in clusters about us, blown in swaying flocks from the rim.

On the third afternoon I came across a moist crack with an angle piton jutting from it. Raising my hammer to reseat it, I heard the croak of a frog. Pulling the loose pin out with my fingers, I found a tiny grey frog inhabiting the fold of steel. Apologizing for the intrusion, I put him aside, slammed the pin and went on my way. What a strange symbiosis: the small creature utilizing a piece of iron placed by man as a shelter against the harsh winter. I'd stumbled upon a fragile, vertical oasis held together by the interaction of trickling water, soil and tiny organisms—a delicate balance, where too much or too little of one factor can turn the oasis into lifeless stone.

The oasis and I, a clumsy oaf laden with forty pounds of jangling junk, bungling into it, severing roots and disturbing the life cycles of creatures I couldn't even see. Reaching the belay, I wondered if our trespass had any justification. It seems that wherever man goes he damages the environment. Even amid 3000 feet of stone he commits crimes against nature. The sunset glows pink with smog; the river below parallels a stream of tar. And inevitably, as man spreads, the wilderness shrinks before him.

A couple of days later the frog had its revenge. Two pitches from the top, on a slightly expanding flake, my mind wandered and I popped a couple of placements and crashed feet first into a flake. Numb at first, I finished the pitch, but soon sharp, rhythmic pain tore at my ankle, which had swollen to the size of a balloon. Matt took the helm for the last few hours as I tried, one-legged, to ascend the rope and clean our pitches. The slightest twitch was agonizing; I feared the ankle was fractured. The final thirty-foot roof was merciless. I dangled and ground my teeth for ages, only to turn the lip and find Matt belayed a mere fifteen feet from the top. The rope had just ended. He led off and hauled me up the last of it. Release from the vertical was like a shot of morphine.

The next day, closer observation showed my injury to be a sprain. With a gnarled stick of hemlock in hand, I began the four-mile hop, crawl and slide down slabs and tearing manzanita to the rappels and the valley floor. The friendly gold-colored stone had showed its mean side. The tales of accidents on the wall and helicopter rescues had only been stories until then. Human error is a reckless luxury in an environment where trespassers are merely tolerated.

By autumn I was locked into the trap that Yosemite can be, lazing by the river and gazing at El Cap's profile. Hanging around the social hub of the valley, the parking lot, I felt claustrophobia building in me. Too long penned between the walls. Just as I felt the roots of stagnation anchoring me to the curb, a hyperkinetic hotshot from the Bay Area named Zachar talked me into a free repeat of the west face of El Cap. He talked so fast I had no chance to refuse.

That's the parking lot, though, a marketplace for partners, gear and simple amusements. People you hardly know will ask you to launch off all manner of routes. All manner of people too. Sometimes the walls echo with the screaming matches of ill-matched teams. Small issues take on huge dimensions on walls.

Sleeping at the base gave us a dawn start and a burst of energy that launched us up pitch after pitch. We took nothing but the clothes on our backs, a small rack of gear, some water and powdered dextrose for energy. The rock was a richly tex-tured brown glaze, eighty degrees steep, with fine incut holds linking hand and finger cracks. It's hard to recollect the climbing, it happened so fast. But even more than before, I felt my subconscious guiding me. Almost as if I weren't thinking, my body performed. It knew exactly where to go.

By noon the pines looked like pencils and by dusk we had scuttled over the final slabs. Once a multiday grade VI nail-up, the route was now a one-day marathon free climb. Refinement of attitudes and techniques had led to the ultimate expression of the form.

Weary after the 2000-foot push, we watched the sun sink into a red Earth. Too late to make a rappel descent and too cold for a bagless bivy, we hiked the eight miles down the Falls Trail, staggering into Camp IV at midnight. Rummaging in the steel locker for a blanket, I heard a snotty grunt from the tree in front of me. Looking up, I saw a bear silhouetted in moonlight, staring at me, a whole three feet away. Behind him was his mother, looking very protective and much bigger. Rational panic prevailed—I grabbed a blanket and slammed the lid just as he made a move for the food box. Foiled, he snorted and continued up the tree to harass a gang of screeching raccoons, no doubt thinking me a strange and scruffy animal as I curled up on a bed of pine needles.

There's always a feeling, after climbing a wall, that it never really happened. It felt inconceivable, then, to wake up in the same old trap a day after starting a route I'd gone up on specifically to escape that very trap. Though completing the route gave me a sudden rush of excitement, it was nothing like the satisfaction of a full-on grade VI. Masochistic as it may sound, there is a subtle beauty in the anxious rope-clutching and waiting at belay to the tune of distant tapping, the gadgetry, logistics and sweating. The tense concentration of climbing an expanding flake, placement by slow placement, your spine tingling with nervous care as the piece you're on shifts as you place the one above it. Then the relief when it holds.

Even the feeling of self-destruction at the end of a route is an integral part of the experience. And the music of steel against steel, clashing and ringing, releasing the pent-up steam of living in the real world. Perhaps this brinksmanship, this contrast of calm and savagery, satisfies our dual egos of aesthete and barbarian, our yin and yang.

A short time later, with a wall-climber by the name of Tim Washik, I made a long, strange journey into the Atlantic side of North American Wall onto the steep and jagged face called the Iron Hawk. Deriving its name from a huge diorite fresco, the likeness of a surreal bird of prey, we found signs of the hawk everywhere. Circling on silent thermals, peregrine falcons watched our every move.

We started from El Cap tree, an eighty-two-foot pine that sprouts 300 feet up the wall. After we nailed a forty-foot ceiling at tree-top level, exposure was total as we swung about in slings, looking at piles of bleached pigeon bones on the ledge below, the morsels of the hawk.

Features invisible from the ground revealed themselves to us as flake led to flake. A rope length of traversing on tipped-in blade pitons led to a pair of curving arches above. Never had we driven so hard on our pins, so steep and insecure was the feeling. Everything jutted out at crazy angles.

On the fifth afternoon we were engulfed in a swirling mass of cloud. That night it rained, a flash flood on the vertical desert. In hammocks under an overhanging arch, we stayed fairly dry. Interludes in the morning cloud cover showed the team who'd been paralleling us on Mescalito, bivied in a water streak, soaked and miserable, climbing to reach the shelter of a ledge. We stayed put and watched the eerie, mist-enshrouded castles and gothic towers of the Cathedral Spires.

During the afternoon the temperature dropped and we donned every stitch of clothing we had. From beneath us we heard music wafting in the breeze. Someone had mounted car speakers toward us and was blaring the Hendrix version of "All Along the Watchtower." The words rang up at us on a gust: "There must be some kinda way outta here...."

As the sun set, a storm front moved in at high speed, interrupting our canned dinner with a wind that filled the waterproof hammock covers like parachutes and lifted us perpendicular to the wall. Before we could batten down the hatches we were being lifted and slammed into the wall mercilessly. This lasted all night. Our hammock covers tore and rain gushed in. The only respite from the beating was to sit upright and pull the flies tightly around us. No one slept that night on El Cap. Above the roaring gale came the staccato chatter of Tim's teeth. Neither asleep nor awake, but more entranced, my mind glowed orange within, while outside my skin shriveled white after thirty-six hours enhammocked in a gale.

By morning we were saturated despite layers of Gore-tex and technology. As the sunset had heralded the wind, the sunrise saw it leave. Numb to the bone, we tried to make the most of the dim sunshine. Tim was still shivering. Our ropes, uncoiled by the wind, looked in bad shape, and pins to which we'd been anchored hung loosely out of the crack. Even our bag of gorp—a granola and M&M mixture—had turned to porridge. We tipped the vile slop out and scree-scrappers below later inquired if we'd puked from fear.

But we were in one piece after a helpless ordeal at the hands of the Iron Hawk. This I felt proved my theory that all bad scenes are transient—it's only a matter of time before the bad part ends.

We decided to climb upward to dry ourselves and escape. Since Tim was wetter he led off on a hard double pendulum and stunt pitch to a corner. By dusk we were back in our damp bags, snowflakes pattering on our tattered hammock covers.

The eighth day dawned clear and warm. As I swung over to a hand crack a helicopter hovered by us. We waved it on; no rescues yet, thanks. Another swing and we were on a small but flat ledge. It was the first thing we'd stood on for a week, and we were determined to sleep on it no matter how small it was. Tim removed his damp socks and produced two wrinkled lumps of flesh he called feet. He plucked a dead toenail from a sock and sat staring at it.

"It was a cruel storm," I consoled, as coyotes howled at a moonless sky and rockfall thundered down Sentinel Gully, dislodged by the first snow of the season.

The last day was warm. Free moves on diorite led to the summit roofs. Tim traversed under them, tensioned right to a fixed pin, clipped it and came hurtling back at me, the pin hanging uselessly from his aider. We had a cursory exchange over this; then an hour later we arrived at the total calm of the summit. Half Dome and the high country were crowned in snow. Suddenly the place was alive with people, friends with food for the starvelings. We told them we were okay—six days' food stretches to ten easily. They poked our ribs and added that 140 pounds drops to 120 just as easily.

Ordeal by piton over, we reached the valley floor to find Tim's van had been robbed. Perhaps our luck was better on the wall after all. Our ways parted after this strange ten-day encounter.

My last hours in the valley saw another storm move in. I wondered what the place would look like next time I saw it. Would it be so free and easy, or would it overdose on law and order and become a grapple for franchises and exploitation, for tourism, telephotos and tinsel?

The walls had been my refuge. A few bolts and pins here and there, a fallen flake every few years, some dabs of chalk on the crags, but essentially they remain unaffected by human erosion, while humans—small things that they are—just come and go.

JOURNEYS

TRAVELING THROUGH THE SQUALOR and color of the Third World, and rambling through jungle, desert and mountain to reach the Himalaya and Karakoram, has always excited me as much as the climbs I've made in those ranges. "The Climb to Shiva's Cave" describes a pilgrimage to a sacred and nearly inaccessible Hindu mountain shrine, a journey I made after an unsuccessful attempt to climb Makalu in 1988. The tale appeared in *Summit* in 1992. Another unsuccessful expedition, on which the whole team fell ill with dysentery, resulted in the cautionary traveler's tale, "The Trouble with Hunza," published by *Rock + Ice* in 1985. The third story in this section, "Baltoro!" is a retrospective on my journeys to the mighty Baltoro Glacier, which cuts a path through the Karakoram. During five expeditions to peaks along the glacier, from 1983 to 1992, I witnessed a slow, manmade alteration of this rugged place. In this piece of wilderness writing I let feelings about the landscape guide my pen, rather than the charged-up emotions that are the glowing afterburn of a climb. It appeared in *Summit* in 1990.

THE CLIMB TO SHIVA'S CAVE

Trekkers avoid Nepal from June until October for a very good reason: the monsoon that turns the country into one big aquarium of humidity and thunderstorms.

Stripped to my shorts on the misty jungle trail and oozing sweat in maximum humidity, I plodded behind Simon, mesmerized by the sight and sound of mud squelching from his boots. Leeches, alerted to our approach by an uncanny invertebrate radar, swayed on the tips of leaves, poised to drop. As we entered a rhododendron grove, insects screeched a maddening, eardrum-fibrillating hum. Above this din rose the rumble of the Barun River, swollen by countless tributaries gushing out of dense forests.

A sudden downpour proved too much for Simon Yates's battered umbrella; it collapsed under the impact, folding over him like a Venus flytrap. "This," he muttered in his thick British accent, "is real wacky explorer stuff."

We were on the trail to Makalu, the world's fifth-highest mountain. Our group of climbers and trekkers had foot-slogged for an eventful week from the tiny airport at Tumlingtar. We'd emerged from the steaming jungles of eastern Nepal, crested verdant ridges, splashed through rice paddies and villages, clambered down and up the steep-sided Arun River Valley and crossed alpine wonderland to arrive at the banks of the Barun River.

The Barun Valley is Nepal at its wildest. Few people, other than religious pilgrims, roaming yak herders and occasional mountaineers, travel there. Prayer flags and walls of mani stones mark the path along the valley. Pilgrims end their journey at sacred Lake Barun Pokhari, fed by the glaciers descending from Makalu. Our destination lay farther and higher, to ice walls, granite prows and, we hoped, the summit of Makalu. Spring and late autumn are more hospitable times to trek toward Makalu, but if you're a mountaineer wishing to reach the mountain and catch the brief spell of calm weather between the monsoon's end and the onset of winter, there is no choice but to brave the wet season. As luck would have it, we encountered a freakishly heavy monsoon. Rain fell in sheets, all day, every day, for a week, dogging us, the lowland villagers and the Sherpas we'd hired to carry our loads. Once in a while, momentary breaks in the clouds let us glimpse the green-terraced hillsides that are Nepal's hallmark.

Since most of the trekkers were English, the full-body water torture of the monsoon really wasn't a problem. In fact, the rain proved to be a sort of cultural catalyst, encouraging the Nepali villagers to invite us into the shelter of every wayside chang house. These are pubs where chang, temba and rakshi—the Nepali alcohol trilogy—are served. Chang, a beer brewed from rice or millet, is the color of washing-up water and is sweetish to the taste; temba resembles chang but is served warm in a bamboo jug and imbibed through a straw. As for the colorless spirit called rakshi, the owner of the bottle from which I first sipped cautioned me: "One man, one bottle: completely drunk."

The rain and the chang-house casualties weren't a problem. It was the earthquake and the leeches that set everyone's nerves on edge. A 6.7 quake hit in the predawn hours of our third day while everyone slept in their sodden tents, quietly growing moss. First we bounced against the ground as if it were a trampoline. Then the boom of landslides filled the darkness. Just as the waterlogged ground seemed about to liquefy and send us sliding into the valley, the quake stopped.

Leeches presented a far more sustained torment. A blood-engorged leech lodged behind the ear or between the toes was little more than an irritation for some of us. Others, though, discovered new dimensions of revulsion. One morning a trekker emerged from his tent, coughing, sneezing and yelling, "Get it out, get it out!" His method of protection had consisted of sleeping in his rainsuit, boots and gloves, then lacing his gaiters, cuffs and hood tightly around him. Inside his tent, he'd zip the entrance shut and then seal the gaps between zippers with wads of toilet paper. Finally, he'd slip inside his sleeping bag and cinch the hood tightly around his neck. His nose was the only exposed part of his body.

Crouching at my tent door, the trekker pointed to a leech embedded inside his nostril. I grasped the slippery creature and tugged, stretching it triple its length, but it kept slapping back into his nose like a strip of Pirelli rubber. The poor man became unglued and frantically pulled at the leech until the doctor brought forth a salt shaker, which caused the worm to explode spectacularly. For a leech, salt is hell.

On the seventh night we camped beside the Barun River at Yangri, a lush pasture used by the Tibetan villagers for grazing zum, a cow-yak hybrid. Waking the next morning, I noticed something odd: rain wasn't pelting my tent. Peering through the entrance, I saw blue sky for the first time in eight days. The monsoon had ended.

The view was worth the long wait. Above the meadow loomed huge cliffs festooned with tropical vegetation and criss-crossed with waterfalls. At the head of the valley the south flank of Makalu rose high and white.

After spending the morning soaking up the sun and drying wet clothing, we set off late. Following the Barun, we passed several crude stupas. These dome-shaped rock stacks decorated with prayer flags flying from bamboo sticks indicate a Buddhist holy place. Prayer flags—cotton streamers printed with Sanskrit prayers—flap in the wind to invoke constant prayer, while passing travelers toss stones onto the stupas to increase their height.

Higher, at a meadow called Mera, we found a veritable forest of prayer flags and shrines. It was easy to imagine why Mera had been chosen as a place of worship, surrounded as it was by crashing waterfalls, green pastures and conifer forests fringed by icy peaks. If Eden or Shambhala ever existed, they surely resembled this valley.

"What is the importance of this place?" I asked Nima Tenzing, a spry sixty-five-year-old from the Everest region who had made a career of assisting mountaineers since the British expeditions of the 1950s. He pointed up at a 3500-foot-high cliff. Two-thirds of the way up the steep wall of moss- and grass-covered granite slabs, a huge triangular rock wedge had fallen away to produce a gargantuan indentation—a cave. Through a fracture in the cave's ceiling fell a cascade of water.

"The caves of Shiva and Parvati," Nima explained.

"A holy place?"

"Oh, yes, very holy. Pilgrim place."

"You mean pilgrims walk all the way up here and climb this cliff to get to that cave?"

He nodded.

The Great Lord Shiva, god of destruction and rebirth, is one of the supreme gods of the ancient Hindu scriptures. Parvati is his consort. Powerful and divine, they are worshipped in every Hindu community.

A trio of toothless old Hindu women appeared on the trail. Barefoot and ragged, they paused to greet us. Several of our porters gathered around the women, including Sharu Prahubati, an Indian member of the expedition who, naturally, spoke Hindi.

"They have been to the caves," Sharu announced.

I looked upward but could see neither a trail nor a safe route through the vegetated slopes and waterfalls. To imagine these grandmothers clambering up sod walls and cliffs was more than I could swallow, but the women insisted they'd made the pilgrimage.

Sharu quizzed them. They'd walked from Khanbari, a week away, and had begun their pilgrimage by bathing in the sacred lake beneath Makalu, two days upriver from where we stood. They'd then hiked down the trail and climbed to the caves of Shiva and Parvati.

"They say there are two caves," explained Sharu. "Each contains a shrine full of the offerings of many pilgrims—piles of coins, crystals and statues of the gods. A hermit guards the caves, they say, and if we go up we must bring money so he can make an offering for us."

"Someone lives up there?" I asked skeptically.

"So they say."

Our porters erupted into chatter. Though none had made the pilgrimage to the caves, each had a story of what could be found there. One claimed the shrine in the cave was paved with precious stones; another motioned that crystals as big as a fist hung from the ceiling; yet another told us the story of a rogue who tried to steal a ruby from the shrine and fell to his death on the descent. The old women nodded. "Great powers protect the shrine," they warned.

"But where did they climb up the cliff?" I asked.

The women told us that there were two paths: one difficult, the other longer but easier. If we wanted to, we'd find the way. Leaving us with this inscrutable advice, they marched off. Again I stared up at the cave. Either there were a lot of pilgrims' bones at the foot of the wall or the old women were spinning us a tale. After all, Nepal is the home of the yeti, which exists more in the imagination than in the flesh.

"Is it true, Nima?" I asked while staring at the play of sunlight on the glistening water spout at the cave's mouth.

"Oh, yes. After Makalu we go up!"

"But you are a Buddhist, and this is a Hindu place."

Nima shrugged, scribing a circle in the air with both hands. "It is all one."

Weeks passed as we tried, and failed, to climb Makalu. Himalayan mountaineering is something of a pilgrimage in itself, an arduous personal journey on which one pushes oneself to physical and mental extremes unattainable within the daily grind of our home lives. Perils confront all pilgrims, and on Makalu one of our members tumbled 1500 feet down the mountain in an avalanche, escaping with minor injuries. After this drama, October's raging winds set in and we quit the mountain. Six weeks after passing through the meadow of Mera, we camped again beneath Shiva's and Parvati's caves, homeward bound.

Emerging from my tent one morning to a cobalt blue sky, I was handed a cup of tea by Nima, who wore his canteen buckled around his waist and held his walking stick, a ski pole, at the ready, evidently anticipating a major hike. "We go up?" he said. It was more of a statement than a question.

Remembering Nima's suggestion that we make the pilgrimage to the sacred caves, I grabbed my camera and a ski pole. Though weeks of humping loads had left us weary, I knew that unless we made the pilgrimage we'd never cease wondering about the tales of shrines and the hermit guardian on the cliffs above.

Nima told me that he; our cook, Pasang; and Pasang Ongde, a porter, would reconnoiter. Four others would follow: Doug Scott, Sharu, Scottish doctor Brian McGowan and me. Thus, our pantheistic pilgrimage included three Nepali Buddhists, an Indian Hindu, an aspiring English Buddhist, and a Scot and an Australian, both of indeterminate religious persuasion.

Pasang led us past fluttering prayer flags to the foot of the wall, where a narrow trail, hidden till we reached it, appeared. Craning our necks upward, we saw the path above—well-worn steps kicked into steep turf by many feet. It weaved between waterfalls and rock slabs and disappeared far above. Pasang turned, smiled broadly and declared we had solved the first problem of the pilgrimage: finding the way.

It occurred to me as I wound up the path that this wasn't the first pilgrimage to a sacred site of Shiva that I'd made. In 1981 Doug and I had walked beyond the town of Gangotri, in the Indian Garhwal Himalaya, to the source of an arm of the Ganges. Along the trail we'd met many pilgrims whose mission was to bathe in the frigid waters and cleanse themselves of sin in preparation for the afterlife. Most Hindu pilgrimages consist of difficult journeys to river sources, such as mountain lakes and glaciers, and on that especially holy trail I was intrigued by the constant flow of people, some so old and sick they had to be carried.

We intended to scale an unclimbed ridge on Shivling, a dramatic-looking peak named after Lord Shiva. Our plans excited the pilgrims, who assured us that we, too, were pilgrims and that it was our destiny to reach the summit of Shivling. Turbaned gurus, wild-haired yogis and saffron-robed sadhus begged briefly for a few rupees to help them along their road to piety and enlightenment.

Like the trek to Shivling, the journey to the caves of Shiva and Parvati is essentially a Hindu pilgrimage. But because Hinduism and Buddhism have coexisted for 2500 years, each religion recognizes the holy sites of the other, hence the enthusiasm of our Buddhist friends climbing ahead of us. Such had also been the case at our Shivling base camp, where our neighbors, who inhabited caves dug into a boulderfield, were hermits of both religions. Their mythology and scriptures share a common geography.

Shared pilgrimages are common in the Himalaya. Another example is Mount Kailas, a 22,028-foot peak on the Tibetan Plateau atop which sits Shiva's throne, according to Hindu mythology. The streams originating around Mount Kailas feed the Ganges; in Hindu myth, these are the matted braids of

Shiva's hair. Buddhists also regard Kailas as a holy site, believing it to be the physical and metaphoric center of the world. A Buddhist pilgrimage to Kailas entails a parikrama, a thirty-two-mile circumambulation of the mountain during which pilgrims meditate on the cycle of life and death. Truly devout Tibetan Buddhist pilgrims may even make the journey in a series of prostrations, literally crawling the entire way.

As the path headed up a vertical rock rib with waterfalls crashing to either side, I began to worry that Pasang's decision to take the direct, difficult path was a mistake. But I needed only a moment's thought to see the method in Pasang's madness and identify the Buddhist metaphor in his decision. By taking the fast, direct, but difficult and hazardous route—like the Buddhist road to enlightenment called Hinayana—we would reach our goal quickly, rather than achieving results by the longer, more methodical route prescribed by Mahayana Buddhism.

We'd grasped our way up a thousand feet of muddy sod- and boulder-choked gully when the wall steepened into a forty-foot bulge. Nima had nearly slipped on a previous rock slab, and I didn't relish the thought of my wet boots flailing against this slick rock.

"We should have brought ropes and climbing gear," I suggested to Doug, figuring that the path had become too dangerous. Then, out of the corner of my eye, I saw barefoot Pasang Ongde saunter up the slab. Pasang followed in delaminating sneakers and then Nima too. Standing on top, Pasang leaned over and offered his hand to Brian, a fearless nonclimber whose scuffling shoes sent shivers up and down my spine. With the nonclimbers on top there was no choice but for the climbers to follow. Hyperventilating with nervous tension, I teetered up the smooth granite, using flexing handholds of sod, trying to ignore the view of the unbroken drop to the valley floor.

Pasang grinned at me and said, "This Nepali climbing expedition."

"Lead on," I said humbly, traversing in Pasang's footsteps to yet another rock band. Again the Nepalis cruised up the slab and waited for us. Pasang, leaning over the precipice as cocky as they come, spied an easier way off to the side. Recommending we follow that route, he pointed to it and said, "That way for yaks." He took off, chuckling to himself.

It was ironic. After seventeen years of technical rock climbing and nine of Himalayan mountaineering, I considered myself a reasonably good climber. But here, in Pasang and Pasang Ongde, were two guys who could literally climb circles around me, yet who'd never "climbed" in their lives. When sixty-five-year-old Nima breezed up the slope, I decided to reevaluate my perception of myself as a climber.

Three hours after we set off, Shiva's Cave came into view. Filled with a strange excitement—the same light feeling in the chest I notice whenever I reach a mountain summit—we clawed up the final brush slope. The first hint of a shrine was a boulder surrounded by prayer flags. Stuffed into a fissure were fistfuls of rupees. We continued till we stood before the gaping, yellow-walled cavern.

The cave, shaped like a Gothic cathedral, was far bigger than I'd imagined. Its roof stood 500 feet off the rubble floor, and the entrance spanned 400 feet. Its deepest recess lay 300 feet into the rock. From its ceiling gushed a curtain of water.

Our Nepali friends strode quickly toward the waterfall, stood in its midst, clasped their hands in prayer and chanted softly to themselves while the water flowed over them. Chanting and the gentle susurration of the waterfall filled the cave. We stood silently, deeply moved, as Nima, Pasang and Pasang Ongde let us observe the ritual of their prayer.

We climbed into the cave to a site marked by prayer flags. No, there was no hermit, nor any jewel-studded shrine—perhaps these were things the old women had seen in their imaginations. Perhaps what we found constituted a treasure nonetheless. Set among the rocks, covered in the dusts of time, were layers of ritual objects: brass statuettes of Shiva and Parvati; pots, oil lamps and bells; a conch shell from the sea; rotting prayer flags and parchment scriptures; rusting tridents that symbolized the Hindu trinity of Brahma the Creator, Vishnu the Preserver and Shiva the Destroyer. Around these lay offerings of coins, kukris (the curved knives carried by Nepalis), jagged lumps of quartz, incense sticks, candles, juniper boughs, faded flowers, handfuls of grain and likenesses of the gods shaped from dough.

Nima made puja, offerings to the gods. He lit several oil lamps and incense sticks and then sparked a blaze of juniper. The rising smoke suggested ascent toward heaven. While we left offerings of cookies and coins, Pasang took up the conch shell and blew a long, proud note that echoed down the valley.

Looking at the meandering Barun River framed by the mouth of the cave and the waterfall splashing before us, I wondered how this remote place had attained such importance. Who came first, and when, are probably unknowable. Hindus have inhabited the lower valleys for thousands of years, but in the mountainous region the population is Buddhist. Perhaps, one spring or autumn long ago, a Hindu wanderer had glanced upward and seen the cave in which we stood. In the chill air he would have seen a tall stalagmite of ice formed by the waterfall set inside a womblike cavern. To our eyes the ice pillar would resemble just so much ice, but the pilgrim would have interpreted it as a natural manifestation of Shiva in the form of a lingam—a phallus. Hindu mythology regards the lingam as representative of Shiva; every temple to Shiva has a lingam as its central point of worship. This dome or column stands for the Axis of Existence, while the chamber containing the lingam symbolizes the womb of Parvati, the life-giving goddess. So, standing in the cave, we stood in a natural temple of the supreme god and of creation itself.

The ice lingam that would form as winter set in is one of several natural lingams found in the Himalaya. These may be mountains like Shivling ("Shiva's lingam"), rock pinnacles or domes of ice. Perhaps the most famous ice lingam stands in the mountains above Kashmir's Sind Valley. Every year, thousands of Hindus make a twenty-nine-mile pilgrimage from the village of Pahlgam, east of Srinagar, to a cave where a water seep forms an ice dome. Pilgrims making this journey brave blizzards and the rigors of altitude, but to die on a pilgrimage, they believe, assures one of a better life to come.

The time came to leave Shiva's Cave. We sidled along a narrow ledge above a precipice to reach Parvati's Cave, where another fountain spattered the rock floor. As the sun neared the horizon, our Nepali friends again made puja. In dimming light we treaded fearfully down, crossing waterfalls and lowering ourselves over cliffs on the roots of shrubs.

Back at the meadow we felt the serenity that follows a safe return from a dangerous pilgrimage. I knew I'd always regard the pilgrimage to Shiva's and Parvati's caves as among the best climbs of my life. For a while I even wondered if our weeks of enduring cold fingers and toes on Makalu were merely a diversion; maybe this pilgrimage was the real objective of the expedition. After all, pilgrimages are predestined experiences—or so believe the Hindus.

Our friends had spent the day lazing at Mera, watching us on the wall. Simon asked what we'd found. I paused. Should I offer a Westerner's literal description of the journey? Or should I tantalize their imaginations?

"A fantastic shrine full of crystals, coins and statues," I replied, echoing the old Hindu woman who'd fired our curiosity six weeks earlier. I told our friends nothing more of what we'd found.

Mystery, myth and mysticism had woven together that day into a strong braid that, for those of us who'd climbed to the caves, connected us as pilgrims. Unraveling and explaining the mystery strand by strand would miss the point of the pilgrimage, for it isn't what you find at the end, but what you learn along the way.

THE TROUBLE WITH HUNZA

Karachi. Dawn. As the sun rises over the slums and fills the velvet sky, the city comes to life for the day. Sounds and visions of Islam form amid the cloying heat.

And smells.

To one side of the truck-rental agency lies an open sewer. Behind it, an acre of fish, drying in ranks. On the other side of the street a car-size mound of offal entombs a bloated beast of burden, lying on its back, its hooves pointing rudely skyward. Bicycles with wobbly wheels zip through the gauntlet of squalor, displacing clouds of flies. The initiates to the Third World in our expedition stand open-mouthed, the cameras around their necks agog, the emulsion shocked off their film.

And the truck: a huge, bed-of-iron Bedford, with six-foot-high steel walls decorated in day-glo dreamscapes, a hookah, a vase of plastic flowers and sundry colorful decorations spread across the dashboard. This "Junga Bus," piloted by two alternating Pakistani drivers, will take us 900 miles to Islamabad and the mountains of the Karakoram, shaking and baking us atop our bags and boxes, buns in the oven of the barren Sind Desert.

Hyderabad, Sukkur, Khanpur and Shujabad slip by in a sunstruck haze. One hundred fifteen degrees. We stop at every Coca-Cola stand and tea house on the way, guzzling and eating chapati and dhalbat curries floating in yellow oil. Mark Miller, a British climber built like a Sumo wrestler, stripped to his underpants, calls them OPEC specials.

Doug Scott, in search of "English-style tea," instructs the waiter to bring us a pot of tea with milk and sugar separate, rather than in the Pakistani style of sugar-tea-sugar-milk-sugar stewed-brewed-boiled together for hours. "Yaar, the mad English," the cook exclaims when he sees us add milk and sugar to the tea anyway. A fat desert toad hops onto the table and plops into a saucer of tea water, looking smug until swatted away.

Lahore. Midnight. The truck makes an unscheduled stop at a back road between nowhere and nothing. Highway robbery? We wake to see the driver disappearing with armfuls of soap, talc and hair oils into the home of his lover, whose father owns the brick factory where we are parked. Around us a Heironymus Bosch-scape of belching chimneys and coke ovens. Monitor lizards with flicking blue tongues and swishing tails police the alleyways between brick stacks. Wood-sandaled coolies lift steel lids on the ground, uncapping hellish holes of spitting fire, and shovel coke into them, while a foreman dumps a glowing ember into a hookah and begins to hubble-bubble the night away. As we roam about we smell burning rubber, then feel burning feet.

Finally, Islamabad. Casualties of the truck ride are admitted to the hospital, too many OPEC specials having wreaked havoc on their stomachs, their brains fried by the sun. Off the truck and onto a bus for a drive up the Karakoram Highway, etched into the banks of the Indus River Gorge.

The bus sways at the hands of our pie-eyed, heroin-smoking driver. Drivers are the renegades of Pakistani roads. The temperature climbs.

Gilgit, gateway to the fertile valley of the Hunza. Terraced fields of vibrant green glow against the barren hills. Veiled women and girls, bent at the waist, pluck the pickings of the fields.

We stagger into a restaurant and sit beneath a swishing fan, ordering Cokes and OPEC specials. A souvenir salesman pesters us with a bandit's sword guaranteed 100 percent to have severed the heads of countless Englishmen on the Khyber Pass. Our drivers cram into a booth, surrounded by friends and friends of friends. Lashings of cokes, tea, dahl, chickens, chapati and rice appear at their table, while unilateral nausea undermines our morale. Mountains? Did we come here to climb mountains?

The bill floats like a butterfly to our table: astronomical. Dinner for ten seems to be on us. Arguments. Gesticulating hands. Managers, waiters, sons of managers, assistant sons of managers, their wives and grandparents and forty children scream at drivers, mechanics and ticket-sellers of the Masherbrum Bus Company. Drivers tear up the bill. Waiters write it again, for an increased amount. I squirm away. Outside, the heat. A mullah chants a Koranic verse from a tower on the edge of town. Stomach in turmoil. I watch a mechanic spark an arc welder to light his K2 cigarette. He grins and I see my cadaverous face reflected in his sunglasses. Then I puke.

Illness reaches a crescendo in Karimabad. We have now left the bus behind in favor of a pair of jeeps. Ibrahim, a one-armed jeep driver, who used to live in London till punks threw him out of the third floor of a flat and crippled his arm, screeches his jeep to a halt in a cloud of dust. The sahibs alight, then puke, or fly in all directions with rolls of toilet paper flapping.

Melons in the stalls swell like bursting footballs under the heat, splitting and hissing with gases and fermenting sugars. Old men with orange beards debate what ails the foreigners and studiously watch our retching. Sweat-and-grime-streaked Miller walks about naked, save for his pink underpants. Bedbug bites dot his torso. A representative of the mayor requests him to clothe more fully, his Sumoesque frame an offense to the townspeople.

In the mountains, we watch avalanches teem off the Ultar peaks. At times, these swell onto the meadows, dragging bleating sheep and goats to their doom. One sweeps so close that we hear the animals' hooves scratching at life, see the near-human disbelief in their eyes as they are carted off by a river of ice. The old shepherd, wheezing with tuberculosis, and whose beautifully lined face I photograph, tells me that each year a hundred tourists take his photograph but no one ever sends him one.

Biboli-Mo-tin, a granite spire, rises above camp. The approach couloir is bathed in sunshine, raked by stonefall and sloughs of mud-snow-ice. The knee-deep upper slopes are poised to avalanche. Tending to our ruined bowels on a safe spur of rock, we are caught with our pants down by a tidal wave of glacial debris. For five minutes it rushes by, like a passing train.

"Safe now," proclaims Scott. We hike up our pants and proceed on up the gully, wading through small sloughs the consistency of lava. Progress slows at a band of rocks and seracs. Nightfall leaves Steve Sustad and I bivouacked on a butt ledge, with car-size blocks thumping down alongside us in bursts of sparks. Scott, Miller and Smith camp on an unstable slope above. Slow step-punching the next day gets us to 18,000 feet, on the col beside Bibo. Heat-wave-loosened rock peppers every inch of the tower. It's out of the question to climb, and we descend.

The next phase of the expedition is ambitious: climb Rakaposhi, a huge mountain reaching into sky and cloud. But ambition has left, replaced by unshakable illness in us all. A combination of dysentery and dehydration flattens me, and I end up back in Karimabad, in the hospital for a day, and I'm prostrate for a week. It was a small thing that entered our guts, bacterial in dimension, but devastating out of all proportion to its size. Our conversation dwells on it. Bowels and intestines. A thousand words for the shits. Miller stops his guts with a plug of toilet paper. Others eat high-powered antibiotics or fast until they look like famine victims. All without success.

Across the river from the friendly town of Karimabad, populated by Ismaeli Muslims, lies Minapin, land of the Nagars, people of the Shiite sect. Our friends in Karimabad warn us that we'll have problems with the Nagars. Everyone has problems with the Nagars. Every year, we are told, the Nagars try to bring their religious ceremony into Karimabad, a procession of wailing and chanting and self-flagellation with whips of barbed wire and spikes. And every year they are turned back at gunpoint.

Our problems begin when the Nagars turn a six-hour porter journey to the base camp for Rakaposhi into a two-day walk, demanding double the wage of any other porter, as well as a goat to eat, footwear, socks and goggles. Sudden bankruptcy. Debate turns to argument, push comes to shove and fifty Nagars jostle and threaten us; then they storm off at our proposal that the matter be settled by the village policeman. They disappear around a bend on the moraine, but, like a horde of charging Tartars, they return, advancing at a run, with sticks and rifles waving, filling the air with shouts. Another bout of jostling, hair pulling and insults and they leave, this time with much of the money they demanded.

News of this reaches the policeman. He reports it to the district commissioner, who sends a memo to the deputy minister for tourism, who mentions it to a colonel, until finally a fat dossier lands on the desk of General Zia himself, the president of Pakistan. Back along the chain goes the outrage, until the policeman at Minapin arrests seven of the ringleaders of the porter riot.

The policeman visits our camp to tell us this and asks if we are pleased. No, we are not. We do not wish these men to languish in prison, their families to go hungry and feel shame. Scott writes a letter requesting the release of the men. It leaves with the policeman, follows the chain of hands to Zia's desk and then returns to our camp. "Sorry, sir, but no one could decipher your handwriting."

The rest of the expedition fades into a non-event. One by one we trickle out of the mountains, having barely scratched the surface of them. As I pass through Karimabad one last time I sit in the tea house, wondering if our downfall had its origins here. The owner suggests a cold Coke. It suddenly strikes me that his

Cokes are ice cold, yet he has no refrigerator. I walk behind the burlap-walled kitchen and see a crate of bottled drinks cooling in the gutter, a glacial stream fed by all the runoff of Karimabad and the sheep-dotted meadows above. A single droplet of tainted water from the lip of a bottle, and the hopes of a summer fell by the wayside.

BALTORO!

Craaack!

The shock wave surges through the ice, passing underfoot, announcing its release with a sharp snap a hundred yards down the Baltoro Glacier. With a sudden jolt, several million tons of ice and boulders creep an inch down the valley. Melon-size rocks topple from sun-sculpted pedestals of ice. They clatter about our feet and splash into water-filled crevasses. Hussein—the old Balti porter carrying my load—clucks his tongue in mimicry of the glacial chatter, beams his toothless smile at me, then shuffles on his way. I follow in his steps, hopping from stone to shifting stone, marching ever deeper into the Karakoram Range of northern Pakistan. A few minutes later, puffing in the rarefied air of 14,000 feet, I pause to rest beside a glacial pond. All around tower ice-clad peaks. Ahead, scudding clouds alternately obscure and reveal the sun, dappling the turbulent terrain with light and shadow, animating the rock-strewn pressure ridges into a pitching chiaroscuro sea. This world appears utterly lifeless until a bumblebee buzzes around me before departing into the emptiness ahead.

Rasul, the Balti cook, joins me. He points to a herd of ibex—the sure-footed wild goat of the mountains—traversing the yellow cliffs of the Trango Towers beside us. With awakening senses I notice tiny yellow and lilac flowers springing up at our feet. Looking more closely at the pond, I see that it, too, is alive, bustling with the frenetic movements of wriggling larvae rising to the sun-warmed surface and minute ground spiders darting onto the pond's surface to seize the larvae.

This life on the glacier amazes me. Tonight, the pond will freeze solid. But somehow the larvae will survive, and, somewhere, the bumblebee will find another outpost of flowers, pollinate them and help sustain a meadow that may germinate in time to fatten the roaming ibex. Above the glacier, though, near the summits of the peaks that thrust into the jet stream, it is still a lifeless world—the solitude broken only when winds from the baking plains of the Punjab blow insects onto the snows, by ravens that fly up to feed on them, and when humans plod toward a frozen summit.

Suddenly, the sound of a Pakistani army helicopter rends the air. Our caravan of porters halts to watch the barrel of a small howitzer swaying on a cable beneath the chopper. In a few days the gun will be lobbing shells onto Indian positions on the Siachen Glacier. Spooked by the din of whipping rotors, the ibex scatter. They would do well to learn even more fear of man.

This is the Baltoro Glacier.

Five expeditions, encompassing more than 200 days on this thirty-five mile river of ice, have left me with a strange affinity for this difficult tract of land and its people. One doesn't easily fall in love with Pakistan or the Baltoro—as one might with parts of Nepal. If the words "lush" and "green" describe the Nepalese mountainscape, the Baltoro equivalents are "barren" and "ochre." No, an affinity for the Baltoro is an acquired taste.

The Baltoro Glacier is a harsh environment. Once you leave the last village on the approach up the Braldu River Valley, little grows that's worthy of being called a tree, save, perhaps, a few gnarled junipers clutching at the sandy hillsides. On the Baltoro, subzero blizzards can rage for a week; the next day, clear skies and scorching temperatures might melt the snowpack, etching sudden streams into the glacial surface. Mountains with mysterious names fringe the skyline, their 10,000-foot faces roaring with avalanches that billow across the two-mile-wide glacier. The Baltoro patiently, relentlessly removes the debris like a natural conveyor belt.

Long before I ever dreamed I'd visit this place, I read of the early expeditions to make the long walk here. Books like *Karakoram,* by Fosco Mariani, described an area so rugged it was barely known by the Pakistani government. Even the local Balti people, hired by expeditions to carry supplies into the glacial wastes, feared entering its deeper corridors. The places on this journey loomed large in my imagination—places such as Bardumal, the windswept plain whose name means "troublesome place"; Rdokas, the fairy-tale meadow; and Concordia, at the intersection of two great glaciers and humbled beneath towering K2, Broad Peak and Gasherbrum IV. When an expedition to climb Lobsang Spire and Broad Peak finally, unexpectedly, delivered me to the Baltoro in 1983, I found a land no less fantastic than that described by the early expeditioners.

Something about this small dot on the map of Asia has fascinated Westerners for more than century. Perhaps the fuss began in 1856, when Captain Montgomerie of the British Survey of India sighted his transit on the highest of the Baltoro peaks—K2, as he named it—and declared to his Indian assistant, "Babu, we have shot the giant." From 128 miles away Montgomerie had triangulated K2 ("K" for Karakoram, and "2" because it was the second in his list of readings), its summit second in height to Everest by only a few lengths of a climber's rope (but, as climbers would find in later years, a summit far more difficult to reach than Everest's). For the rest of the century a handful of explorers would try to penetrate Montgomerie's distant cluster of peaks.

One of those explorers, Francis Younghusband, using his Balti guide Wali's unwound turban as a makeshift climbing rope, crested an icy, 17,800-foot pass at the head of the Mustagh Glacier and looked over the Baltoro. In so doing, Younghusband became the first Englishman to link the known world to the Baltoro Glacier and the still-medieval villages of Askole, Chakpo and Chongo below it. That was scarcely more than a hundred years ago.

Atop the Mustagh Pass, Younghusband—a Kiplingesque political agent of the British Raj of India—gazed over the jagged peaks of Masherbrum, the Gasherbrums and K2. He was no stranger to Himalayan mountains, but the startling symmetry of the Baltoro skyline struck him in the same way that would captivate subsequent generations of alpinists. So spectacular is the layout of the Baltoro that an element of design seems to be at work.

Today, at first appearance, it seems little about the Baltoro landscape has changed since Younghusband's travels in 1887. Yet the Baltoro is no longer a solitary experience. With Pakistan's embrace of tourism in the late 1980s the Baltoro became that country's version of Nepal's popular Everest trek. Lured by the talismans of adventure and high altitude, trekkers today tour the valleys and villages, and climbers flock to the challenges of K2 and its massive neighbors.

But the booming tourist trade has overnight propelled the tribal people into the twentieth century. The sudden influx of visitors is squeezing the land and its wildlife. An undeclared war between India and Pakistan—known as the Siachen Conflict—ravages the mountainous border just a few miles from the trekking routes. With the dawning of the 1990s, the Baltoro stands on the verge of great change.

In Younghusband's day, maps of the Himalaya were filled with blank spots, but few were blanker than this branch of the Karakoram. The nation of Pakistan didn't even exist; it was still part of Indian Kashmir, divided into numerous, often warring, tribal regions. Of these quarrelsome tribesmen, the frontliners of the Raj regarded there to be no less reliable a band of brigands—yet conversely, no more loyal breed of man—than the Balti from the valleys around Askole and Skardu, where modern Baltoro treks begin.

Early explorers told tales of treachery, strikes and desertion among Balti porters; the terrain was difficult enough, but the inhabitants could make it hell. Today's Balti remain a tough, feisty bunch, molded by a lifelong struggle with the seasons in an unyielding land, and by centuries of conquest by Buddhist Ladakh, Hindu India, perhaps even by the Greeks under Alexander—and, most recently, by conquering Kashmiri Muslims, who converted the region to Islam several hundred years ago. The Balti are poor farmers, traditionally illiterate, since the people have no written language of their own. Their origins are vague, though their spoken language—an archaic Tibetan dialect—points to a Tibetan ancestry.

For Younghusband's trouble of crossing the Mustagh Pass and then wandering into Askole, the explorer was run out of the valley. Villagers were enraged that a foreigner had discovered the secret of their isolation, for the trade routes and passes to Ladakh and Hunza that converged on the Baltoro Glacier were closely guarded secrets. Today, the great-grandchildren of those villagers are the porters, cooks, guides, jeep drivers, shopkeepers and hotel clerks who vie for the business of trekkers and mountaineers visiting Baltistan.

As progress creeps up their valley, this once-reclusive people have become the measuring sticks of change. In 1989, when I last entered the cobbled streets of Askole, it seemed that half the village turned out to try and sell their wares. Women working the wheat fields had already halted us on the edge of town, shouting, "Hello! Hello!" and waving jewelry and embroidered caps made from homespun cloth.

Just a few years earlier, village women had veiled their faces and fled at the sight of us; now they were driving hard bargains. I looked over a few of the trinkets. The caps were decorated with found objects, such as zippers, battery caps, beads and old coins, some Indian, stamped with the head of England's King George VI and dated before the partition of India and Pakistan in 1947.

Among the jewelry—mostly composed of plastic beads—were a few bits of coral, turquoise and Xi stones, all common in the Sherpa valleys of Nepal. The stones attested to a bygone trading era between Ladakh and the Braldu Valley that only the grand-parents of these Balti women would recall.

In the village it was the men's turn to ply the market with us. In the house of Haji Medi, Askole's mayor, we drank tea and negotiated the price of a goat for our porters to eat. Haji spoke of the improvements to Askole since my last visit—a medical clinic across the river and a resident schoolteacher—and of future plans, including a radio for emergencies and, of course, the road, moving up the Braldu Valley only slightly faster than the glacier moves down.

"But do you think the road will really come this far?" I asked skeptically, thinking of the gorge and the landslides that frequently erase the old path.

"Yes," Haji insisted, and to prove his point he took me into another room, where he proudly displayed an incongruous item for this village where yaks still plow the fields with wooden plowshares: a brand-new mountain bike.

"When the road comes," explained Haji, "I can ride to Skardu."

Sometime in the future, an archaeological report on the approach to the Baltoro might read something like this: "The boulder-strewn valleys between Skardu and the Baltoro Glacier are littered with the rock peckings of Baltistan's earliest visitors. Chipping through the desert varnish covering the boulders, artists predating the birth of Christ and through the second millennium A.D. left symbols of their daily lives: hunting scenes, Buddhist stupas, Shivaite tridents, Chinese characters. By the mid to latter half of the twentieth century a different range of relics appears: the sardine tin, the empty gas-stove canister, the Kodak film wrapper, worn-out boots, double-ply toilet paper. These artifacts abound along the glacier and toward the summits of 8000-meter peaks. The wheeled period of mountain exploration began in 1987 A.D. with the first penetration of the glacier by mountain bike by a Swiss expedition. Bicycle spokes and brake grips from this period have been discovered near the Dunge Glacier, while automobile relics are common along the road to Askole."

Explorers of the nineteenth century faced a months-long overland journey through India to Baltistan's capitol, Skardu. From there, they could finally set out for the Baltoro. Even by the 1950s, when aircraft delivered expeditions to Skardu, the walk to K2 took eighteen days and involved river crossings by rope bridge and zahk—a raft made from inflated goat bellies. By the 1980s bridges and jeep roads had halved that time from Skardu. By the mid-1990s, at least according to plan, the dangerous Braldu Gorge—once Askole's best defense against invasion—will be tamed by jackhammer and blasting powder, so expeditions will drive directly to Askole.

The villagers eagerly await the road and the prosperity expected to follow in its wake. Villagers who have been to Skardu and have seen its thriving bazaar, its hospital and the luxuries of electricity—lights, appliances and, if they've peeked into the K2 Hotel, television—know how a road can change a village. They know that the jeep drivers and hotel and tea house owners who cater to tourists are wealthy men.

Until the road's approach in 1987, the Balti had shunned Western culture, in marked contrast to the mimicry of Western tastes that runs rampant in Nepal. Disinclined to outside influences, and too poor to afford modern luxuries, places like Askole remained time capsules of a medieval lifestyle. The Balti sluggishness to cash in on the tourist trade stemmed largely out of a disdain for things foreign. The Balti, who are devout Muslims, had their Koranic sensibilities so shocked by brash Western behavior and dress that the villagers were relieved when foreigners left town.

But now Haji Medi has given up politely asking trekkers passing through Askole to wear trousers rather than immodest shorts. Such things may seem unimportant, but they forecast changes of glacial impact. Progress offers the Balti solutions to many problems. Health care will solve the high infant mortality rate and ensure that simple ills do not become life-threatening. Winters, when Askole is snowed in, need no longer be desperate and hungry, as jeeploads of food and kerosene can be easily stockpiled. But progress will also dilute their ancient culture. "Young men don't know the old songs anymore," our cook Rasul lamented one day. "They listen to radio instead."

Yet Askole is just one stop on this road of change; the real reason the highway is being built is to allow the Pakistani military better access to the strategic passes at the head of the Baltoro Glacier. The Siachen Conflict is the highest-altitude war in history. Though both sides keep their own casualty counts classified, they admit that as many soldiers have fallen to altitude maladies and Karakoram storms as have to bullets. Since 1984 the Baltoro experience has included army camps, daily helicopter sorties and the distant thunder of artillery strikes.

The conflict erupted in the early 1980s when Indian forces established bases on the vast Siachen Glacier, adjacent to the Baltoro, and placed outposts on several passes straddling the two glacier systems. The border hereabouts is vague, with both nations claiming the region. Pakistan sent troops to remove the intruders, but the Indians, convinced of their ownership of the land, held fast to the high ground. Both armies dug in for a long siege under torturous conditions.

It's a war in which the skin on a soldier's finger freezes to his rifle trigger, in which long stays at 20,000 feet sap the strength and sanity of even the most disciplined trooper. Storms that ground helicopter—or porter—support can leave outposts starving. Opposing trenches are sometimes separated by only a few hundred yards. Snipers fire on anything that moves. Artillery rounds often fail to explode on impact in soft snow, so fuses detonate shells in midair, scattering a deadly rain of shrapnel. Assaults on foot at 20,000 feet degenerate into desperate uphill trudges where the gasping attackers make easy targets. Occasionally, mountain passes change hands, but usually whoever holds the high ground maintains. Trench warfare at its worst.

All this bloodshed over control of a few empty icefields seems curious, until you look at the conflict's roots. Pakistan split from India in 1947. Problems on the populous plains used to keep India and Pakistan preoccupied, and neither cared much about their vaguely drawn, shared borders in the vastness of the Karakoram, where boundaries ran along unreachable mountain ridge crests and glacial valleys. In 1965 and 1971, however, the two countries fought for control of areas along the length of their borders. In the end, cease-fire lines drawn in the north left many Muslim-settled parts of Kashmir under Indian (Hindu) control. Meanwhile Pakistan claimed valleys opening onto Indian territory.

Efforts to resolve boundary claims proved fruitless. Maps of the north drawn during the British rule of India left many uncertainties. Entire areas were unsurveyed; maps of some northern areas simply received a wash of color and the notation "undetermined."

Indian army mountaineering expeditions ventured into the Siachen region for years before the current conflict erupted; they found no one to counter them. When Pakistan finally did challenge the Indians, neither side envisioned the long, costly war that would follow. But neither side will relinquish its claim over an inch of land—not even uninhabitable ice and snow. If any issue might close the Baltoro to tourism, as happened during previous wars with India, it is this struggle.

The road, the war, the tourists; sounds of jackhammers, smoke on the horizon, trash on the trail. Intrusions, yes, but I wonder just how much the Baltoro's stubborn spirit of wildness has really diminished. I suppose each of my visits to the Baltoro has attempted to find again that ephemeral state of being I've encountered when luck and weather have allowed me to reach high on a mountain. The very things that make high-altitude climbing so dangerous—oxygen deprivation and the short-circuiting of body chemistry—also heighten one's awareness of the mountains and one's place in them.

I remember scratching out a snowcave with two companions at 26,000 feet on Gasherbrum IV in 1986. Night was approaching, the temperature plummeting. The concept of surviving a bitter bivouac wearing nothing but the clothes on our backs seemed tenuous at best; the very thought released a switchblade of adrenaline inside me and spurred feverish digging. Catching my breath between pawing handfuls of snow from our shelter, I looked down on the Baltoro. Alpenglow spilled over the west face of our mountain, setting our snowfield alight; a sudden calm settled in.

Here we stood, at the apex of all symmetries, or so it seemed. Eleven thousand feet below, at Concordia, the glacier forked in a perfect Y. Parallel lines of rubble ribbed the glacier along its length, and waves of ice blue mountains paralleled its flow. Distant monsoon thunderheads loomed over Indian Kashmir, but the Karakoram sky remained cloudless, divided into star-pocked bands of cobalt and pink. On my one side was the ascending moon, to the other the setting sun.

The chaos of colliding tectonic plates suddenly assumed a perfection of proportions. The mountains, I realized as never from below, defined the glacier, while the glacier, whittling away at the mountains, defined the architecture of the range. Radiating from this, all aspects of the mountainscape marched upward in equilibrium. So exact did this balance appear, it seemed there was neither one grain of sand too few nor one too many.

As expected, the bivouac was frigid. But we summited the

next morning, and a week later I was back on the Baltoro Glacier, stumbling over scree, with only the recollection of those thoughts and sights from the mountain. As we hiked home we caught up with a commercial trek, sharing the trail with them and enjoying their friendly company.

When the trekkers heard that we were low on provisions after two months on the Baltoro, they generously shared their excellent imported food. I complimented the cooking, and they told me I'd missed the best of the eating, as they'd dined on ibex the previous week. "Delicious, if you know how to cook it," I was told. At first I thought they were joking, but then they informed me that their guide had shot an ibex for them on the meadow above the campsite called Lillego.

"Don't you know that all wildlife is protected here?" I asked one of them later, mentioning the sign by the bridge at Dassu proclaiming that very fact.

"I don't recall any sign. Anyway, the fellow wanted to shoot it as a gift for us. I didn't want to offend him by refusing," replied the trekker.

Speechless before the fundamental ignorance of his answer, I realized that the sight of an ibex and the pawprint of a snow leopard—always present but so elusive as to be invisible— would soon be things of the past. I tried to fathom the mindset that would take such an encounter and turn it into a hunt. The villagers may be entitled to take a few ibex during the year, as they are the real owners of the land; one could argue that the army, defending Pakistan, are also entitled to the ibex they shoot. But for foreign trekkers to use the herds as a food source is inexcusable.

Growing human pressure is upsetting the natural balance on the Baltoro. When I first set foot on the glacier, in 1983, I shared it with fourteen climbing expeditions and a handful of trekkers. On my next visit, in 1986, nine expeditions were camped at the foot of K2 alone, with sixteen other climbing expeditions and a seemingly endless stream of trekkers dotting the Baltoro's length. Every year, the barren hillsides get scoured ever cleaner for firewood, while rubbish piles up in campsites and wayside stops such as Paiju, which have become giant, open-air latrines.

Though slightly bruised, the Baltoro still reigns magnificent. A full-blown Karakoram storm or the white chaos of an avalanche reminds us that nature still controls here, that man's visitations are temporary stains easily buried in the ice. The threat isn't so much what we leave there, but what we take away.

The Gasherbrum trek over, I reenter civilization just in time for video night in Skardu. In the lounge of the K2 Hotel, German, English and American trekkers, freshly returned from or about to embark on forays into the Karakoram, gather around a television. The warm glow of the cathode ray tube attracts a few jeep drivers and hotel staff too. They are watching an incredibly bad, American-made sci-fi flick.

Through the window beside the TV, I glimpse the waxing moon surmount the hills that flank Skardu and channel the mighty rivers that roar out of the Karakoram. Suddenly, below the hotel, the sprawling delta of the Shigar and Indus rivers lights up bright as a pool of mercury. It's a beautiful last look at the Karakoram before I jet out on the morning flight, but somehow my eyes can't leave the trash on the television. All too soon, it seems, I've reentered the global village. My two months of wandering and climbing on the Baltoro Glacier suddenly seem distant.

Conversation among a group of trekkers catches my ear. A woman, just returned from the mountains, laments that the Balti will never be the same after the road is built. Isolation, she argues, has preserved them from the corruption that has turned Nepal into a land of rupee sharks; progress will do the Balti no good. She would, it seems, prefer that they remain pickled by poverty, culturally embalmed exhibits in a private museum. I wonder if she'd be so keen on living life without a doctor or raising her own children in a dirt-floored hut.

She looks toward me for support and says, "If the road reaches Askole, will you help me blow it up?"

The trekker, so well intentioned, yet so naive with her fantasy of Third World monkey-wrenching; the Balti of the Braldu Valley, so eager for the good life—these people epitomize the double-reflection of the romantics and the aspirants, those who look back and those who look forward. The trekker may envy the simplicity of the Balti way of life, but not as much as the Balti envy our prosperity. What the Balti dream, we live, and what the Balti live, we dream.

MEETINGS WITH REMARKABLE MEN

CLIMBING IS AS MUCH ABOUT PEOPLE as it is about mountains. A fortune of my expeditions in the Himalaya and elsewhere has been to encounter some of the climbing legends of our time. Writing their profiles proved to be among the hardest assignments I have tackled. Being a climber myself, and in some cases having shared extreme moments on mountains with these people, gave me a unique perspective to view them from. *Climbing* published three of these pieces. "Seeking the Balance" profiles Doug Scott, the famous British expeditioner who invited me on my first Himalayan climb and with whom I made four expeditions in the 1980s. A climber not as well known to Americans, yet who influenced the trend in lightweight ascents of Himalayan peaks every bit as much as Reinhold Messner did, is the Pole Wojciech "Voytek" Kurtyka. We met at K2 base camp in 1987. His profile is called "Between the Hammer and the Anvil." In "Party of One," I profile an enigmatic and little-known American big-wall soloist named Jim Beyer. Two profiles appear in this anthology for the first time. "A Climb with Roskelley" sketches the famous, controversial American climber and sportsman John Roskelley. The story takes place in 1989 during our attempt to climb a Tibetan peak called Menlungtse. "Working-Class Hero" remembers the late, legendary Don Whillans, the hard-drinking British mountaineer who was as famous for his caustic wit, wisdom and one-liners as he was for the peaks he scaled.

SEEKING THE BALANCE:
A PROFILE OF DOUG SCOTT, THE GREAT SURVIVOR

The year was 1981 and the setting a peak named Shivling in India's Garhwal Himalaya. Doug Scott and I were huddled in a rocky corner at 20,000 feet, sheltering from the wind and the falling ice that our two companions above were dislodging. We'd been climbing for twelve days, our food and fuel were finished and the weather was deteriorating.

It was my first Himalayan climb, Doug's umpteenth. I began to whine about my hunger and the cold. "You'll never find enlightenment on a full stomach," Doug merely said; then he swung onto the rope and headed up the wall. Scott—a man designed to fell mountains—was in his element. For him, Shivling's summit was only one step on the journey; the experience was the essence of the climb.

Today, after twenty-five expeditions, the tenacious Briton remains one of the world's most active high-altitude climbers, still cramming two or three Asian jaunts into every year. With a career spanning three decades, Scott has watched the Himalayan scene change dramatically. Not surprisingly, he has given much thought to the philosophies and tactics of high-altitude climbing. Since he summited on Everest as part of a large team in 1975, Scott's thinking about mountaineering has evolved dramatically. For the past decade, he has approached his summits with small teams, moving fast and light, and relying on instinct, ability and commitment for success and survival. His message is that of the alpine-style prophet.

Scott, forty-seven at the time of our interview in 1988, has outlived most of his generation of Himalayan climbers. High-altitude mountaineering is a dangerous game that claims many of its players, but Scott, like Italy's Reinhold Messner, has lived a charmed life, touching the void more than once, yet always returning. Good luck or good instincts? Scott believes that it is the latter that brings him home from each trip. The loss of instincts—the ability to tune into oneself and the mountain—is, he believes, behind many recent climbing tragedies.

Still stocky from his rugby-playing days, Scott has greying hair frequently worn shoulder-length. His beard is shot with silver. Round, wire-rim glasses give him a John Lennon look, not inappropriate, as Lennon and Bob Dylan are still his favorite lyricists. A vegetarian, Scott also has interests in Eastern mysticism, homeopathic medicine, organic gardening and the philosophies of Gurdjieff. He's been known to make decisions by throwing the I Ching.

He speaks often about following the middle path in life, a Buddhist philosophy of avoiding extremes; yet Scott is famous for what can only be called extreme climbs. He is careful with his words, pausing often to choose the right phrase, but he also has a burly, tempestuous side that is intolerant of fools and false prophets. One journalist likened him to a Hell's Angel.

After five Himalayan expeditions with Scott, I finally cornered him for an interview in a ramshackle bar in Tumlingtar, Nepal, in fall 1988. We had just returned from his fourth (and my first) unsuccessful attempt on Makalu. While chickens strutted across the floor of the bamboo shack and a goat was bloodily quartered beside us, I plied him with Star beers and found that when looking back on thirty-four years of climbing, the great survivor has more to reflect on than just the mountains he's climbed.

The son of a Nottingham policeman, Scott began climbing on the gritstone edges, or cliffs, around Derbyshire. By age thirteen he was cragging on weekends and wintering in Scotland; at seventeen he was climbing in the Alps. In 1962, at twenty-one, Scott hitchhiked to the Atlas Mountains in Algeria and got the taste for big peaks and vagabonding that has kept him on the move ever since.

Working as a schoolteacher in the mid-1960s, he put his summer holidays to good use, making low-budget climbing trips to Chad, Kurdistan and Afghanistan, often traveling overland in ex-army trucks bought for about fifty dollars. Big-wall climbing, from the Cima Ovest to the Troll Wall, to Baffin Island and El Capitan, preoccupied him during the early 1970s and was the subject of his classic book, *Big Wall Climbing.*

His Yosemite sojourn marked a turning point in Scott's attitudes. There, embracing the free and easy atmosphere of the valley's heyday, he tossed aside his nerd glasses for the Lennon look, grew his hair long and adjusted his pace of life. Scott gave up teaching in order to pursue climbing full-time. It was a fortuitous decision, for previously unthought-of opportunities soon presented themselves to him.

"I had no interest in Everest until spring 1972, when out of the blue, Don Whillans invited me to the southwest face on the European expedition," says Scott. "I reached 26,000 feet, becoming snowblind in the process." But he also acclimatized without much trouble, and the unclimbed southwest face piqued his interest. And so began Scott's Everest years.

In autumn 1972 he joined Chris Bonington's first southwest face expedition, reaching 27,000 feet with Dougal Haston before turning back in the face of bitter winds. Three years later, on Bonington's brilliantly organized second expedition, Scott and Haston became the first to climb the southwest face, and the first Britons to climb Everest by any route. During their descent the pair ran out of daylight and oxygen and bivouacked in the open, above 8000 meters, enduring a desperately cold night without sustaining frostbite. It was an important lesson for Scott, showing him that it was possible to survive high bivouacs under severe conditions.

A day after Scott and Haston's summit climb, Peter Boardman and Pertemba Sherpa reached the top in deteriorating weather. As they descended, Mick Burke passed them en route to the summit. While Boardman and Pertemba waited for Burke near the lower South Summit, clouds rolled in and darkness fell; they finally had to descend in order to save their own lives. Burke was never seen again.

Though the expedition had been laced with tragedy, the ascent made Scott and Haston household names in Great Britain and opened doors usually closed to climbers. They even rubbed shoulders with royalty. Visiting Buckingham Palace, the Everest team met the queen. She remarked that they were the first climbers she'd ever met, to which, as Scott tells it, "Mo Anthoine replied that she was the first queen he'd ever met."

That Everest ascent in 1972 was also Scott's first meeting with Dougal Haston, a climbing partner Scott has found few equals to. When speaking of the late Haston, Scott's tone softens in admiration and nostalgia. He describes the legendary Scottish climber as a very self-contained man. "He didn't give much away, yet he didn't take much from you either. He just expected you to do your bit." Scott feels that such self-reliance is essential to Himalayan climbing. "The best team will be two people hardly conscious of each other, functioning equally well," he says. "Worrying about each other only drains your energy."

The pair climbed a new route on McKinley's south face in 1976, cementing what seemed to be an invincible partnership. But in winter 1977, Haston was killed in an avalanche while skiing near Chamonix. Scott took the loss of Haston hard. After everything they'd been through together, he found it incredible that Haston should die in what was virtually his own backyard. Scott finds it more than coincidental that Haston died shortly after completing the manuscript of his novel *Calculated Risk*. "In the book," says Scott, "the hero triggers an avalanche while skiing a couloir in Chamonix, but he outskis it and lives. Dougal triggered an avalanche in the same couloir, but it overwhelmed him." In Scott's thinking, life and death are governed by more than capriciousness.

In later years, with the deaths of Nick Estcourt and Al Rouse on K2, Georges Bettembourg and Roger Baxter-Jones in Chamonix, Alex MacIntyre on Annapurna, Peter Boardman and Joe Tasker on Everest's northeast ridge, and Don Whillans—the hard-drinking old friend who gave him his start on the big peaks—to heart failure in England, Scott watched his closest friends disappear. These deaths stripped away an entire era of British mountaineering, leaving behind an ethos of wild, on-the-edge living and climbing.

Scott has had cause to consider his own mortality many times. Describing his thoughts in the seconds after being pulled into an avalanche behind Estcourt during an attempt on K2's west ridge in 1978, he says, "I realized I was about to die and suddenly thought that it wasn't such a bad thing. I didn't want to die, but I had no fear of it." Scott used up one of his nine lives that day when the fixed rope he was clipped to snapped, freeing him from the snowy vortex that consumed Estcourt.

Such events are cause enough for some to give up climbing, but Scott has returned to the Himalaya many times since. "There seemed no point in giving up," he says simply. Shaping an attitude about death is essential to Himalayan climbing, Scott believes. "In order to climb properly on a big peak you must free yourself of fear," he says. "This means you must write yourself off before any big climb. You must say to yourself, 'I may die here.'"

With the mountaineer's beast of ambition—an ascent of Everest—finally tamed, Scott realized the potential of an untapped Himalaya and eagerly participated in its development.

In 1977, Scott and Bonington made the first ascent of the Ogre, a 24,000-foot granite massif in the Biafo region of the

Karakoram. Their descent from that climb is one of the great epics of survival.

Rappelling from the summit, Scott was forced to make a tension traverse to the next set of anchors. At the end of his rope, he couldn't quite reach over to the crack. Rearranging his feet in the evening's gloom, he unwittingly stepped onto a thin veneer of ice and fell, swinging wildly through space before smashing into the summit headwall. Both of Scott's ankles were broken, and the climbers had to bivouac a few pitches lower.

Descending the peak's upper icefield the next morning, Scott was forced to crawl down, assisted by Bonington; they were joined by Clive Rowland and Mo Anthoine, who had stayed at the team's top camp. A major storm moved in, complicating the descent even further. They soon ran out of food and fuel, and after five days, during which Bonington rappelled off the end of a rope and broke several ribs, they feasted on the contents of a lower camp's rubbish dump—frozen rice, tea leaves and cigarette butts.

On the eighth day of descent they reached the glacier, and Scott crawled the remaining four and a half miles of ice and moraine to base camp. When they finally reached it, the camp was abandoned, their other teammates having presumed the foursome dead. Then, after walking out to the nearest village, Anthoine and Rowland got a stretcher party to Scott. Balti porters carried Scott out to Askole and, thirteen days after the accident, he was helicoptered to Skardu. The helicopter crashlanded in Skardu, leaving the injured Bonington still stranded in Askole for seven days until it was repaired.

Scott plays down the magnitude of his endurance with typical British understatement. "To be up there," he says, "one must be fit. All I wanted was to get home. It may sound trite, but when the press found me in Nottingham Hospital, I was embarrassed that I was so daft as to break my legs.

"Everest southwest face showed that you can do anything with enough good climbers, good organization, Sherpa support, oxygen and fixed rope," Scott points out. In using minimal fixed ropes on the Ogre, he was moving toward an ideal of total self-sufficiency on even the biggest peaks. Jumaring ropes on Everest was a relatively risk-free role compared to the freedom of his first expeditions. "You haven't left the ground if you're still tied to it," he believes. "I learned a lot with fixed ropes, but at the end of the day it's a hollow victory compared with the cut-off feeling of being a million miles from home."

In 1979 Scott took a step closer to his ideal on Kang-chenjunga, when he and Frenchman Georges Bettembourg teamed up with Peter Boardman and Joe Tasker for an ascent of this peak's north ridge. In some ways this is Scott's most interesting climb, not only for the achievement—a new route accomplished with lightweight tactics on the world's third-highest peak—but for the personal dynamics within the four-man team.

"I first met Georges in Skardu, after he'd done Broad Peak," says Scott. "He came rushing toward me and said, 'I am going to climb with you.'" Scott immediately took to the warmth of this Latin and asked him to Kangchenjunga. "He was a good balance," says Scott. "It was quite a formidable thing to be with Pete and Joe."

Books and history paint Boardman and Tasker as an insepa-rable climbing pair, but Scott found a lot of competition be-tween them. "Neither wanted to be the weaker of the two," he says. "I think that attitude brought the best out of them both. But it might have been what killed them on the northeast ridge of Everest."

Scott measures personality in terms of the mixture of "male" and "female" characteristics that comprise an individual. "Male" characteristics, such as aggressiveness and its twin, ambition, can be useful in pushing unwilling flesh up a mountain, but Scott feels that an overdose of either can be hazardous. "If all one can think about is the summit and one loses touch with one's intuition," he says, "there's a good chance you'll get killed."

Scott's solution is to encourage what he calls the more intuitive "female" characteristics.

Nonetheless, his views on women climbers in the Himalaya may be controversial to some. "I think women are up against it in alpine-style Himalayan climbing, mainly because they can't carry the same weight as men," says Scott. "They're certainly capable of Sherpa-assisted siege ascents, but it'd be a very exceptional pair of women who could climb one of the five highest 8000-meter summits totally alpine style."

On Kangchenjunga, intuition worked for Scott. On the final push, Boardman, Tasker and Scott were on the verge of retreating from their snowcave at 26,000 feet, discouraged by hurricane winds. But Scott awoke at 3:00 A.M. with the compelling feeling that they should continue to the summit.

"The feeling came from the chest," he says, "not from the head." Stepping outside at 5:00 A.M., he found that the winds had dropped for the first time in five weeks. "On that occasion the feeling was to go for it, but many times the inner voice has advised me to go down," he concludes.

Rivalry is common among successful climbers, and despite the trip's success, there were wounds from the aftermath of Kangchenjunga. "I inevitably was the one the press gave prominence to, simply because I was well known from Everest," says Scott. "In fact, only Pete and I were mentioned in the first news bulletins. Joe was completely left out—he felt I was in the way of the publicity and recognition that were his due."

During the summer of 1980, Scott returned to the west ridge of K2 with Boardman, Tasker and Dick Renshaw. Rather than fix the whole mountain, they tried to leapfrog up this difficult route with only 2000 feet of rope, pulling their lines up and reusing them above as they established higher camps. Scott found that this experiment in "capsule-style" climbing involved even more drudgery than conventional siege tactics. In addition, his relationship with Tasker was deteriorating, and their partnership soon dissolved. "The atmosphere between us was so bad I quit the expedition," says Scott.

After K2, Scott moved toward his ideal trip, seeking out partners gifted with more intuitive than aggressive traits, and made no more concessions about his pure alpine-style tactics. From 1980 onward he never used fixed ropes again.

Autumn 1980 was the first of Scott's four expeditions to Makalu. His companions were Bettembourg and Roger Baxter-Jones, two climbers who had what Scott felt was the right balance of ambition and intuition. They intended to go up the unclimbed southeast ridge and descend the southwest ridge, the original line of ascent on Makalu—six miles long in all, with much terrain above 8000 meters. High-altitude traverses, Scott believed, presented the next frontier in Himalayan climbing.

The southeast ridge is a committing route, involving a descent into a huge cwm from which escape is difficult. Baxter-Jones likened it to "putting one's head in a noose." The trio came close to Makulu's summit, but a storm drove them down in an epic retreat.

Despite the lack of a summit, Scott regards this as one of his most successful trips because of the human element. He speaks fondly of Baxter-Jones and Bettembourg, in whom he not only found able ropemates—Scott calls Baxter-Jones the strongest climber he's ever known and Bettembourg brilliant on mixed terrain—but warm companions.

Scott's ideal of commitment reached its zenith on Shisha Pangma's west face in 1982. In terms of style, Scott regards this 9000-foot new route on an 8000er as his best climb; it was made with Baxter-Jones and Alex MacIntyre, both of whom shared Scott's alpine-style vision. Shisha Pangma came as a progression: Nuptse's north face in 1979 showed Scott how fast a high peak could be climbed, while the 1980 multiday marathon attempting Makalu and thirteen days on the east pillar of Shivling in 1981 showed him just how long one could be self-sufficient.

"By 1979 there was no other way I wanted to climb," Scott explains. "I knew I wouldn't always be successful, but climbing alpine style was immeasurably more satisfying than spending three months like an ant, working away with other ants constructing a route."

Two weeks before our talk in Tumlingtar, Doug and I had been cramponing up the northwest face of Makalu. Around us stood three of the last great problems of the 8000-meter peaks: the interminably long northeast ridge of Everest, attempted by Scott in 1987 and climbed in 1988 to its connection with the north ridge, but so far not to the top; the south face of Lhotse, which resisted many sieges until 1990; and, beside us, the 10,500-foot west face of Makalu, a huge ice face capped by an El Capitan-size wall. Looking at these enormous climbs, I had wondered if it would ever be possible to climb such extended routes in alpine style.

Scott admits that the idea of a pure alpine ascent of the 3000-foot vertical wall capping Makalu's west face may be a pipe dream, but he hopes that such objectives are left to future generations. With improved gear and fewer psychological barriers, climbers fifteen or twenty years from now might accomplish what we currently consider impossible. "If climbing is about facing uncertainty, what is the point of sieging?" says Scott, defending his idealism.

Many Himalayan climbers today apparently agree, but this philosophy is not without its inherent risks. Increasingly, the urge to succeed on an 8000er and accrue kudos and economic opportunities has become so all-important that climbers seem willing to accept enormous risks. The events of 1986 on K2 reflect this trend, as does the impressive, yet tragic, lightweight ascent of Everest's southwest face in 1988 by four Czechs, who climbed that vast face but perished near the summit.

The go-for-it attitude of one of those Czechs may exemplify the current "fate-of-the-art" mentality. Sharing their permits with a small group of New Zealanders, the Czechs intended to make an ascent of Everest's neighbor, Lhotse, in preparation for the southwest face. New Zealander Gary Ball, a veteran guide, dug a snowpit and found suicidal avalanche conditions. In his judgment, continuing was not only personally too risky, but unjustifiable, as an avalanche triggered by his team would likely wipe out a lower camp occupied by other expeditions. Ball descended, while his Czech teammates continued to the summit in appalling snow conditions.

In base camp after the climb, Ball extended his hand to congratulate one of the Czechs. "You lose," the Czech replied coldly. But a few days later these same bold, brilliant Czechs became the losers: after reaching Everest's South Summit in a push characteristic of modern speed-alpinism—with minimal bivouac gear and provisions—one member struggled to the top, while his ailing companions waited at the South Summit, broadcasting a final radio message. Some of them were blind, either snowblind or from altitude. They never came down.

How does Scott react to such all-or-nothing efforts, particularly on a route he pioneered? "The Czechs lost totally," he says. Citing the fact that there were 300 people at Everest base camp in 1988, he also notes that with the clamor to climb the 8000ers the Nepalese and Pakistanis allow any number of teams on a peak. "Never again will one set off from base camp totally isolated," he says. "In the back of everyone's mind now is the thought that if they blow it someone will bail them out.

"I don't want to go anywhere with big crowds, and this now means the 8000ers," Scott concludes. "There's no longer the adventure there was. I may sound like an old man looking back to the golden age, but the media hype of Messner and Kukuczka's race for the 8000ers has changed Himalayan climbing completely. I'm not objecting to people going to the mountains— I just don't want to meet them!"

Just as rock climbing has become infused with competition, so, too, has Himalayan climbing; there has been a virtual explosion of people vying for status summits such as Everest. Many climbers have high expectations of themselves, Scott feels, but are unwilling to go through the long apprenticeship necessary for both success and safety on the big peaks.

And without such an apprenticeship, he worries that the intuitive balance needed to survive in the Himalaya won't be developed. "Finding the inner voice doesn't come without a struggle," says Scott. "Letting go of ambition is the key. If you can't do that, you'll only hear ambition."

A telling example is the case of the Swiss sausage-maker and climber, Marcel Ruedi. Scott first met him while descending Broad Peak. It was Ruedi's third 8000er in three months, and his first words were, "Ah, Scott, how many is it now?" Since Scott wasn't interested in the race to collect the 8000ers, he took a while to catch Ruedi's drift.

Three years later, Ruedi was close on the heels of Messner and Kukuczka in the 8000er race, having climbed nine of the fourteen summits. He planned to climb Makalu, Lhotse and Everest that season. Ruedi helicoptered into Makalu base camp, and seventeen days after leaving Zurich he reached Makalu's summit but died of altitude illness on the descent. In Scott's opinion, Ruedi's death is "the ultimate negative statement about collecting 8000ers. Poor Ruedi died trying to beat Messner."

For Scott, fixating on the 8000ers is a very restrictive habit. "It's highly dangerous, unnatural," he says. "Climbing is about pioneering new routes, exploring new ground, facing the unknown." With countless fantastic routes still to be done on lesser peaks, the Himalaya offers a nearly boundless climbing arena. "Those hooked on climbing the normal routes on the 8000ers will miss all that," Scott believes. "They are wasting the best years of their climbing lives."

Nevertheless, few can argue that Everest or a string of 8000ers is a good career move for a climber. Everest, after all, is the foundation of Scott's own reputation. But the idea of mountains as status symbols with commercial and media value troubles him.

While he earns his living from lecturing about his climbs,

Scott has resisted lucrative offers of company directorships; we have yet to see his name endorsing any product. He deplores the backbiting that often results from climbers competing for sponsorship. "I once came across a French expedition that broke into different camps depending on their sponsors," he relates. "I see the same thing happening in Britain among competitive rock climbers. I'd be disappointed if I noticed my climbing being directed by the finances my climbs would generate."

In one well-publicized incident after the Ogre climb, Scott was nominated by a gambling club for its "Most Courageous Man in Sport" award. He refused to accept it. "I didn't think it had anything to do with climbing," he says. "I'd done a good job of surviving, but courageous people are those who have a choice. Mo or Clive, who helped me down, were better candidates in my opinion."

Then an official of the club told Bonington that there was 25,000 pounds (about $50,000) in the award. At the time, Bonington and Scott were lecturing all over Great Britain to raise money for the Mount Everest Foundation; hearing about the cash, Scott decided to accept the award and put the money into the MEF. He had one additional condition: that the award be presented "to all of us, as a team."

He thought nothing further of the matter until just before a TV interview, when he was told that the award, in fact, consisted of a golden orb worth 5000 pounds and a laurel wreath worth 6500 pounds that would be taken back after a year. "Well, I couldn't melt that down for the MEF," says Scott, "so I told them, 'No, thank you,' and left."

The headlines the next day—HERO DOUG SPURNS AWARD—were the opposite of the praise Scott had received after Everest. "Suddenly everyone thought I was a cad," says Scott. The incident hurt, he admits, but even when, a week later, he was offered one last chance to accept the award, Scott refused again. "They didn't care about me or climbing," he says. "All they wanted was publicity for their club.

"You learn as much about yourself after an expedition as

when on an expedition," Scott says. "Reading about yourself in other people's books, listening to others' views, handling publicity, is always quite revealing. The lesson from the Ogre's aftermath was that I realized I had a lot of pride and needed people to like me."

By 1983 Scott had mastered the art of acclimatization by practicing a program of gradual adaptation to altitude by climbing several peaks of increasing height—the multipeak expedition.

The theory had worked well on his 1980 Makalu attempt and on Shisha Pangma in 1982. In 1983 Scott returned to K2, warming up on Lobsang Spire and Broad Peak first. In a completely alpine-style push, he, Baxter-Jones, Andy Parkin and Frenchman Jean Affanassieff reached 25,900 feet via a new route on the south face.

With only one bivouac to go, it looked like Scott would climb K2 at last. But just below the shoulder of K2's Abruzzi Ridge, Affanassieff developed cerebral edema, losing his sight and his orientation. Three weeks earlier, the expedition doctor, Pete Thexton, had died on Broad Peak from pulmonary edema. From their position the foursome could look across the Godwin-Austen Glacier to Broad Peak, to the camp in which Pete's body lay; with that fact sharp in their minds, there was no time to lose getting Affanassieff down K2.

Floundering through cascades of spindrift as storm engulfed the mountain, they lowered and shepherded the Frenchman down 8000 feet. On the second day of descent they reached a 2000-foot rocky barrier. Baxter-Jones led the way, hammering in anchors for the rappels; Scott brought up the rear, finding Baxter-Jones's piton placements so dubious that he could pluck them with his fingers. When Affanassieff chided Baxter-Jones for his questionable anchors, "Roger told Jean that he should perhaps take up golf, instead of climbing," Scott recalls. The four reached base camp safely a week after leaving it.

The following year, using Chamlang and Baruntse as stepping-stones, Scott, American Steven Sustad and Affanassieff returned to Makalu's long southeast ridge. After a week of good progress, the trio passed Scott's 1980 high point. High on the final ridge they discovered a figure sitting among the rocks—it was the body of Czech climber Karel Schubert, who had reached the summit in 1976 and expired on the descent.

The next day, only about 300 feet from the top but faced with a long descent down the north face, their physical conditions dictated retreat. So it was back into the cwm, where the noose tightened around their necks. Swirling spindrift consumed them; Sustad survived an avalanche; and so fatigued was Affanassief that he kept falling asleep in the snow. Severely dehydrated and out of food and fuel, they found a can of tuna left en route, opened it, but found it frozen solid. In desperation they tried to melt the fish with a cigarette lighter.

After eleven days on the mountain they struggled back into base camp, so exhausted they'd had to stop along the glacier every few yards to rest. In a lifetime of close calls, Scott regards this as the closest he's come to dying.

Makalu in 1988, like K2 in 1987, eluded Scott for a fourth time. The October winds had hit earlier than we anticipated, and we'd burned too much energy rushing up to 23,000 feet to rescue our friend Rick Allen, who'd been avalanched from 26,600 feet during his summit bid. Rick's head was a bloody mass of gashes and bruises, and he'd sustained some frostbite, but he was walking away with his life. For that much we were glad.

Back in Tumlingtar after the trip, the chickens rooting around our feet grew restless as Doug pondered yet another of my many questions. Soon, the sound of an airplane approaching the runway told us it was time to finish our beers and bribe our way on board, but not before Scott considered one final question about his future in the Himalaya.

"I'm finished with the big ones," he said, referring to Makalu and K2. I detected a tone of regret—after all, he'd spent more than a year of his life camped at the bases of these two mountains. But as he emptied his glass he was talking about his next climbing trip, to the Siachen Glacier in India, and about plans to return to Bhutan. With an endless sea of peaks to explore, Doug Scott has no intention of slowing down.

Between the Hammer and the Anvil:
A Profile of Poland's Voytek Kurtyka

I first met Voytek Kurtyka at K2 base camp in 1987. He and Swiss climber Jean Troillet, his partner on an intended new route on K2's west face, had invited our expedition to their well-appointed, family-size base camp tent for lunch. We had taken to calling this pair the "Odd Couple."

Lounging in Nero-like repose, Jean leisurely stirred a bubbling fondue, while Voytek, anxious that his guests be suitably primed, flung open the liquor cabinet and poured us first vodka, then anise.

He turned to dash about the kitchen, whipping up a chocolate mousse, setting the table, slicing bread and advising Jean about the status of the simmering pots on the cooker.

As Jean declared the fondue ready, Voytek slipped a tape into their tape deck. A world-weary female voice sang out of the speakers.

"Marianne Faithfull?" I asked.

"Yes. You know her music?"

"A little. Is she popular in Poland?"

"Not really. I was given this tape several years ago by Alex MacIntyre," said Voytek, smiling at the thought of the famous

English alpinist killed on Annapurna in 1982; the two had been great friends.

"When I heard this tape for the first time," Voytek explained, "I was very interested. 'What kind of person is this woman with her sad and angry words?' I asked Alex. 'It is Marianne Faithfull,' Alex said. 'She is like the history of Poland: everyone has been there and everyone has done great damage.'"

Poland is not the easiest country from which to launch a Himalayan expedition. It is a nation damaged by the tides of history: the savage Nazi occupation of World War II, the postwar years as a Soviet satellite, the 1980s government crackdown on the Solidarity movement as martial law brought social unrest and economic chaos.

Quick to cite the failures of socialism, the American media dwelled on Poland's agonies: the bloody battles in steel mills and coal mines between striking workers and police, the huge rallies protesting runaway inflation, arrests of Solidarity leaders, the Soviet troops massed on Poland's frontiers. Even after the collapse of the Soviet Union and Poland's shift to democracy, commodities we take for granted—bread, meat, butter—are still in such short supply that people anticipating a shipment of goods bivouac overnight outside stores to be at the front of the long lines that will snake down city blocks by morning.

Expatriate Poles assure us that these were, and still are, facts of Polish life. Yet instead of sapping the people of their will, such trials gave birth, at least in the case of Poland's climbers, to a breed of canny, tenacious escapists who live, according to an old Polish saying, "somewhere between Debussy and the devil."

In Poland, hard currency is almost impossible to come by. The Polish zloty is worth little more than pennies. Modern climbing equipment is virtually unavailable and is unaffordable anyway: the average monthly income of a Polish worker in 1989 was the equivalent of $30, or less than the cost of a No. 1 Friend. By comparison, an ambitious Balti porter in Pakistan can earn

$120 in a month carrying loads to base camp. Consequently, to fund their expeditions, the Poles have become creative financiers.

Several years ago Reinhold Messner described Himalayan climbing as the by-product of an affluent, leisure-loving society. He evidently wasn't including his brothers and sisters in Eastern Europe. Given that Poland's domestic situation has made it one of the world's fastest submerging nations, it is doubly remarkable that among Poland's greatest exports is the Himalayan mountaineer.

Wanda Rutkiewicz, Jerzy Kukuczka and Wojciech (Voytek, or Voy, is his nickname) Kurtyka—three of Poland's most successful mountaineers, and the ones best known to the West— battled for many years not just against high mountains but also against seemingly insurmountable economic barriers. By the mid-1980s, the three had carved reputations and were invited on well-heeled European expeditions, but in earlier days they could barely reach the foothills of the Himalaya.

All found a different way to fulfill their dreams. Rutkiewicz made climbing more viable by making mountaineering films and exploiting her role as probably the world's leading female high-altitude alpinist, with ascents of the 8000-meter peaks Everest, K2, Gasherbrum III, Nanga Parbat and Shisha Pangma to her credit. Kukuczka is legend in Poland and Europe as the man who nearly beat Messner to the title of collecting the fourteen 8000-meter summits, and was, like Messner, awarded a silver medal by the Olympic Committee in appreciation of his contribution to sport.

Voytek Kurtyka, though, has taken a different tack. The race for the 8000-meter peaks never interested him, nor has he ever felt pressed to try Everest. Voytek climbs a mountain for its geometric beauty and for the promise of adventure that it may hold. His idealistic approach has drawn him to the great un-solved problems of the Himalaya—huge frozen faces, multipeak high-altitude traverses and technical big walls. His career is that of a dedicated alpinist with an eye for routes futuristic, artistic and bold. He regards his climbs as the expression of his deeper self. In sum, Voytek could be described as the last of a breed of mountaineering romantics. As to style, he is fanatic in his devotion to unsupported small-team climbing, with no fixed ropes or fixed camps.

Kurtyka, forty years old when I met him, looked five years younger. The lean, soft-spoken Pole speaks and writes Russian, German, French and English, the latter fluently. His father was a noted Polish author; one of his two brothers was a Solidarity activist. Voytek has found work as an electrical engineer, an importer and recently as a lecturer and writer on climbing. Born in the small town of Skrzyka in 1947, he has made his home for many years in Krakow, a city of scholars and stately buildings.

In Voytek's mannerisms are evidence of great patience and powers of observation, but also an element of high tension, of physical energy and thought pounding for release. It is this controlled tension that has fueled Voytek's climbing since, as a teenager, he first stepped up on the rock of his native country.

From this beginning on the crags, Voytek spent several winter seasons mountaineering in the Polish Tatra Range. Then, in the late 1960s, he secured a difficult-to-obtain visa for France and visited the Alps. There, even today, the only alpinists more poorly equipped than the itinerant English are the Poles. Despite his antiquated gear, Voytek made several notable ascents, including a new route on the Grandes Jorasses.

During a lightning storm on the Walker Spur, Voytek experienced one of his closest calls, shared with the American climber John Bouchard. Feeling electricity humming around them, Voytek and his partner were hurrying to top out and descend the other side of the peak when suddenly a lightning bolt struck the rocks above Voytek. "It felt like being hit by a hammer," says Voytek. "When I came to a moment later, I smelled something burning."

Bouchard, just below his partner, had caught the worst of

the strike. The shock traveled through his hand and out his leg, leaving him stunned and temporarily paralyzed. Seeing Bouchard slump in the snow, Voytek began to shout for him to move up before another strike finished them. "John crawled up on one hand and one leg, and I pulled him up and over the top. There was electricity everywhere. I was more scared there than at any time since," says Voytek.

Bouchard recalls that in the confused instants after the strike, when he asked if Kurtyka was all right, Voytek still had the wit to call back, "I okay. I only hit in head."

In 1972 Voytek made his first foray to high altitude, to the Hindu Kush of Afghanistan, with a large Polish group. With one other climber, Voytek broke away from the main group to make an early alpine-style first ascent of the north face of Acher Chioch (23,048 feet) and to do a new route, alpine style, on Koh-e-Tez (23,015 feet) by its unclimbed north ridge. Though technically rated a modest 5.6, Acher Chioch is a big wall, huge and dangerous. The idea of two climbers scaling it in a single push was practically unheard of at the time.

In 1977 Voytek returned to the Hindu Kush to try a much more ambitious objective—the 8000-foot northeast face of Koh-e-Bandaka (22,533 feet). This expedition brought Voytek together with one of the luminaries of British climbing, Alex MacIntyre, and with the American expatriate John Porter. The two had been invited after they had met an exchange group of Polish climbers in Great Britain.

Porter described the route on Koh-e-Bandaka as "a massive face—ugly, yet compelling," adding that "rockfall was so continuous that it rarely deserved comment."

The ascent lasted six days, the route steepening from sandstone into massive fluted walls of metamorphic rock, to end in a 2000-foot icefield capped by seracs. It stands in Voytek's mind as his first taste of total commitment: "We were very worried about the rockfall. When we got to the point where it would be very difficult to go down, we had a discussion and decided to continue. As soon as we crossed that point we had no more fears and felt very calm."

Though few climbers have ever heard of Koh-e-Bandaka, the sixty-pitch Anglo-Polish route was one of the most difficult climbs done in the Himalaya as of 1977. Inspired by the notion of climbing Himalayan big walls with alpine-style tactics, the trio made for the south buttress of Changabang in India, in 1978.

Changabang, in the Nanda Devi Sanctuary, is regarded as one of the most technical Himalayan summits; defended by 5000-foot granite walls, the 22,520-foot peak offers no easy routes. Two years earlier, Peter Boardman and Joe Tasker had climbed the west face, using fixed ropes. Now, in a single push on the south face, Voytek and his countryman Krzystof Zurek, with MacIntyre and Porter, climbed what some believe is a more difficult route, using no fixed ropes or camps, and spending nights in hammocks against the granite walls or on hacked-out ice ledges.

By the end of the trip, Voytek's convictions about how to climb in the Himalaya were firm. He had been on two large expeditions prior to Koh-e-Bandaka and Changabang—the 1974 Polish Lhotse south face attempt and the 1976 Polish K2 east ridge attempt—and had seen both sides of the expedition coin. He decided Lhotse and K2 would be his last encounters with big expeditions. He refers to those trips as "bad experiences" and was unhappy about the competition and the jockeying for position among the many climbers, and the use of miles of fixed rope, fixed camps and oxygen. "But," says Voytek, "at the time, I had no way to visit the Himalaya except to join these expeditions. Because of money, it was simply not possible to launch small expeditions from Poland in those days."

Even now, Polish expeditions hustle for money in many ways. Government sports associations help sponsor some expeditions, and the many climbing clubs in Poland have arrangements with industry to hire climbers for highly paid dangerous work, such as erecting scaffolds and building towers. Foreigners who can pay their expedition contributions in cash are also often invited on Polish expeditions.

But usually a Polish group has no choice but to assemble a large team to break down its unit costs. With money so tight, creative financing becomes a skill as important to a Polish Himalayan climber as the ability to use crampons.

For instance, in the climbing markets of the Thamel district of Kathmandu, Nepal, it is not uncommon to see Polish climbers peddling such goods as running shoes, titanium ice screws or down gear, which they can procure cheaply and in bulk in Poland.

Nepalese government customs agents are so aware of Polish expeditions traveling overland in trucks laden with gear for sale that they often impose tariffs on the equipment. And the Poles are such well-known traders in Delhi, India, and Istanbul, Turkey, that many shops display signs reading "Polish spoken here."

With their earnings, Polish climbers can then buy duty-free electronic goods or liquor in ports such as Singapore, or cheaply manufactured jewelry or cotton clothing from the Delhi markets, for resale at home. Such transactions provide not only a way to pay for expeditions, but of financing a lifestyle back in Poland. In an economy where a dollar can buy sixty eggs or a hundred pounds of bread, a few dollars goes a long way. Expeditions, then, are an economic boon to Poles, and they are canny traders. "There is a famous story of a Pole," says Voytek with a smile, "who left Poland with a pack of chewing gum, sold it in India and then bought and sold goods as he crossed borders across Asia and back to Europe. When he returned to Poland he had a Mercedes Benz."

In an article called "Broken English" in *Mountain* magazine, Alex MacIntyre described receiving a postcard from Voytek in 1980 that showed the east face of Dhaulagiri. The picture was "obscured by a mass of lines, spot heights, arrows and exclamations that may have had meaning for the author," MacIntyre wrote. "The reverse side held a clue. 'Dear Alex, Great chance for great days on the face you see on the card. See you in Kathmandu, March 10th. Love, Voytek. P.S. Bring a partner.'"

The beauty of small expeditions is the freedom and speed with which an expedition may be launched. MacIntyre gathered up his gear, met Voytek and his Polish friend, Ludwick Wilczycznski, and the Chamonix guide Rene Ghillini in Nepal and trekked into Dhaulagiri in March.

Dhaulagiri's east face is a sweep of icefields and snow-covered rock slabs that lead to the summit of the sixth-highest mountain in the world. Prior to 1980, there had been few alpine-style attempts on the 8000-meter peaks; Messner and Habeler's 1975 climb of Hidden Peak was the first. In 1980 the concept of "alpining" the 8000ers was still experimental, but the prospects for this bold style of ascent to succeed on Dhaulagiri were good. Like the Messner-Habeler route on Hidden Peak, the line on Dhaulagiri was direct and uncomplicated. Since speed was everything, bivy sacks replaced tents, and the climbers carried minimal gear and food, soloing most of the route.

Two attempts, both under severe conditions, were required before the four summited. MacIntyre later wrote of a night on the face that he and two others shared a single two-man bivy sack in a "claustrophobic, oxygen-starved atmosphere endured in a variety of cramped, tortuous positions" while Voytek, alone, was "perched on crumbling snow and half slumped in slings with a bivy sack over his head and unable to get inside his sleeping bag, all on a face awash with wind-driven powder."

Voytek calls the Englishman his first strong partner. At the time the pair were climbing in the Himalaya, alpine style wasn't common. "We had the same ideas about climbing," Voytek recalls. "He was very imaginative in the mountains, would try anything. His favorite tactic was to drink heavily the night before a climb, to approach the great things in his life with a hangover. He regarded this as good training for high altitude."

MacIntyre's wild but unflappable nature complemented

Voytek's character. "Alex was very calm," he says. "I like to be with a partner who radiates calm. I'm much more nervous. I worry about many potentialities."

After two consecutive seasons in 1981—pre- and post-monsoon—attempting the unclimbed west face of Makalu in Nepal with MacIntyre and Jerzy Kukuczka, Voytek made plans for the trio to traverse Hidden Peak and Gasherbrum I in the Karakoram Range in 1983. But tragically, in the autumn of 1982, MacIntyre was killed by stonefall on Annapurna.

Voytek learned of MacIntyre's death just a week before they were to meet in Kathmandu. He later wrote in *Mountain* about his friend, remembering how, a year before, he had watched Alex walk away down the Barun Glacier after their defeat on Makalu: "I'd watched for a long time, until the small shape disappeared amid the glacial mess. Will I ever see you again? Oh yes, in a week I'll see Alex with all his dominating tranquility and confidence, which, when I look back through my mountains and even more through my anxious returns to the plains, I was always so lacking and longing for. I'll see him again and he'll make me believe for a while that I can seize this tranquility as well."

From 1982 to 1984 Jerzy "Jurek" Kukuczka was Voytek's sole partner in ascents of the 8000ers—Broad Peak's west face, a new route on Hidden Peak's southwest face, the traverse of Gasherbrum East to Gasherbrum II via a new route and, finally, the first complete traverse of Broad Peak. Often, on these expeditions, the pair lived completely alone in the midst of high mountains for weeks at a time. Kukuczka has been described as "a kindly, reticent bear" and "a man who can subsist on a diet of Himalayan rocks." As with MacIntyre, Voytek found that Kukuczka's aggressive nature in the mountains was a perfect counterpoint to his more careful, detail-oriented personality.

These were the days before Kukuczka had embarked on the race to beat Messner in climbing all the 8000ers, and he and Voytek were just two struggling Poles bartering and scamming their way overland to Asia, always on the verge of bankruptcy, with only the shared dream of a mountain propelling them forward.

"We had to make our expeditions by very tricky ways," says Voytek of those days, grinning. "It's probably better not to print it. But imagine, for example, for the Broad Peak traverse, leaving Poland, thinking all the time about this very serious objective— a traverse over three summits, two of which are above 8000 meters—and arriving in Islamabad with only a third of the money we needed. As soon as we got our cargo from Poland we feverishly sold it in the city, counted our money and then sold other goods till we had enough. Only at the last moment was the expedition possible." This sort of tension, as well as the obvious tension spawned by the climbing objectives, both prevailing beneath a beating Asian sun, fanned their fires of commitment.

The 1983 ascent of Hidden Peak by a new route was a tribute to pure brinksmanship, pulled off only at the eleventh hour. The two climbers were well acclimatized after having made a fast traverse of Gasherbrum East and Gasherbrum II, but then twenty days of storm pinned them down in base camp. Only the day before the porters were to arrive did the clouds part. Hastily, Voytek buried their passports and money to protect them from being pilfered and, to explain the pair's intentions, drew a picture of Hidden Peak with two climbers on its face on a piece of paper for the porters to find. Setting out before dawn, the pair climbed into a huge, potentially deadly basin laden with fresh snow. Wrote Voytek of this crossing: "We switched off our brains and moved steadily into danger. Ten minutes later we emerged."

Two bivouacs later the pair was searching for a path through the final headwall to the summit. The route was complex and time evaporated, forcing them to rappel down to an unplanned bivouac. As Voytek descended he heard Jurek cursing in Polish and noticed out of the corner of his eye one of his own crampons disappearing down between the rocks.

It was more than 8200 feet to the valley. Carefully the pair descended to a bivouac, contemplating the dangers of Voytek descending with only one crampon. The next morning they decided to carry on to the summit nonetheless. As they retraced their footsteps from the previous evening, Voytek heard "the familiar and joyous cursing of Jurek, and instantly I knew it was good news. He had found my crampon! Unbelievably it had caught in the soft snow on our tiny trail!"

They reached the summit. Later, in *Mountain,* Voytek eloquently summed up the abstract and fleeting rewards found at altitude: "When I looked down over the rotting mountains of Sinkiang to the distant snowy hills I sensed a vague but familiar affinity to something great and enormously calm. I could never track it down, or identify it inside me, and this time it remained shapeless as well. I felt this affinity intensely, though I couldn't see more than reddish, distant mountains, motionless glaciers and clouds silently coming up the valleys."

The following year the same pair assembled at the foot of Broad Peak, a neighbor of the Gasherbrums, planning to climb in a single push the North Peak (24,934 feet) via the unclimbed northwest face, then continue along the undulating ridge to climb the Central Peak (26,290 feet) and then the Main Peak (26,400 feet). Descent would be by the original 1957 west face route, which they'd climbed in 1982.

Two and a half days of difficult climbing to the North Peak placed the pair on the ridge crest. From base camp the entire ridge had looked rocky and technical, but upon reaching the ridge they were elated to find snow on the east side of the peak. After the two dropped into the saddle before the Central Peak, their level of commitment rose: should a storm hit now, retreat would probably be impossible.

After climbing to the Central Peak's summit they rappelled for five rope lengths into the col between the Central and Main summits. This was the scene of a Polish tragedy in 1975, when three of five climbers fell to their deaths in a snowstorm after making the first ascent of the Central Peak via the west face. While Voytek and Kukuczka rappelled off shaky pitons and broken rock flakes as anchors, a fierce wind drove clouds between the ridge pinnacles. "We felt as if we were rappelling into hell," Voytek wrote later. One hundred twenty feet above the col, sticking out of the snow like a cross, was the ice axe of the first Pole who fell in the 1975 tragedy. In blasting winds, Voytek and Kukuczka reached the summit of the Main Peak the next day and then descended.

Voytek calls the five and a half days and seven miles of climbing and traversing "the most relaxing climb I've done." Not that there was physical or mental rest, for the audacious route was extended and committing. But he and Kukuczka found an inner calm, something they'd been seeking for a long time. "I decided that the route was so beautiful, that commitment was so necessary, that I would continue, even though if the weather changed we would be trapped," explains Voytek. "Internally I was willing to accept the possibility that though I might sacrifice myself, I would be happy with whatever happened. It turned out that these were some of the best moments of my life. I find great motivation in the routes of greatest commitment."

Voytek and Kukuczka began plans to return to Gasherbrum IV's 10,000-foot-high west face, a daunting and coveted route largely believed impossible for a two-man team. But the mountain was a hair beneath the magic-number status; at 7925 meters it was one and a half rope lengths too low to be of use to Kukuczka, who was now openly competing with Messner to be the first to climb all fourteen 8000-meter peaks. Instead Kukuczka went to Dhaulagiri, Cho Oyu and Nanga Parbat, leaving Gasherbrum IV to Voytek and the Austrian Robert Schauer.

The split disappointed Voytek, not only because he had lost a fine partner, but because Kukuczka's choice represented an ethical parting of the ways as well. By challenging Messner in the race for the 8000ers, Kukuzka had stated that he was a competitor in a sport.

"For me mountaineering is not just sport," says Voytek adamantly. "Jurek just wanted to go for the 8000ers. I was looking for objectives for which I have total conviction, because when I have the right objective my motivation is doubled."

To him the attitude that the 8000ers have more significance than other peaks is ludicrous. If converted from meters to feet, an 8000er becomes a 26,240-foot-high peak: where, asks Voytek impishly, is the magic in a clumsy number like that? If 26,000 feet were the hallmark of a notable peak, then the collectors would have twenty-seven summits to climb (twenty-eight if one stands on someone's shoulders on the summit of Kangbachen in Nepal).

If Voytek can be said to have a chip on his shoulder about anything, it is the metrically based Euro-fad for collecting summits. Writing in *Mountain* on modern Himalayan developments, he diagnosed peak-baggers of the highest summits as "pathological victims of emotional consumption," explaining that, "If there is such a thing as spiritual materialism it is displayed in the urge to possess the mountains rather than to unravel and accept their mysteries."

He lamented the use of a number—the fourteen peaks above that magic height—that has transformed the highest mountains from being symbols of extremes in Himalayan and human endeavor to mere commercial measures of mountaineering fame. "Numbers are simple and understandable, even by those who have never had cold fingers," he concluded.

Voytek also saw that in Kukuczka's quest for the 8000ers his old friend was beginning to lose sight of another facet of mountaineering that Voytek holds dear: partnership. "Kukuczka didn't care so much about who he was with," says Voytek. "He just wanted one more 8000er."

Physically and psychologically, few high-altitude climbers have ever approached the enduring toughness of Kukuczka. As the gap between him and Messner closed, Kukuczka accepted ever greater risks, often joining large expeditions comprised of people he barely knew. By the mid-1980s Kukuczka was a big star in Eastern and Western Europe, and Polish expeditions were actively assisting him in reaching his goals by inviting him to participate in multiple expeditions. He hopped from one 8000er onto another, going from Dhaulagiri to Cho Oyu in the same month in winter 1984, creating the sort of situation that Voytek always rejected. "The reason I dislike big expeditions is that the relationship with your partner is not always good," he says. "If you are with strangers, which is common on big expeditions, it is difficult to care about them."

Indeed, several who tried to keep up with Kukuczka in those competitive years did come to grief, despite being strong climbers. Kukuczka was faultless in those deaths, but Voytek detects a dangerous chemistry among climbers who mix their love for being in the mountains with national and personal competition. The result is sometimes a wartime-like callousness toward life.

This is why Voytek is so particular about climbing with close friends in small teams. "The event of an alpine-style ascent has a very deep, ethical reason. I would go only with someone very dear to me," he explains. One tribute to his twenty-year experiment in the human dynamics of mountaineering is that he has never lost a partner.

In the winter of 1986, Voytek joined Kukuczka on Manaslu in Nepal. A few weeks earlier, Kukuczka had witnessed his partner, Tadeusz Pietrowski, fall to his death while the two descended from a bold new climb on K2's south face. The attempt on Manaslu was under appalling conditions. "Kukuczka was ignoring dangers," says Voytek. On all sides avalanches were pouring down, but Kukuczka wanted to go, go, go."

Voytek quit the trip and a few weeks later Kukuczka summited. Though immensely fond of each other, Manaslu was their final parting of the ways. "Our climbing partnership is like a broken marriage," Voytek explains. "We no longer find each other attractive."

Gasherbrum IV is Voytek Kurtyka's enigma. It is the mountain of his greatest obsession and the mountain for which he is best known and lauded. Yet, he says, "it is my greatest disappointment."

To see the west face—a symmetrical triangle of ice and marble that glows bright amber at sunset—looming above the Baltoro Glacier, it is hard to imagine that two men could make any impression on its vastness. But that is exactly what Voytek and Robert Schauer did in July 1985, surviving everything the west face could throw at them, but not claiming the summit.

Much has been written about Gasherbrum IV. It is one of the few mountains to rival K2 for beauty and is difficult by any of its three existing routes. For several years parties had made little headway on the rocky west face, getting bogged down on a shallow rib near the center of the wall.

Voytek, however, chose a line farther right, beginning with a huge couloir leading to a series of snow ramps and rock steps. Though subject to danger, it could be climbed quickly if conditions were good.

The 1985 Karakoram season was characterized by long fine spells and comparatively little snow on the west face. Going light as usual, with only bivouac sacks over their sleeping bags for shelter, Voytek and Schauer made rapid progress at first, but slowed when confronted with the unprotectable compact marble in the center of the face. At times they ran out rope lengths with neither belays nor runners.

Eventually the pair had overcome most of the difficulties, reaching the final slabs and snowfields beneath the summit. But during the night, at 25,000 feet, snowfall engulfed them, building up around them as they sat tight. Food and fuel began to run out as they waited all the next day for the storm to break. As dehydration and hypoxia set in, the two began to drift into a world of semiconsciousness and dreams.

"Retreat was impractical," says Voytek. "To rappel down we'd have needed many pitons, and we only had ten." There was no choice but to wait for the storm to break and then climb to the summit ridge and descend the northwest ridge, which they'd reconnoitered to 23,000 feet two weeks earlier. When the storm ended they ploughed slowly through deep snow toward the summit, weakened by altitude and dehydration, yet in a seeming paradox, feeling more alert for the understanding that death was at hand. As they struggled upward they experienced the ability to read what the other was thinking before he said it and shared the constant sensation of having been joined by another presence lingering nearby but always just out of sight.

The pair veered away from the summit, knowing that to survive they had to shed altitude and reach a cache of fuel and provisions on the northwest ridge.

During their long descent hallucinations persisted. While slumped on a ledge during the rappels, Schauer watched a raven hovering in front of him. The longer he stared at the bird the more he became the bird, until he felt utterly convinced that he was it, looking back on himself, a poor human wreck high on a mountain face.

During the final stages of the descent Voytek experienced the strongest hallucinations. "Persistently, I saw faces of people I'd never seen before—an old Greek man, a scene of children playing with a ball," he says. "The children were shouting to each other to throw the ball higher; then one of them said to throw it to me!"

Voytek calls such experiences "the sounds of the human machine breaking down." He adds, "Whatever the explanation, there are things stored in the brain that only come out in extreme situations. Himalayan climbing is important because it gives one access to parts of the mind that are usually inaccessible."

Even though the pair missed the summit, most climbers regard the ascent as the high point of a decade of Himalayan mountaineering. "If I went to the summit I'd be happier," Voytek says with a shrug. "It would be more artistically complete. But there are cases in literature or music of unfinished works—*The Castle* by Kafka is unfinished, but it still is great."

In recent years Voytek has again found two partners who share his ideals. The Swiss alpinists Erhard Loretan and Jean Troillet—who have, among many great ascents, climbed Everest via the Japanese Couloir in forty-four hours round-trip—sum up the qualities of partnership, vision and commitment that Voytek extolls. He is excited by the promise of adventure that this new Polish-Swiss trinity offers him in the Himalaya.

In 1988 Voytek and Loretan climbed a new route on the east face of Nameless Tower (20,508 feet), a vertical-walled granite spire of the Trango Group in Pakistan's Baltoro region. On this 3000-foot wall, the pair climbed twenty-nine rock pitches during fourteen days of leading, hauling and moving up and down between storms. Voytek feels the ascent demanded a greater physical effort than any of the 8000-meter peaks he has climbed.

What, then, makes the Poles, and Voytek Kurtyka in particular, so successful on such difficult routes? Western climbers have long thought that Poles are willing to accept more pain than other climbers; ascents such as the first winter ascent of Everest, by a Polish expedition, as well as the climbs of Kukuczka and Kurtyka only shore up this impression.

"It is something in our nationality," says Voytek. "Under the Germans and the Russians we've lived between the hammer and the anvil. Because of the struggle in Poland for freedom at home, most Poles feel a sense of being tough. The sense of defeat on a mountain is greater for a Pole, so the last thing a Pole wants is to fail on an expedition. In the end, we are better at the art of suffering, and for high altitude this is everything."

Like every Himalayan climber, Voytek has experienced defeat in the mountains—he's been beaten by K2 five times—and because of the mountains. "Climbing has definitely affected my personal life," he says. "The best proof of this was my divorce after thirteen years of marriage." However, he remarried in 1987. His wife, Halina, bore a son, Alex, in 1989.

Voytek also has a lyrical acceptance of defeat. I recall visiting him late one night in K2 base camp in 1987. Weeks of high winds made it unlikely that anyone would climb K2, and the mood of all the expeditions at K2 that season was frustration. Seeing Voytek's tent illuminated by a candle, I crossed the rubble and found him reading, studying French. As we spoke of our disappointments he smiled and asked, "But how can we turn defeat into victory?"

"When you are totally defeated you begin again to enjoy the small things around you," Voytek later explained. "Just going again to the mountains, not for victory or glory, but to enjoy nature or to enjoy fine people. If you always succeed you enjoy the admiration of many people. Being defeated means being limited to the basic existential choices of life. If you can enjoy the quiet evening hours it is beautiful; a hero who always succeeds may not have time to enjoy such things."

A Climb with Roskelley

On the east ridge of a Tibetan mountain called Menlungtse, in the spring of 1990, John Roskelley and I emerge from a tiny tent perched at 20,000 feet to watch a storm build around us. Our tent occupies a narrow ledge on a sharply etched ridge. On either side huge cliffs drop into a landscape of frozen lakes and glacial wastes.

In the west a grey lenticular cloud hovers over Everest, thirty miles distant. It quickly consumes the great mountain like a protozoan swallowing a chunk of food. Eastward, welling out of Nepal and mushrooming over the walls of the mountain Gaurishankar, clouds as blue-black as a bruise and pulsing with lightning roll toward us. The top of Menlungtse disappears in a haze of shimmering ice crystals. Detonations of thunder echo off mountainsides. It's going to be a humdinger of a storm, and we're smack in the middle of it.

"We'd better get out of here," I say, feeling a tingle of urgency.

"Let's wait and see if it blows past," Roskelley says, finding optimism at a porthole of blue sky above.

So we sit, watching and waiting.

Right then, a crackling sound like radio static discharges in the air around us. The sound modulates to a buzz, like the hum of a generator. Roskelley's Nikon, which sits on the snow ledge beside the tent, begins snapping pictures by itself. Its motor drive churns over and over, as if a ghost is pressing the shutter release.

"What's going on?" I shout.

"It's the electricity in the air."

"That does it. Were outta here, NOW!"

"Maybe we'd be safer here," Roskelley suggests. "We could sit on our foam pads. They'd insulate us from the lightning."

I ponder the option of squatting all day and night on the two-foot-by-five-foot strips of half-inch-thick rubberized foam that we sleep on. It doesn't sound very restful, and I doubt the integrity of the insulation of the flimsy pads against a bolt of lightning.

The more I think about it, the more I picture our bivouac site as a Grand Central Station of electricity. Metal ice screws and ice axes anchor us to the mountain. They poke out of the ice like lightning rods. The ridge is sharp, and our bivouac site is notched into the very crest. Electricity travels along ridge crests, flowing downhill like water, following the path of least resistance. It trickles through cracks and leaps over obstacles like climbers, zapping anything in its way.

"If it's a choice between staying put and being a sitting duck," I tell him, "or going down and being a moving target, I choose to be a moving target."

He nods. A static buzz like a cloud of flies hovering over a carcass lingers around us now, attracted to our sling of carabiners, ice screws and pitons. Roskelley kicks the sling to the end of the ledge, uncoils a rope and begins the first rappel.

While I watch him descend, I make the mistake of leaning out and poking my head above the ridge crest. Instantly, electricity swarms around me, setting my hair on end inside my helmet. My heart flutters, like a power surge hitting a pacemaker. Fillings in my teeth hum. A metallic taste settles on my tongue. I am a conductor of electricity, and I don't like it.

Roskelley, now a small dot at the end of the rope, hammers

two snow pickets into the ridge, clips himself to them and then calls for me to descend. The pickets at my anchor vibrate like tuning forks and emit a bluish aura as I leave the ledge. I'm genuinely terrified. My breaths come in rapid spasms.

We keep moving for a thousand feet, rappelling and traversing the side of the ridge in a crouching, crablike crawl, keeping our heads low. Waves of power wash along the crest. It crackles like a high-tension cable. When I touch the pick of my steel ice axe I recoil with a mild shock. Snow begins to fall, and everything turns grey.

All the way, Roskelley remains in front, hunting out the route. He likes to be in front, hates to be behind. It's been like a blind date coming on this expedition with him—we'd never done more than shake hands together before traveling to Tibet—but right now I'm glad of his calm company.

Not many people had heard of the peak we'd just been driven down from. It goes by two names, Menlungtse and Jobo Garu, and it has two summits. The highest one—the one we were aiming for—was unclimbed and more than 23,000 feet. It sits in a seldom visited region beside the Nepal–Tibet frontier, near Chang bu Jiang, a little village not easily found on maps.

Menlungtse is a striking mountain shaped like two pyramids built side by side, their summit towers linked by a broad saddle of snow. It stands like an island, unattached to surrounding peaks, as if it were thrust up through the earth's crust like a double-pointed spear. Ice cliffs ring Menlungtse's summits, and the whole massif is surrounded by glaciers and lush meadows inhabited by marmots, blue sheep and the occasional snow leopard.

Few Westerners had ventured into the Menlung Valley. One who did, the legendary British explorer Eric Shipton, came away from his jaunt in 1951 to the Menlung Glacier with a photograph of a yeti footprint. Some believe the photo was a bit of mischief on Shipton's part, a joke that ended up being taken seriously. Others think the print of a massive foot proves the yeti's existence.

The first climber to try to scale Menlungtse, in the early 1980s, was a New Zealander named Bill Denz. Denz was something of a loner who, on a mountain, felt as comfortable and self-contained in his own company as with a climbing partner. He'd soloed serious alpine routes in New Zealand, where he was a local hero, and in Nepal. To reach Menlungtse, Denz followed Shipton's route, trekking with his girlfriend through the Rolwaling region of Nepal and over a pass called the Menlung La. He didn't have official permission from the Chinese to climb Menlungtse; it was a pirate attempt, and his expedition consisted of whatever he and his girlfriend could cram into their rucksacks. But sickness, an arduous approach and the realization that Menlungtse is a steep-walled layer cake of ice cliffs that regularly fracture off and fill the valley with billowing clouds of ice spicules soon shut Denz down. He and his girlfriend barely made it back over the border.

In the late 1980s the British entrepreneur of expeditioning, Chris Bonington, led two attempts on Menlungtse. He persuaded British television and newspapers that there was a chance of seeing the yeti, and, well funded by the media, he set up camp in the Menlung Valley. His team never saw a yeti and didn't reach the true summit. One member was struck by lightning, yet lived to tell the tale. However, on the second expedition they climbed the west peak. This is just slightly lower than the east summit Roskelley and I would attempt, but is separated from the higher summit by a half-mile-long plateau.

In 1990, as Roskelley, Jim Wickwire, Jeff Duenwald and I drove across the Tibetan Plateau to approach Menlungtse by means of a caravan of yaks, we bumped into Alan Hinkes, one of the Brits who'd made the difficult climb to the lower summit on Bonington's expedition. When we met him, Hinkes was accompanying a French team planning to climb Cho Oyu and Shisha Pangma, two 8000-meter peaks. Their sponsor was a computer company, and they planned to set up a radio satellite dish, computers and fax machines at base camp to send high-altitude bulletins to the boardroom of their sponsor.

In the town of Tingri, over a breakfast of fried peanuts and something with the taste and consistency of boiled dog's nostrils—typical Chinese fare—we chatted with Hinkes about Menlungtse and yetis.

"There were all these reporters around, all bursting for a photograph of the yeti," Hinkes said. "I warned them that if it did exist, it was very rare and the chances of seeing it were remote. But they pointed out that a picture of the thing would be worth a fortune, so it was worth the chance.

"Every time they saw a set of tracks in the snow they'd want to investigate it, and I clambered up hillsides everywhere, guiding them along these tracks. Invariably the tracks were wild sheep. The best part was at base camp. They set up cameras and flashes on tripods and strung the perimeter with trip wires, in case a yeti came prowling around camp at night. All they got were some climbers in their underpants taking a midnight leak."

I had been flattered to be asked to climb with John Roskelley, America's most famous Himalayan alpinist and the veteran of seventeen Himalayan expeditions to summits such as K2, Dhaulagiri and Makalu, and to lower, technically fierce peaks such as Tawoche. I was also nervous. Stories of his hot temper and his redneck diatribes against fellow climbers were legion.

Yet most of what I knew about Roskelley was a jumble of journalistic impressions, screenwriters' distortions and second-hand climbers' gossip. Plays, television and movie dramas about climbing had used him as a model for the bad guy. Once, at a gathering of a chapter of the American Alpine Club, I'd heard the mere mention of his name inspire a loud hiss from the audience.

Roskelley's fiery reputation—a reporter once described him as the John McEnroe of climbing—is rooted in his unabridged honesty, his short temper and perhaps his huge appetite for nerve-twitchingly strong coffee. Conversationally, he is blunt. He likes to speak his mind, to call a spade a spade. On a mountain, if someone isn't pulling his weight, he'll tell him to his face that he has no business being there, even that he'll probably die if he keeps going. Roskelley treats climbing partners the way some bosses treat employees: the boss expects a professional performance or the employee is fired. "John sees everything in black and white; there are no shades of grey," one of his friends told me before I headed off to Menlungtse.

Roskelley is tall and lanky, like a character from a Sam Shepard play. On his ranch on the outskirts of Spokane, Washington, where he runs horses and mules, he and his wife, Joyce, a schoolteacher, raise two children. A patriot who once aspired to join the CIA, Roskelley also told a magazine writer that he climbed for America, the way an athlete represents his country in the Olympics. He hunts, with rifle and crossbow, and knows as much about the art of stalking deer and bears as he does about cramponing up alpine slopes. Guiding, mule-packing, consulting for the outdoor industry and writing earn him a living, though he is self-conscious about this patchwork career. "I've never had a real job in my life, and I'm forty," he told me in his self-deprecating manner.

Roskelley had written a book, *Nanda Devi: The Tragic Expedition*. Reading it, I thought, would be a good primer before climbing with him, a man who seemed to know how to push all the wrong buttons with people, but who had earned the respect and loyalty of a select few. The book had received a lot of negative reviews in the climbing press, because in it Roskelley came down hard on some of the icons of American climbing. Nanda Devi had been an expedition fraught with personality conflicts, yet when I read the book, I thought Roskelley's tone about events was level-headed. I found myself agreeing with him that there were people climbing on a big, hard mountain who lacked the judgment or abilities such an undertaking demanded.

Some reviewers had criticized as unsympathetic his treatment of the death on the mountain of Willi Unsoeld's daughter, whose name was, prophetically, Nanda Devi. She was ill, but insisted on going high on the mountain. Roskelley warned the expedition leaders that she would die if she went high; she went high and died. In Roskelley's opinion the foolishness and idealism of the young woman and her elders had killed her, and he said so in print, with minimal diplomacy or delicacy.

Roskelley's bad-boy image grew after Nanda Devi, and for a time it almost outweighed his reputation as an ambitious, capable pioneer of hard new routes in the Himalaya. Because he is controversial, outdoor magazines sought his opinions frequently, and often gave him enough verbal rope to hang himself. His knack for crafting shock-value, even tactless comments became quotable copy. Asked once, in *Outside* magazine, whether he would attend the prestigious annual American Alpine Club meeting, he quipped, "I've got better things to do, like floss my dog's teeth."

Knowing what I knew about John Roskelley, I realized that the challenge for me on Menlungtse, a mountain with no easy way up, was more about shaping up to Roskelley's rigorous standards as a climbing partner than about climbing a mountain.

On May 11 we return to the ridge, and three days later we reach a rocky promontory at 21,200 feet. There, in a swirl of cloud and light snow, we scurry about, looking for a bivouac site. The ridge is narrow and without ledges. It begins to look like we'll spend the night sitting in shallow troughs. Then Roskelley swings around to the east side of the ridge.

"Hey, man, we're in fat city," he shouts, announcing he's found an ice cave.

The entrance is small, but when I peek inside I see a spacious, wind-hollowed womb. We smash open a doorway through the ice with our axes and enter a quiet, translucent chamber of blue-green light. The tunnel winds back for twenty feet, and there are natural benches to sleep on. Stalks of dry grass lie on the floor, blown in by the substantial winter winds.

Then I look at the ceiling. My mouth gapes open, as if I'm seeing the Sistine Chapel for the first time. Covering it are thousands of ice crystals, delicate as feathers, each shaped in some unique variation of a pentagon. Some are fist-size; others droop down like daggers or leaves. As we chop into the ice benches to flatten our sleeping platforms the crystals dislodge, tinkling around us and shattering, like ornaments of finest glass.

"I feel like a vandal. This place is like a museum," I say, and I think of the Buddhist monastery we'd visited, in the valley below, robbed by Chinese soldiers in the 1960s, its buildings and Buddhas dynamited and raked with bullet holes, its prayer flags scattered across the floor where they'd fallen three decades ago.

Roskelley smiles. "I call it home. Get a brew on, McChild!"

He's happy. The last two days have been up and down for us. Though the climbing hasn't been hard, our progress has been slowed by our heavy rucksacks, loaded with gear and food needed for the long, corniced ridge ahead. We both have doubts about the next 2000 feet of snowy crenellations and ice gargoyles. Maybe we just can't climb the ridge. Maybe it's too long. Maybe those frozen whipped-cream shapes won't even support our weight. The thought of being caught in another lightning storm, in the middle of the narrow ridge, weighs heavily upon us. Much of our climbing has been done in a hazy, foggy funk of cloud, weather Roskelley calls "Pooh." Once, he'd erupted into a classic Roskellian tantrum, not at me, but at a tangled rope. His rage came and went, like a passing storm. Yet I'm nagged by a feeling that I'm just not up to par in his eyes.

He's strong on ice, this Roskelley. Even with a heavy pack he kicks his way up steep ice with speed. I try to match him for output, but when I look at his face for some hint as to how I'm doing, I don't get a positive vibe. So I defer to my elder, letting him make the decisions and lead the hard pitches. At least that way he can't complain if I'm moving too slowly. Yet even after a month in Tibet, he still smiles at me.

This afternoon in the ice cave, we lie in our sleeping bags. Roskelley takes two photos of his children from his pocket and spends the last hour till dark looking from one to the other, telling stories about the wonder of watching a child being born and the pride of teaching his son how to fire a rifle. They mean a lot to him, these kids. The stories are less for me than for him.

At sunset I peek out of the cave. Everest is partially clear, a good sign. I tell Roskelley, and he grunts. "Another dozen probably climbed it today," he says disdainfully. At base camp a few days earlier we'd tuned in to Radio Nepal. The news reader announced some twenty ascents of Everest, a summit Roskelley had tried, without oxygen, three times, but to his chagrin had never bagged. "If I hear about one more ascent of Everest I'm gonna puke," he'd said, then repeated his intention to retire from climbing after we climbed Menlungtse.

The next morning—our fourth day on the route—we climb onto the sharply corniced ridge. Instantly, doubt pervades the air. I hold the rope as Roskelley ploughs through a soft cornice. He leads away from me, twenty feet, forty feet, and then stops, floundering in a bottomless formation of snow that has the consistency of a sculpture of wet sugar. It's taken a half-hour for him to traverse that short distance. Ahead are 2000 feet of the same. It'll be like a tightrope walk the whole way.

"I hate it to come down on my shoulders," he shouts, "but I don't think I can get through this cornice. Want to try?"

I think for a moment. "I'd probably come to the same conclusion," I say. "You're better at this than I am anyway."

He looks at me, seemingly embarrassed. He hates defeat, but he also hates senseless risk, and going on at this pace, with so little food and gear, on such unstable snow, does seem senseless. Earlier, we'd discussed trying to climb other lines on Menlungtse, up the ice faces by weaving a route between the seracs. He scoffed at the idea, regarding such routes as death traps. That's what has kept him alive these twenty years—his refusal to expose himself to the extremes of objective danger that shorter-lived alpinists might accept.

So, with barely a word, we go down, into a whiteout. Roskelley rappels in front, hunting out the way, the way he likes it. That way, if my anchors aren't to his liking, he can't complain.

A day before leaving base camp for home we see a herd of wild sheep. Cameras in hand instead of rifles, Roskelley and I creep up on them like predators. He motions silently for me to follow his moves. We stay upwind so the sheep can't smell our scent. The forty-strong herd senses something is up, but the old ram with the big, curved horns—the leader of the herd—cannot see us or smell us. We crawl and drift from boulder to boulder across the meadow, stalking now, like the snow leopards that hunt the sheep. Roskelley had seen one of those big cats near the foot of Menlungtse. It had bounded away from him across a frozen lake on the glacier, moving like lightning and disappearing in seconds.

Suddenly Roskelley leaps up in front of the sheep. The herd frights, and we snap photos as they gallop away. He grins from ear to ear, and I decide that this willful, contentious legend of American climbing is more like a sheep in wolf's clothing than the predator his reputation has made him out to be.

PARTY OF ONE:
A PROFILE OF JIM BEYER, AN AMERICAN SOLOIST

I first encountered Jim Beyer from a distance, in Yosemite Valley, in 1977. He was 2000 feet above me, on El Capitan, making the first solo ascent of the Shield. I stood among a group of climbers in El Cap meadow, watching spring storm mists swirl around the wall and Beyer. I still recall the patter of rain against our raincoats, the beat of the Grateful Dead playing from a tinny portable tape deck and the awe that the sight of El Cap filled us with back then, glistening wet and gold as it did that day, like a fearful, shiny beast. It was the year a drug lord's plane had ditched in a frozen lake in the high country, and bales of weed were still being hauled out of the ice. Life in the valley was deliciously deranged, we were young, our hair was long and we lived and breathed climbing.

The sky darkened as a Sierra Nevada thunderhead regrouped to pelt the valley with another assault of sleet. On El Cap, climbers, sodden, cold and had-enough, could be seen rappelling off the Nose and Tangerine Trip. Only one remained, going up, not down.

"Who is that guy up there?" I asked.

"That's Jim Beyer," someone replied.

"He must be freaking out in this weather."

"Nah. Beyer can handle it. He soloed the Dihedral Wall last year. He likes it up there alone."

I filed the name—Jim Beyer—in my memory. It would keep cropping up in years to come, attached to news of bold solos on big walls.

Clouds engulfed El Cap and we departed to our clammy nylon abodes in Camp IV, leaving Beyer, with two-thirds of El Cap beneath him, to press on.

The headwall of the Shield is so overhanging—ten degrees beyond vertical—that rain doesn't touch it, but, in the gloom of storm, it's cold and very exposed. By afternoon Beyer had nailed the crux, called the Triple Cracks, anchored his rope, rappelled the pitch and was jumaring back up and hammering out knife-blade pitons when he began inexplicably sliding down the rope. He was stung with the adrenaline shot. Something was dreadfully wrong, but what? When his jumars jammed and he jolted to a stop, he looked up to see a big-wall climber's nightmare.

The sheath of his lead rope was cut through, neatly circumscribed from rubbing against a sharp burr on a piton. His weighted jumars had stripped the sheath down the rope, causing his slide, and exposing several feet of white nylon core, at which, strand by strand, the piton was sawing.

With no one but the misty sky to bitch to about it, Beyer looked up at the rope. Every movement caused the piton to cut another millimeter into the core. Later, he told a friend, he begged God's help. "When nothing happened," Beyer said, "I knew there was no God."

Beyer had put himself in this situation, he knew, and he alone would get himself out of it. He muscled aside fear as he jumared the fraying rope toward the haul bag and spare lead line. It was as if these adrenaline-thumping moments were a test of his physical and mental training, a test to see if he really had the stomach for the life of soloing he'd mapped out for himself. The test was simple: the rope snaps, Jim dies; jumar past the fraying strands, he lives. Years later, on other walls, in other ranges, the tests would become harder.

This, then, is the story of Jim Beyer, America's most accomplished big-wall soloist. It's the story of a reclusive man on a twenty-year solitary odyssey that took him quietly yet triumphantly up a score of American monoliths, but that ended in agonizing defeat in the Karakoram Range of Pakistan. It's the story of self-discovery through extreme climbing and, by the end, of an alchemical metamorphosis of purpose.

But who is Jim Beyer? Most readers of climbing magazines will draw a blank on the name, for he is not the doyen of the climbing print trade. He doesn't pen articles about his climbs, save for understated accounts in the back pages of the *American Alpine Journal.* Never before has a photo of Beyer appeared in a magazine. He possesses neither the lean, leonine leotards nor physique of the sport-climbing set. Beyer is a house-builder who dresses in well-worn, sawdust-scented work clothes. His Falstaffian physique is built for endurance rather than sport. He is a soloist in more avenues than climbing: he kayaks whitewater solo, and even the spec houses he builds for a living are mostly Beyer's work alone.

Beyer is suspicious of anyone who basks in the glow of fame in climbing. Magazine profiles are anathema to him. Sponsored climbers and sport-climbing heroes are "posers." Thus, it took some convincing on my part to get him to discuss his career. But talk he did, on a winter weekend in 1991 in Boulder, Colorado, in the half-finished shell of his latest spec house, and in Eldorado Canyon. "My agenda in spilling my guts to you," he told me, "is to show there are traditionalists left in climbing." That was his conscious agenda. If he had an unconscious agenda, then it was to unburden himself of himself, for in the world of a soloist there are few people to listen.

Jim Beyer's brand of climbing—solo big-wall climbing—is not everyone's cup of tea. It's a slow and laborious process, a mental and physical marathon. It is, essentially, aid climbing for pitch after pitch up huge cliffs, using a roped self-belay system. Such climbs might take two weeks, and on them the climber must carry masses of hardware, bivouac gear, food and water. The endeavor means hauling loads weighing hundreds of pounds; it means complex ropework and sleeping in porta-ledges. On a hard pitch, the climber might nail fragile flakes, make multiple moves on skyhooks or step off an A5 aid placement to begin free-climbing into unknown territory—with no one at the other end of the rope to whimper to. To embark on a solo climb, the climber must be driven to succeed and fueled by a deep belief in himself. Thus, for a soloist, defeat comes hard because there is only himself to blame for failure.

Born in Florida but a longtime resident of Boulder, Colorado, Beyer, now thirty-six, made his big-wall solo debut at age seventeen, with Sunshine (VI 5.9 A3) on the Diamond Face of Long's Peak. The route was a first ascent—remarkable for a youngster—and it set the course of his climbing: inevitably solo, usually first ascents, unsupported and unpublicized to the extent that few people knew where he was, and he placed bolts only as a last resort.

The original premise of climbing—that all routes should be climbed from the ground up, without previewing—is, to Beyer, both ethic and religion. His traditional convictions are bred of twenty-three seasons in Yosemite, ten in the Tetons and three in the Karakoram. He despairs of, and endorses guerrilla warfare on, the gridwork rap-bolting practices of sport-climbers. Like the Earth First! environmentalists who creep into forests to hammer mill-saw-wrecking spikes into old-growth trees, he has, under cover of darkness, erased several efforts of the Bosch generation. "Anyone has the right to place a bolt wherever he wants," he says, "but anyone is also free to remove it." In a letter to *Climbing* magazine, he challenged its editors to publish a "how to" article on bolt removal to balance the plethora of advice on bolting, hangdogging and sport-climbing techniques filling today's magazines.

But the story of Jim Beyer, student of traditional ethics, pales against the tale of Jim Beyer, graduate of the school of hard knocks.

The year Beyer soloed the Shield he left Yosemite to climb in the Canadian Rockies, driving a VW Bug crammed with his possessions. In Banff, while hanging around a parking lot outside a pub with a friend, Beyer was accosted by a man wearing a leather jacket. "He grabbed me by my sweater and cranked me up close to smell my breath. Then he flashed a police badge," says Beyer.

Ordered to empty his pockets, Beyer produced an apple. The undercover agent was disappointed; he was looking for contraband. But Beyer's back pocket contained a joint. His survival instinct took over. Beyer backed out of his sweater, leaving it in the agent's hands, and ran. Cutting his losses, the narc arrested Beyer's friend. After a cold bivouac in the woods, Beyer traded himself to the police for his buddy's release and spent a week in Spy Hill Correctional Institute.

On his first day there, he recalled, Elvis Presley had just died, so the radio stations played nothing but Elvis songs. After hearing "In the Ghetto" for the eighth time, everybody was yelling, "Turn it off, turn it off!"

This youthful debacle ended when Beyer was deported, handcuffed, from Canada as a persona non grata. Across the border, he sped back to California, visited his girlfriend, found their relationship had ended and proceeded to the haven of Yosemite. Near Merced, at 2:00 A.M. he parked and entered an orchard to sleep. When he awoke his car was gone; while he'd slept it had been burglarized, torched and then towed to the scrapyard. Beyer had lost everything he owned.

Beyer quit climbing for a couple of years after that. "Jim's epic on the Shield really scared him, and a run of bad luck hit him hard," says Steve Quinlan, a climber and carpenter from Wyoming and one of Beyer's oldest friends. "I think it shocked him to discover his capacity for getting himself into hot water."

So Beyer filled his life with other things. For a time he drifted with radical pro-environmentalists. Later he earned a place on the U.S. National Kayak Team as a flatwater racer. Curious to examine left-wing politics from the inside, he visited Nicaragua after the Sandinista Revolution with an American group to help harvest the coffee crop. Beyer did not adapt well to his new surroundings, however, and tired of the endless political lectures, barracks living and constant surveillance. Instead of kowtowing to the propagandists, he argued with them. One day he rented a car and went to the beach without official permission. Such independent thinking didn't sit well with his Sandinista hosts: he was deported from Nicaragua by armed escort. Authority and Beyer did not mix.

Beyer's own tales to me create a picture of a loner. But people who know Beyer reveal another side of the man.

"Jim Beyer is the most politically aware climber I've ever met," says Quinlan, who told me of Beyer's support of environmental and political causes over many years. On one occasion Beyer marched with a group across Utah, from Moab to Salt Lake City, as a protest against a planned nuclear dump in the desert, near North Six Shooter peak. As for Beyer the climber, Quinlan affectionately describes a curmudgeonly reactionary traditionalist who refused to use the modern camming gadgets, Friends, for several years and who, till recently, often didn't report his routes, especially those in the Wind River Range.

By 1982 Beyer quit believing he could find a more significant purpose in life other than climbing. If he had abandoned climbing because he suspected its tunnel-visioned lifestyle made him unsuited to normal society, then he returned to it because it was the most gratifying life he knew. And when he returned to Yosemite it was to activate the plan he had been nurturing since his earliest solo walls: to embark on a series of climbs that would harden him for his ultimate dream—a new route, solo, alpine style, boltless, in the Karakoram Range.

Methodically he ticked off a succession of new Yosemite walls. On Heading for Oblivion (VI A4+) on Leaning Tower he copperheaded his way up tenuous seams just forty feet right of the original Harding route. But, unlike Harding, Beyer did little drilling. He regards this as his hardest Yosemite wall. Later, on a twenty-three-and-a-half-hour solo roped repeat of El Cap's west face, he accomplished the monolith's first one-day solo.

Solid Yosemite granite polished Beyer's technical skills, but to harden himself against isolation and pure fear he turned to the vertiginous Fisher Towers near Moab, Utah. These lonely, weirdly eroded sandstone spires of crumbling rock, says Beyer, are "an alien, hostile environment, perfect for training for the Karakoram." During the 1980s he forced himself up five new 900-foot-high solo routes there.

To describe these routes he coined a term—"shakefest," a climb that reduces the leader to a state of quivering terror. Beyer's route names reflect his mindset at a given time. Sandinista Couloir and Revolutionary Crest from the Tetons in the early 1980s show his political period. In the Fisher Towers, his route names reflect a darker mood: Run Amok (VI 5.9 A4a), World's End (VI 5.9 A5a), Death of American Democracy (VI 5.10 A4d) and Deadman's Party (VI 5.10 A5c). On these, he conditioned himself to climb alone and never give up, no matter how scary or awful. On Run Amok, in 1979, he climbed a pitch-length curtain of vertical dirt by chopping steps into it with a hammer. He looked at Deadman's Party for five years before finding the gumption to try it. On it he discovered the use of copperheads in soft rock. Such placements, aid-climbing aficionados will attest, provide all the security of walking on thin ice in a heat wave. On Intifada, his masterpiece on the east face of Cottontail Tower, Beyer quivered enough to rate the route A6—making it the world's most severe aid route. He summarizes its delights as "thirty-eight hook moves, a crux of stacked blade tips in rotten flakes and a lunge to the summit."

Beyer's Conradian obsession with Fisher Towers scared not only him, but those close to him. "During those years," he said, "every girlfriend I had told me I'd die there."

The Fisher Towers attuned Beyer so well to the subtleties of aid placements that he subdivided aid ratings from the usual five into fourteen. In this system, A1 through A3+ describe aid in a way most climbers who have stood in etriers would comprehend. Beyer's system divides A4 and above, though, into four degrees, a to d. Hard, or "psycho aid," commences at A4d, a rating that indicates the risk of a forty-foot fall with injury potential. A5a sports sixty-foot fall potential. By A5d a fall could rip out a full pitch, including the anchor. Beyer describes A6a as having "extreme death potential involving more than two pitches with possible 200-foot falls." Cruxes are cutting-edge technical aid. No bolts can be used for protection or belays, meaning that in the case of fixed ropes below, a fall could rip out lower anchors too.

Though Beyer always climbed alone, and quietly, word about these routes got around the desert. Were his routes as extreme as he claimed? One veteran desert rat, Kyle Copeland, a climbing guide and guidebook author from Moab, knows Beyer and the nature of his routes. "There is no doubt that Jim has done the hardest nailing routes on Utah sandstone," he says, "but I don't always agree with his choice of line. He looks for incipience and difficulty rather than aesthetics."

Charlie Fowler, the peripatetic all-around climber from Telluride, Colorado, has known Beyer since the 1970s. "Jim has become a role model to many Yosemite big-wall climbers," he says. "He pushes hard on his routes. The few who know him find his single-mindedness inspiring."

But if Beyer's determination has earned him admiration, his intensity also scares people. "I'd be nervous to climb with Jim,"

Copeland says. "He might push me beyond my limits." Furthermore, though Beyer's routes are established from the ground up, sometimes he stretches traditional tactics.

John Middendorf, a big-waller with many hard desert and Yosemite walls to his credit, says, "Jim's tactics are unusual. He sometimes fixes ropes till the final ascent, bivying on the ground rather than the wall. And his free tactics are questionable. He sometimes aids a pitch first, then subsequently frees the moves while hanging on jumars from fixed rope."

Beyer admits to these methods in accounts in the *American Alpine Journal.* On Intifada in the Fisher Towers he states that "the 900-foot climb took nine days and one night on the wall." On a new route on El Capitan left of the west face, Reach for the Sky (VI 5.11d A4d), he records his tactic of working a pitch free from fixed rope. "My only question about climbing like that," Middendorf says, "is that subsequent leaders are unlikely to find themselves on-sighting 5.12 when the only protection are A3 copperheads that the first ascent placed on aid but subsequently removed."

After his sagas on the Fisher Towers, Beyer noticed something an impartial observer might call strange: he was more comfortable climbing alone than with a partner. "On multiday aid routes," he explains during our Boulder meeting, "you need mental stamina to focus on the technical situation. Being with another person breaks my concentration."

With the dream of a Karakoram wall of rock and ice in his mind, Beyer spent hundreds of hours running, weight-lifting and biking. He crafted his diet to create physical bulk to sustain his body on long walls. Even on a simple pitch in Eldorado, he always shouldered a full rack to stay used to carrying the heavy gear needed on long routes.

In the mid-1980s he began experimenting with a form of sports meditation or self-hypnosis. "It's mental preprogramming," says Beyer. "It helps me cope with instances when I need an automatic reaction to survive." He would visualize himself in dangerous climbing situations and store survival responses. Long before a climb, Beyer would be psychologically ready, for he had already visualized the worst a climb could present—even hideous injury. By indoctrinating himself with planned, automatic escapes from every situation he learned to push himself harder. "Some people buy insurance; I train mentally and physically to stay alive," he says.

By 1989 Beyer deemed himself ready for the Karakoram. He arrived at the base of the Grand Cathedral, a lofty, 19,245-foot-high granite layer cake of walls overlooking the Baltoro Glacier. With only a cook at base camp as support, Beyer set off on his dream climb. At just about the same time, Mark Wilford and I stumbled out from a thirteen-day nightmare of storm and failure on Trango Tower. Once again, as in Yosemite in 1977, I found myself on the ground watching Beyer, who appeared as a dot on the wall. Beyer's cook, a Balti, handed me a cup of tea, and we sat on a boulder watching him solo a searing crack line. "Jim good man," said the cook, "but little bit crazy."

Fifty-four pitches. Thirteen days. The Beyer Route on Grand Cathedral was no pushover, but it went smoothly in good weather. Beyer rated the experience VII 5.10 A4+. Perhaps it was a fantasy realized too easily, for in 1990 he was back in the Karakoram, this time in the Hunza region.

"On some of my climbs I've gone for the summit at all costs, exceeding what could be called intelligent actions. This might compromise my credibility with some people," says Beyer as he begins to tell me the story of his solo of Bib-O-li-Motin, a 19,685-foot rocky fang above the village of Karimabad.

I, too, knew the peak well. I'd attempted it in 1985, but fusillades of stonefall from its couloirs and 2200-foot walls sent me and my companions running, as it has many other expeditions since then. The only previous ascent when Beyer tried it in 1990 was by Patrick Cordier's French party in 1982, via the mixed east ridge. The stupendous southeast face was unclimbed, and that was Beyer and Pat McInerny's goal.

Beyer had befriended McInerny, a climbing guide, that year in Moab. To prepare for the Karakoram the two climbed a new route on the Diamond (Steep Is Flat, VI 5.10 A4+) and had an impressive season in the French Alps.

On Bib-O-li-Motin, the pair spent twelve dangerous days dodging rockfall, while fixing rope and load-carrying up a 200-foot ice cliff in the approach couloir, before dumping their gear at the foot of the wall. Avalanches are common in this region—two Japanese attempts on Ultar, beside Bib-O-li-Motin, have ended tragically this way, and in 1985 I'd seen slides rake the gullies and flow over the meadows, sweeping away sheep and goats with them.

The night Beyer and McInerny set off, they found their fixed ropes piled at the foot of the ice cliff, having been shredded by an avalanche. Undeterred, Beyer patched a makeshift line together from bits of five-millimeter and nine-millimeter cord and headed back up the ice cliff. At the final overhanging lip, Beyer, totally without protection because all their gear was beneath the wall, struck rotten ice that he couldn't get his ice tools to stick in. Each time he struck or kicked a crampon into it, chunks blew out and his placement skated. A shakefest began that Beyer called "worse than A6." Says McInerny, "It was the most incredible thing I've ever seen. For five minutes Jim would dangle from one ice axe, get the other in and then the first would pop out, along with his feet. He was gasping desperately. If he'd fallen he'd have gone 200 feet, and the rope would surely have snapped."

But Beyer got them over the bulge. They reached the wall in a storm and began to climb. Two days later it was still storming and they were 500 feet up, climbing rotten rock. Cold numbed their hands. McInerny dropped a rope. As he rigged a rappel to fetch it from a rock snag, his doubts about the sanity of their adventure welled to the surface. "Maybe I'll just rap down to the rope and keep going and let you solo this nightmare," McInerny said.

"Why don't you do that," replied Beyer calmly, and the pair divided some gear for McInerny to descend.

The partnership they'd begun on the Diamond was hard for McInerny to break. "I felt bad leaving Jim," McInerny later told me. "I wanted to be there, but I was way out of my depth."

As McInerny began the first rappel, Beyer smiled at him reassuringly, to let him know he bore no grudge. "Don't worry, dude," he said in a fatherly tone. "You're like 99 percent of the people: you're afraid of dying."

By day six Beyer was near the top, having climbed a dozen ice-coated free and aid pitches. But three days later he hadn't moved, trapped in his bivy sack as a snowstorm raged around him. On the ninth day he pressed on in frigid weather. Beyer's resolve and equipment were now wearing thin. His ropes were frozen cables, his ice hammer had snapped at the head, food was dwindling and the weather, by the tenth evening, was again deteriorating. The whole time Beyer climbed, a Japanese expedition on nearby Ultar deemed the weather so bad they didn't move out of base camp.

"Every hour or two," says Beyer, "I'd stop and shout into the storm, 'Do I really want to go on?'" Each time he decided he did, he'd swallow a caffeine pill and continue.

Sixty feet from the top he found himself stemming free up a rime-coated dihedral, his boots skating. Suddenly the snow blobs forming his footholds collapsed, and he was hurtling through the air.

Self-belay falls tend to be long and often messy, and Beyer could ill afford such folly. His mental programming kicked into gear. He rotated and lunged for his last piece of pro and caught it with both hands. Had this catch been in a baseball game, Beyer would be in the Hall of Fame, but where he was, his only reward was survival. Grappling with the corner again, he thrashed up and over the summit rim to find himself in darkness and storm, without headlamp or bivouac gear. He was not, however, on top, but on a rubble-strewn slope below a thorny crown of possible summits.

The situation was deflating. "My adrenaline rush had long gone," says Beyer. "The survivor in me said, 'No more.'" He turned around.

Bitter thoughts wracked Beyer on the descent. He felt he no longer cared about summits. He hated mountains. But by the time he reached the meadows and McInerny two days later, he realized that, although he hadn't stood on the highest pile of rubble on top, there was an element of success to his climb: he had completed a wall that had thwarted four expeditions, and he and his partner were going home alive.

By 1991 Beyer figured he was ready to climb the hardest big-wall route in the world. Using money from a spec house he built in Boulder, he organized an expedition to Trango Tower (also called Nameless Tower; 20,463 feet) in Pakistan and, since he was in the land of the 8000-meter peaks, Gasherbrum II (26,360 feet). Two solo "training routes," in 1989 and 1990 in Colorado's Black Canyon of the Gunnison—Like a Psycho on the Painted Wall and Black Planet on North Chasm View Wall, both boltless and rated VI A4d—had put him in good stead.

Perhaps Bib-O-li-Motin had left a residue of fear in him. Shortly before departing for Pakistan, Beyer visited Yosemite to seek a partner for Tango Tower. John Middendorf was keen. Though Middendorf had seen Beyer around for years and knew he was a master big-wall climber, they'd never climbed together. "Jim was always an outsider to the cliques of Yosemite," says Middendorf, who suggested they climb a wall to get acquainted. "But I couldn't get him up on a wall. It was as if he was scared of committing to climb with another person." Beyer and Middendorf's Pakistan plan never got off the ground. Perhaps in the solitary constellation of Beyer's universe, the idea of climbing with a partner had become more disquieting than soloing.

Beyer arrived alone in Islamabad a few weeks after the defeat of Saddam Hussein's army. Many climbers had canceled their trips to Islamic Pakistan, but not Beyer. He called his expedition the "1991 Karakoram Shakefest." He wanted an experience beyond any of his other climbs. This he got, but not in the way he planned.

His problems arose in Islamabad. Says Beyer, "A paperwork mixup between my expedition and some other group had led my young liaison officer (LO) to believe three women were on my team. His first question to me was, 'Where are the ladies?' When I explained there was only me, his fantasy of a vacation in a base camp of women was shattered."

To fathom Beyer's further fiascoes one must understand that Pakistan's mountaineering rules in 1991 required expeditions to have at least four members. Through negotiations with the Ministry of Tourism, Beyer solved this glitch by hiring three Pakistani high-altitude porters to be his partners. It wasn't an ideal situation, and was costly, but it got Beyer moving to the mountains. The problem was, though paid and contracted to do so, this trio refused to carry loads. During the approach along the Baltoro, these paid members and Beyer's other porters held daily sit-down strikes, demanding better equipment and more pay.

But Beyer's main conflicts arose from the bad chemistry between him and his LO, whom Beyer paints as a rigid martinet who protested at every opportunity. "Jim, you'll take 101 risks on this climb, but I will not take a single risk," said the LO at the start of the trip. "Every rule must be followed exactly." Things went downhill from there, says Beyer, beginning when the LO, while examining the expedition clothing provided by Beyer, found he was getting used long-johns and other hand-me-downs from Beyer's wardrobe. The combination of the LO's intractability and Beyer's distrust of authority figures and naivete on how to interact with his Pakistani hosts created an explosive situation.

Perhaps Beyer had preprogrammed himself for the showdown that followed on the Dunge Glacier. On the final day of the approach, trouble began within sight of the granite bulwark of Trango Tower. Beyer attempted to pay off and send back one of his three paid members. This plan—intended to save him money and endorsed by the Ministry of Tourism, says Beyer—precipitated an argument when the member refused to leave. He wanted to stay to earn more money. Backed up by the LO, the others quit in sympathy, leaving Beyer with six regular porters to shuttle his ten loads to the peak. Beyer left the four bickering on the talus fields and set off, happy to be rid of them. An hour later, sweating under a heavy load, Beyer heard the LO behind him hailing the group to stop.

Awaiting the LO's arrival, Beyer instructed the porters to remove their loads and pile them in a heap. "No man approach me," he ordered and positioned them ten feet away.

"The expedition is over," declared the LO. "We return to Skardu. Porters, pick up your loads and follow me."

"Don't touch the loads. Everyone stand back," Beyer countered.

The LO cited a technical point: because three members had quit, Beyer was no longer the team of four stipulated by the rules. Also illegal was the fact that the team had split into two groups. Such details are commonly overlooked by LOs, who usually do their utmost to help an expedition climb its peak. But in this case expedition justice became perverted.

A war of words ensued. Beyer made it clear he was staying. Essentially, he was in the right—the rules state that the expedition leader is the ultimate leader of the trip, and if he disagrees with an LO's decision he must state the nature of the disagreement in writing, but need not follow the LO's orders.

Meanwhile a witness appeared out of the rubble: a Spanish climber heading up to jumar his ropes on Great Trango Tower. "He seemed torn between his climb and this crazy spectacle," says Beyer. "I said, 'Hey, man, wait a few minutes and you'll see the biggest fistfight of all time.' I knew I couldn't fight off ten guys, but a witness might be useful."

Despite the offer of a ringside seat, the Spaniard left. With a cry of "Porters, follow me," the LO charged at Beyer, who pushed the enraged soldier onto his back. Successive charges—unaided by the flabbergasted Balti porters—ended identically.

The LO screamed, "You assaulted a Pakistani army lieutenant! I vow you will never leave this country. You will go to jail. I will see that a helicopter returns to forcibly remove you from this mountain."

Beyer considered, then stared into the LO's eyes and said calmly, "The decisions you make today might have a great effect on your career, lieutenant, because if a helicopter comes up here they'll never take me alive."

While relating the tale to me, Beyer grinned, as if in hindsight he had found a soft spot for the LO. "We were similar in a way. We're both fearless." The stalemate ended when Beyer agreed that everyone except him would return to Skardu. He gave the Pakistanis food and a goat, but retained everything else.

Alone, Beyer couldn't shake off the feeling that his enemies were hiding in the rocks, waiting to steal his gear the moment he left camp. So he hid his loads under boulders across the glacier then carried them upvalley by night to a concealed camp, where he hid by day from the threatened helicopter, which never materialized. After a week of load-carrying to the base of the 3000-foot wall, Beyer was in position to begin the greatest climb of his life. He had gone through the awful and the ridiculous to get there; now it was just himself and the wall. In a fit of jubilation he stood atop a boulder and declared the Dunge Glacier an independent country and himself its king.

But, as Beyer climbed the couloir the next evening, he was flooded by doubts. "With every step toward the wall a voice inside me kept saying, 'Dude, you are one step closer to death,'" Beyer says. The insanity of the previous weeks and the isolation were playing on his nerves, but Beyer knew the value of intuition. To add to his burdens, he had twisted his ankle (the injury was later diagnosed as a fracture) and walked with pain throughout the week of load-carrying.

Beyer groped for words to explain his snap decision to quit Trango Tower. "I spent a lot of time in my tent, thinking. Climbing had always been something I'd done for my own amusement," he says. "But this time I'd found myself fighting for the very right to do it. Every step of the way things had gone wrong, and I began to have very negative thoughts about my chances under the emotional circumstances. One morning I woke up with a complete change of thought. I would cross the glacier, find some people to talk to and head on to a fresh start and another adventure: to climb an 8000-meter peak." He thought first of Gasherbrum II.

Masquerading as a trekker hurrying to catch his friends, Beyer and a single porter he hired on the Baltoro Glacier trail crept through base camps to arrive beneath Broad Peak (26,400 feet), the world's twelfth-highest summit. He abandoned the idea of Gasherbrum II, as it was two additional days upvalley. Beyer planned a clandestine ascent, using fixed ropes and camps others had left on Broad Peak's west face. He began climbing the day after his arrival, just as storm clouds appeared. It was late in the season and his camp had minimal provisions. Beyer gambled that he could climb faster than the storm would advance.

Carrying only a bivy sack, he raced up the slopes. At about 23,000 feet he encountered three Frenchmen descending because of the impending storm.

"Who are you?" one asked, shocked to see a new face on the mountain.

"I can't tell you my name, but I'm a friend," said Beyer, still edgy about being captured by the army.

"American?" quizzed the Frenchman.

"A friend."

"You have no permit?"

"I'm a friend. Tell me what is above."

"There are some Mexicans, but their tents are full."

"I have no tent, no sleeping bag," explained Beyer.

"You must go down!" shouted the Frenchman.

"Not till I reach the summit."

"You are crazy!" The French climbers left.

At the Mexican tent a gale howled. Beyer, desperately cold, shouted into the door, "*Buenos días*. I'm in bad shape out here." He had weighed the possibilities of this moment. What if the Mexicans refused him entry? Would he beg them, bribe them, use violence? He didn't have to worry. Two hands reached out and dragged him in. For an hour Beyer languished in exhaustion— he hadn't eaten or drunk all day and had climbed 8000 feet.

But soon the tent began disintegrating in the hurricane wind, and the Mexicans urged him to get out and escape with them. When he looked at the wind plume raging off the summit, Beyer realized that climbing up was impossible and began descending. His first few steps told him that his body had, as endurance athletes put it, "bonked," or used up every molecule of available energy. Hallucinations and leg cramps plagued him. He staggered, sobbing with the pain and frustration and fear that his body wouldn't carry him out of the blizzard. Beyer became convinced he'd die. The Mexicans urged him on, but the snows were nearly smothering them and they didn't even know who he was. The only thing that kept him moving during that ten-hour descent to Camp I were his caffeine pills, each one equivalent to four cups of coffee.

"I'd always prided myself on being a survivor, and it was those skills, that willpower and all my training that got me down that afternoon," says Beyer. "But I also realized something else, and that was how much I love life. Anyone who didn't want to live as much as I did would have died, regardless of his training."

At Camp I Beyer flopped in a tent while the Mexicans descended to base camp. Thirty hours of constant movement had wrecked him. He stayed awake long enough to melt some snow and drink it. At dawn he awoke to a churning gut. The snow—polluted by many climbers over many seasons—had given him explosive diarrhea. "The stomach cramps were terrible. I fouled the tent, my suit, everything." He forced himself down the last of the mountain, shit welling up the legs of his altitude suit. At base camp he collapsed, until the Mexican team's doctor rendered assistance.

Oh, were it over then: he had yet to face the music in Islamabad after walking out. Needless to say, the Ministry of Tourism's officials didn't view the "1991 Karakoram Shakefest" as a triumph in U.S.–Pakistani relations. Wisely, they'd vetoed the LO's demand for a helicopter mission to arrest Beyer, but when Beyer asked for a refund of his helicopter rescue and environmental protection bonds (amounts totaling $5000), matters got sticky.

At the ministry, a high-ranking official told Beyer, "The good news is we won't stop you from leaving the country. The bad news is your LO says your porters did massive environmental damage on their hike out by burning firewood and not disposing of a goat carcass in a hygienic manner."

Pressed to sign a document accepting responsibility and forfeiting $1000, Beyer refused, calling the charge bogus. An argument ensued and became so heated that Beyer's Pakistani trekking agent, who was also present, shouted, "I hate Americans! George Bush kills innocent Iraqis!"

Finally Beyer consented to pay a small fine. "Well, Mr. Beyer," said the Ministry of Tourism official as the troublesome tourist left his office, "I don't think we'll be seeing you back in Pakistan again, will we?"

My weekend with Beyer was classic Colorado, with cool winter sunshine. He took most of a day to relate his tale of Pakistan, and by its end he looked exhausted. In what he'd told me I found much that was shocking and askew from my perceptions of human nature. Though I admire Beyer in the same way I admire climbers such as Voytek Kurtyka, Doug Scott and Mugs Stump, his cult of solitude was unsettling in a visceral way. But then I had never visited the spiritual and physical hinterlands of self the way he had. Beyer has many layers, and I had only scratched the surface of getting to know him. Though his adventures as a soloist defined a personality separate from those around him, at my last question he revealed a newly emergent individual.

"I'll ask you the question I'm often asked after an expedition," I had said to Beyer. "Are you a different person than you were before that ordeal?"

It sounded like a dumb question, and I expected to hear plans of more solo brinksmanship. Instead Beyer said, "I left the old Jim behind the morning I decided to quit Trango Tower. It's not that I psyched out, but for the first time I admitted to myself I was wrong. My whole psychology believed it was right to cultivate risks to achieve success. This led me to take terrible chances. Because I was soloing, in my self-centered world I could talk myself into it. Without being conscious of it, I behaved as if summits were worth dying for. I don't buy that anymore."

I hadn't counted on this dimension of Beyer—sobered, humble, sated. When he saw I was surprised he simplified his reasoning: "I guess I just saw clearly that someday a hook was going to pop when I was soloing and that would be the end. I still want to climb hard and climb traditionally, but I want to share it—with partners."

WORKING-CLASS HERO

In the high-performance climbing scene of today the name Don Whillans is probably an anachronism, but those who spent time with the legendary hard man of British climbing still gather together to recount his exploits as if they happened yesterday. Clusters of Whillans aficionados are easily spotted. They zero in on each other at pubs and parties, below cliffs and in base camps beneath remote mountains in the Third World, and try to outdo each other in resurrecting his abrasive wit and imitating his singular delivery of the one-liner.

Standing in a circle, they typically clutch glasses of ale and sway slightly. As the evening progresses they jut their bellies forward, mimicking the Whillans swagger. Simultaneously, their speech lazes into a nasal, monotone whine, and their tone becomes deadpan, ironic and sweetly derisive of acquaintances.

Whenever the urge to imitate Whillans overcomes me I see puzzled gazes appear on the faces of friends who knew nothing of the taciturn old Brit. They stare at me as if I'm speaking in tongues, or as if I'm just plain drunk. But the well-traveled and wider-read among them recognize the affected Lancastrian accent, and they know I'm giving them a gobful of Whillans-speak.

Although he died in 1985—from a heart attack in his sleep, brought on by steering his motorbike through a rainstorm from Chamonix to Wales—his life still inspires biographers, and

Whillans stories still make the rounds. Open a score of mountaineering books and there is Whillans, speaking directly at you. His incisive, morbid, brilliant wit endures in British climbing, even if the impact of his climbs has been forgotten by a harder-climbing generation.

I met him in 1981 on my first Himalayan expedition, to Shivling in India. We didn't talk much on the flight over. He seemed more interested in reading a book on keeping tropical fish as pets than in talking to me, a mere kid half his age. He was a short man of hippopotamus proportions in his nearly fiftieth year, yet still he looked powerful, with hamhock-size forearms honed the hard way, by years wrestling with pipe against wrench as a plumber. His lips were cast in a perpetual state of near-frown, and grey stubble forested his chin.

Studying his aggressive profile—he was a man who always looked ready for a fight—I tried to reconcile his portly stature with what I knew of him. I'd read his biography, *Portrait of a Mountaineer*, before embarking on the expedition. It had left me with an image of a hard-boiled and earthy individualist, blue-collar to the bone, quick-tempered yet soft-hearted. His laconic wit and philosophic gallows humor were phenomena of the British climbing scene, and his one-liners were extolled in climbers' pubs from Wales to Chamonix. He had invented a waist harness that bore his name and which, back then, was worn by climbers across the world, while his tent—the Whillans Box—was an invincible hermitage designed to endure ferocious Himalayan storms. For a time, in the early 1970s during his obsession with Everest, he had spent more time at high altitude than any other human being, chain smoking his way to 8000 meters on several occasions.

When younger, he had sported a frame as buffed as any modern sport climber's. During the 1950s he and Joe Brown had left a trail of rock climbs across Britain that still inspired full-bodied, trench-warfare–style physical effort. One Whillans route, an overhanging groove called Goliath, on a gritstone edge called

Burbage in Derbyshire, still holds a very respectable difficulty rating of E4 under the British system. The day before boarding the Air India flight in Heathrow, London, I had visited another gritstone crag and climbed a wildly exposed ceiling crack called Sloth, another Whillans test piece. On the plane I asked him if he remembered it. He turned from his book, gave me an icy look, said "Aye," and then resumed reading about fish.

Like a character actor who drifts onto the stage for a cameo role and upstages the main players, Whillans figured in several climbing books I had read. He appeared in Bonington's 1966 book, *I Chose to Climb;* the two had made ascents in the Alps like the Central Pillar of Freney on Mont Blanc. They climbed the granite cracks in gym shoes, or plimsolls, as they called them. In Bonington's *Annapurna South Face,* about the breakthrough ascent of the 26,545-foot Nepalese mountain's massive south wall in 1970, Whillans was a key player, reaching the summit with Dougal Haston. Haston's own book, *In High Places,* describes Don as "practical, without a romantic dream in his head." Whillans had tried reading Haston's copy of the J. R. R. Tolkien fantasy *Lord of the Rings,* but had cast it aside, muttering "fuckin' fairies."

Doug Scott, who does a very passable Whillans imitation himself, and who sat on the other side of Don on the flight to Delhi, loved to recount the time on the International Everest Southwest Face attempt when the German climbers heard on the radio that they had beaten the British soccer team in the World Cup Final. Doug described the exchange, which went like this:

"It seems ve haf beaten you at your national game," said one proud German to Don.

"Aye," Don nodded, "and we've beaten you at yours, twice."

Droll comments like these, as much as his exploits on Annapurna or Everest, in Patagonia or the Alps, shaped the Whillans fame. To be on the receiving end of a Whillans barb was to be cruelly gored, but it was also the highest honor, because it guaranteed some form of immortality in the climbing ethos. So I hung on his every word, hoping to hear one of these famous comments. He continued to ignore me.

Outside Delhi airport while we sat on our baggage, waiting for a truck to carry us into town, a young Indian boy positioned himself beside Whillans. He asked if we were a mountaineering expedition. "Aye," Don told the boy, who was sizing Whillans up carefully.

"But are you not too fat to be a mountaineer?" the boy brazenly asked. By any comparison, Don was. "Some people tell me I've got a problem with eating," he'd sometimes say; "I don't know what they mean. I eat everything." His athletic body long gone to seed, Don attributed his now Buddha-like physique to his wife Audrey's incomparable cooking, and, perhaps, a bit to his grand capacity to put away beer.

The Indian boy's audacity made Don turn his head. He stared into the lad with iceberg eyes, then he gestured toward me and the other members of the expedition.

"Perhaps I am too fat," he told the boy, with chilling seriousness, placing careful emphasis on every syllable. "But by the end of this expedition I'll be skinny and they'll be non-existent."

There it was. I had heard my first Whillansism, and I had, by association, been a part of it. It was a significant day in my climbing career.

He hailed from Manchester, a grimy industrial city known for smokestacks, mills and soccer hooligans. Don was the second Mancunian I had met. The first was a tough teenage emigrant to my school in Australia, who, on being taunted by the school bully to display his mettle as a fighter, head-butted said bully into unconsciousness, then drew a switchblade on the adolescent crowd. Manchester bred tough knucklemen, and Don, though only five-foot-five, had learned to account for himself with fist, tongue, tooth and claw. Thus, many a tale of confrontation concluded with Whillans saying "and so I 'it him."

Don carried himself like a working man, though he was too proud to be a minion and never worked long under a boss's schedule. In Doug Scott's book *Himalayan Climber*, Whillans enters a theater to present a slide show. "I'm Don Whillans," he tells the crowd. "They say I'm working class but I'd like you to know I've not worked for twelve years." He disliked Britain's blue-blood upper class for its snobbery and establishment climbers who had made big reputations, though he enjoyed the small privileges that came his way. His commentary on elitist folk was like a scythe slashing at smug, tall poppies.

A week after arriving in Delhi, we were trekking toward Shivling along a branch of the Ganges River. Strange-looking mystics—gaunt, turbaned and toting iron tridents and brass pots of Ganges water—shared the trail with us, heading to the sacred source of the river. Whillans, rounding a bend, came face to face with a yogi. They stared at each other for a moment, then the yogi stretched out his palm for Whillans to drop a coin into, as it is the custom for men of means to give alms to those traveling along the paths of enlightenment.

"Hmm," said Whillans (who was something of a guru of negative realism himself), "are you on some sort of sponsored walk?" Then he grasped the yogi's hand and firmly shook it, utterly confounding the Indian.

Incidents like this amused us, but by base camp the eight-climber group had learned first-hand Don's famous capacity for idleness.

"Old Don won't carry a load," protested one of the group during a discussion at base camp. "He fills his bloody pack with his sleeping bag. If you ask him to carry something he says, 'It's not the weight—it's where to put it!'"

"Well, Don's getting on in years. He has trouble with his

knees," countered Doug in defense of his canny old friend. Don had decided long ago that his seniority excused him from carrying heavy loads.

"And he wouldn't brew you a cup of tea if your life depended on it. He expects us to do all the bloody cooking," snarled another climber. Doug smiled these complaints away.

"Ah well, I warned you about Don and cooking before we left. It's his generation, his upbringing. There are certain things he won't do, and cooking is one of them. He thinks it's woman's work, or something like that. On Everest I spent a week with him in a tent cooking all his meals. I finally told him, 'Don, I'm not your mother!' He just sat there and said, 'You're not one of those types that moans about a bit of cookin', are you?'"

But if Don's idiosyncrasies flustered us in base camp, his stories and his sheer presence galvanized us all. At midnight a yell from his tent roused the camp.

"Hey, wake up! I just realized it's me fiftieth bloody birthday!"

By the light of a full moon we gathered together in the cold, passing round a bottle of Irish whiskey. It wasn't really his fiftieth birthday—it was his forty-eighth—but he liked the well-rounded, half-century figure and claimed it as his own. The night wore on, the bottle grew empty, prompting Don into nostalgic reminiscences.

"After we came down from the summit of Annapurna, somewhere on the way out, we had a victory celebration. I don't know how many bottles of whiskey we polished off, but it was quite a few. The Sherpas watched us get wilder and wilder. Dougal disappeared for a while—he'd fallen into the latrine and couldn't get out. By morning we were sick as dogs—a terrible sight. The Sherpas loaded us onto a tarpaulin, dragged the entire expedition to the river and dumped us in it. As I woke up I remember one of the Sherpas shaking his head at me in disgust, saying, 'Sahibs like buffalo!'"

On Shivling Doug, Georges Bettembourg, Rick White and I climbed for thirteen days and reached the summit by the previously unclimbed east pillar. By the end, Don's prediction that we'd end up skinny as yogis became a fact. We had run out of food, had been spanked by storms and were thoroughly done in. As we wearily descended Shivling's west side, a small dot sitting on the glacier, awaiting us, took on the unmistakably rotund form of Whillans. I daydreamed of the tea he would surely be brewing, and the biscuits and other goodies he must have brought up. Beneath that coarse exterior, I had learned, Don had a heart soft as 22-carat gold.

I arrived in time for Don to shake my hand, say to us, "Well done, lads, you made it back," then turn his back and waddle down the glacier. We had taken so long to reach him that he had gotten hungry and scoffed the biscuits and flask of tea he had brought. "Well," Rick said, "it's the thought that counts."

For his part, Don tried the west face of Shivling, but he'd felt out of place climbing in the fast, lightweight "alpine style" adopted by our expedition. Don was accustomed to an era of siege climbs that used big teams of climbers and vast amounts of rope and material to beat Himalayan peaks into submission. The notion of our alpine-style ascent of Shivling—with its commitment to venturing into uncharted territory, carrying only what we could cram into our rucksacks, and traversing the mountain without an escape route of fixed ropes—was, to Don, reckless, and our method of acclimatizing to altitude by scaling Shivling's neighboring peaks was haphazard. Don derided this approach as being "up and down, like a bride's nightie." Doug's famously loose leadership of the expedition, which let events take a casual, even unpredictable course, was haphazard to Don. "This lot couldn't organize a fuck in a brothel," he scolded us in base camp one day.

Such talk led Doug to tell me, "Don may be the most selfish person I've ever met." Yet Doug felt a debt of gratitude to the older man, since it was Don, in 1971, who had lobbied for Doug to be invited on the International Everest Southwest Face expedition. That expedition, though a failure, revealed Scott to be a brilliant performer at altitude, and he went on a few years later to make the first ascent of that coveted frozen wall, with Dougal Haston, and to achieve a lasting place in British climbing history. Don, however, had been left off the list for the successful 1975 expedition, led by Chris Bonington. It seems that the Whillans idiosyncrasies we celebrate as humorous today—irascibility, recalcitrance, bone laziness—had outweighed the value of his wit. To some, Whillans was a royal pain in the rear.

Outwardly, Whillans deflected the rebukes of his peers without a flinch. Inwardly it was another matter: "Not being asked along on Everest in '75 hurt him immensely," said Doug.

History will note that Whillans was neither the pushiest climber, nor the bravest, boldest or fastest. Those epithets belong to a newer vintage of climbers. A conservative bent regarding the acceptance of danger led him to turn away from many summits. He regarded climbers who habitually courted great risks as fools. Survival and life were, to Don, the ultimate goal of mountaineering, and he had a host of maxims to prove this point:

"The mountains will always be there. The trick is for you to be there as well."

"I don't mind fighting my way out of trouble but I'm damned if I'll fight my way into it."

"There are two types of climbers: smart ones and dead ones."

In fact, the human race on every level could be divided into two types of people, according to Don. Once, during an argument between us in Islamabad, following the death on Broad Peak of our friend Peter Thexton, and immediately after Don had drunk dry the liquor cabinet of our British Embassy host, he tried to categorize me in similar fashion. Leveling his finger at me he began, "There's two types of people in this world, youth..." but I cut him off before he could finish. I've always wondered on what shelf of the human race Whillans had placed me.

A trait for rebelliousness and a taste for drink—supping, he called it—were part of the Whillans aura and, doubtless, part of his downfall. His propensity for ale, which he could pour into himself all night, distended his dimensions, and his moods.

"People ask me why I drink so much," he would quip. "It's because of a morbid fear of dehydration." A local newspaper once published an account of a drunk and disorderly Whillans running afoul of the local constabulary for some trivial offense. At the beck and call of no man, he obstinately refused to be arrested. It took a squad of coppers to uproot him from his stance and load him into a paddy wagon.

Whillans liked the company of wild drinking men. Where alcohol was concerned, he could outpace anyone, even the stratospheric partner from Wales, Al Harris, whose house—which was grand party central in the British climbing scene until Harris's death in a drunken car crash—was not far from Whillans' own Llanberis Pass cottage and guesthouse. Don also supped with a shadowy figure he simply called Kershaw, who Whillans swore could crunch up with his teeth and devour a pint beer mug, just to get a rise out of a crowd.

Alcohol was the inspiration behind many Whillans stories, but, like other wits or writers who have used booze to oil their imaginations, it came at a price. He let himself go physically, became bloated with booze and often moody. Yet still, he climbed occasionally, and many sought his acquaintance, accepting his barbed tongue and forgiving his indiscretions.

Upon rereading this I have to wonder what the person who never knew Whillans would make of him. "Why," they probably would ask, "would anyone deify this apparently cynical, verbally uncharitable roughneck larrikin?" That's a hard question to answer. Maybe a Whillans story is only valid to those who knew him. Perhaps you had to be there, to see and hear the man deliver the maxim, with a hand-rolled cigarette perched on his lower lip and his finger aimed like a dart, pointed at the target of his wit. There was something about Whillans that a generation of climbers can't forget, and it has little to do with his climbs. It's his presence we remember.

And, like that literary smart-aleck Oscar Wilde, Whillans could only have been born of England, for the citizens of the island nation have perfected a talent for self-effacing, irreverent humor. "Taking the piss," they call it. It's a humor born in that cozy village watering hole, the local pub, to which the British climbing scene is eternally wedded. A British expatriate climber, Adrian Burgess, once told me, "The difference between British expeditions and American expeditions is that in Britain expeditions are hatched inside pubs, and in America they are organized on the phone."

Since the earliest days of British cragging, a day on the rocks is followed by a night in the pub. In pubs the British climbing scene blows off steam, loses restraint. To become a gibbering, raving, furniture-wrecking lunatic is de rigueur in the British pub and climbing scene. In the last year of his life Whillans was a guest speaker at the annual dinner held in a pub of an association called the Black Pudding Team. After his talk, proceedings degenerated into the usual British celebration of life, and there was Whillans with the lads, rolling around on the beer-soaked floor, wrestling, crashing into tables and causing as much mayhem as when he had been a teenage rebel.

In the wake of Whillans's life we are left with a thousand— no, ten thousand—little stories. Everyone who crossed his path has a tale, as if it were an endowment or a gift given by the man in the knowledge that like a work of art each would gain value with time, and could be traded like currency. Not long ago in a Boston pub, a climber named Barry Rugo introduced me to a transplanted British rock climber, Craig Smith, who had once been very hot.

"Craig knew Whillans a bit in his last years," Barry announced.

"Yeah?" And so the Whillans stories began to flow, like ale from a tapped keg.

In the early 1980s, Smith was climbing well and getting a fair bit of attention in the climbing press. As one of the New Wave of punk rock climbing, Smith also sported a Mohawk haircut. Whillans acknowledged the existence of the obviously talented, accomplished Smith by simply referring to him as "Bog Brush," a reference to his hairdo resembling one of those spiky cleaning brushes kept beside the toilet.

Said Smith: "He'd fix that gaze on me in a bar, shake his head a bit as if in disgust, then say, 'Hey Bog Brush! Get me a beer!'"

And Leo Dickinson, the British adventure filmmaker, balloonist and parachutist, is a connoisseur of Whillans stories. He tells of Whillans at an airfield, about to take his first parachute jump: "After studying the aerial antics of parachutists all day, Don decided it was safe to try," said Dickinson. So Whillans signed up for a jump with an instructor, who, in turn, had been studying Whillans, as he wasn't the usual shape for parachuting.

"When about to jump out of the Cessna, Whillans turned to his instructor and asked, 'Have you ever seen a falling safe?' The instructor replied he hadn't. 'Well, you're about to,' Whillans replied, and leaped into the sky without another word.

But nobody captured the essence of Whillans as precisely as the late Tom Patey, the famous Scottish climber and wit. In a story called "A Short Walk With Whillans," about an attempt on the Eiger Nordwand with Don in 1962, he wrote, "Don has that rarest of gifts, the ability to condense a whole paragraph into a single, terse, uncompromising sentence. But there are also occasions when he can become almost lyrical in a macabre sort of way."

Patey recorded some vintage Whillans gallows humor in that tale. In one instance, the pair are rushing down the mountain in a deadly looking holocaust of storm and lightning when they encounter two Japanese climbers:

"Going up?" queried Whillans.

"Yes, yes," they chorused in unison. "Up. Always upwards. First Japanese ascent."

"You may be going up, mate," said Whillans, "but a lot 'igher than you think!"

Whillans' commentary was always decisive, always blunt, but it wasn't devoid of a strange kind of compassion. On Everest in 1971, the Indian climber Harsh Bahaguna was suddenly, rapidly overcome with altitude and cold while descending from a high camp in a storm. Bahaguna dangled on the rope for hours, his life ebbing away. A rescue team including Whillans reached Bahaguna when he was all but dead and tried to help him, but the storm threatened to freeze the rescuers, as well. A difficult decision had to be made, and Whillans made it, deciding that trying to save Bahaguna would endanger the whole team.

"I'm sorry, Harsh, old man. You've had it," Don said, then the group turned, leaving Bahaguna, and fought their way down the mountain in raging storm. Callous, the faint-hearted would mutter; Realist, those who know the game of climbing would counter.

I made a second jaunt into the mountains with Don, this time to the Karakoram, in 1983. We went high on Broad Peak together. His gargantuan belly and age slowed him, but he ambled into the thin air steadily, happily.

During those days we talked a lot. He told me stories—not Whillans stories, but life stories, about people he had met, about his journeys to peculiar places. Like the time, after climbing a 25,000-foot mountain called Trivor, that he had ridden a motorbike 7000 miles from Pakistan to England, fending off border guards with backhanders and baffling backchat. Or about the cavern-riddled, lost-world summit of Roraiama, atop a lofty vine- and tarantula-festooned wall in the Venezuelan jungle. Don wasn't known for his sensitivity—he had alienated a lot of his early acquaintances with that combination of laziness and gruff selfishness—but he spoke here in a way I hadn't heard before.

"Don, these are great stories. You should write a book," I said as we lay in a frost-encrusted tent on the Savoia Glacier.

"Oh, no, youth," he said. "Never write anything. You'll only regret it."

Weeks later Don and I hiked back down the Baltoro Glacier to the dusty town of Skardu. While passing time there, Don asked me to accompany him on a stroll alongside the Shyok River. He seemed to be looking for something. When I asked him what it was he told me that he thought that somewhere around these parts was the place where he and his friends had buried a companion who had died during an expedition to Masherbrum in 1957. Don had nearly gotten to the summit, but another companion had grown gravely ill from altitude and Don had escorted him down.

"But Don," I said. "That was back in the same year I was born. We'll never find an unmarked grave after all that time."

"Aye, a bad year was '57. Herman Buhl was killed, we missed out on climbing Masherbrum, my mate died and you were born."

Still, he insisted we look. We roamed about, Don sheltering from the scorching sun beneath a black umbrella, looking for something amid the drab landscape to jog his memory of twenty-six years before. Luckless, we gave up and sat in the shade of a rock, looking across the brown river valley.

"Ah," he sighed, "it's a good life, providing you don't weaken."

"What if you do?" I asked.

"They bury you."

"Wait a minute," I said. "Isn't that one of your lines from Tom Patey's story, about when you two were on the Eiger?"

"Well-read little bugger," he muttered, parting his sun-cracked lips in a rare chuckle, and getting up to waddle back along the riverbank.

MYSTERIUM TREMENDUMS

The nether world, the spirit world, death, superstition and unexplainable phenomena are the subject of the two stories in this section. "The Other Presence" is an essay about that mysterious feeling, experienced in extreme moments by alpinists and explorers over the ages, of being accompanied by a ghostly companion who often comforts and guides one to safety. *Backpacker* published the story in 1989. A sobering encounter with death on a glacier in Nepal prompted "Meeting with a Stranger," which is an unapologetic meditation on death in mountaineering. It is published here for the first time.

THE OTHER PRESENCE

It was 1933, at 28,000 feet on Mount Everest's north ridge. As British climber Frank Smythe paused to rest, he gazed across the Rongbuk Glacier to the golden hills of Tibet. He pulled a piece of mint cake from his pocket, broke it in two and offered half to the companion who had been with him all day. Smythe found himself trying to share the snack with thin air. He was alone, as he had been the entire day.

Long before my own Himalayan climbs, I had read about Smythe's encounter with the "other presence," that eerie visitation by a ghostlike entity that accompanies some mountaineers. The "presence" may be visual and auditory, or it may be simply a gut feeling. "It" arrives unobtrusively, usually when the going is toughest, and often at altitudes above 20,000 feet. The presence is never menacing. Smythe called it "strong and friendly. In its company I could not feel lonely, neither could I come to any harm."

Accounts of such encounters are tantalizingly brief. Just as airline pilots seldom admit to UFO sightings for fear their colleagues will think they cracked under pressure, climbers are often guarded when speaking about strange experiences that are usually the result of altitude and isolation. But enough accounts of the other presence are sprinkled throughout mountaineering folklore to make you wonder. What goes on in your mind at high altitudes when there's only thin air to breathe?

By my second Himalayan expedition in 1983, I'd read

many accounts of this phenomenon but heard few interpretations. I never expected to meet this unsettling visitor personally, but then, I never anticipated what would happen on Broad Peak.

Pete Thexton and I stood at 26,000 feet after descending from Broad Peak's foresummit, 380 feet above us. We'd forsaken the main summit—a half-hour farther on—because I feared my headaches and hallucinations were the onset of cerebral edema, the altitude-induced and potentially deadly accumulation of fluid on the brain.

The sun was low in the sky. To either side of us the rocky Main and Central summits reared up. Behind us was a sheer drop into China, while ahead was the descent route in Pakistan. It was 2000 feet down to our tent. Though my condition improved as we descended, Pete was soon immobilized by pulmonary edema, another altitude-induced fluid buildup, but in the lungs. Within minutes he could barely breathe or move. Since the only remedy was to lose altitude, we continued down despite the clouds and darkness closing in.

At 10:00 P.M., Pete lost his sight. An hour later, he could only crawl. By midnight I was dragging him through the snow and lowering him down slopes on a rope. A windstorm engulfed us, and huge ice cliffs were all around. Our tent was the proverbial needle in a haystack, and we were completely lost on the vast west face of the world's twelfth-highest mountain.

Earlier, near the summit, I had felt a peculiar sense of disassociation from myself, as if I were outside my body looking on. But there was also a strong feeling that someone was peering over my shoulder. Lower, while struggling through blinding spindrift and darkness, I felt that someone was leading the way. I later wrote: "The sensation of being outside myself was more prevalent than ever. My watcher checked every move and decision. I kept turning around, expecting to see someone."

The feeling of traveling with a third presence was powerful and calming. I felt confident Pete and I were being led to our tent. Indeed, we did find our camp, at 2:00 A.M. But reaching shelter was not enough. Pete's condition worsened. At sunrise he died. I descended the mountain with a heavy heart, and many questions.

Years later, my thoughts often return to that time. Often, too, I wonder about the vivid sense of being accompanied down Broad Peak. While perusing climbing literature and speaking to other climbers, I have been made aware of many experiences like mine. It seems remarkable that so many climbers have had similar encounters. Skeptics might lump them in with Sasquatch tales, or Castaneda's sessions with the Yaqui mystic Don Juan, or, perhaps justifiably, merely pass them off as hallucinations caused by oxygen deficiency.

But those who have encountered the other presence describe it in a serious tone. They don't speak of an imaginary presence; they speak of a flesh-and-blood being. Seeking a solution to the mystery of the other presence is like being a detective stalking the invisible man; there is no fingerprint, no solid evidence at all. The clues lie deep within us.

The other presence plays a historic role in the ethos of adventure literature. Though almost all the tales are from mountaineers, the earliest recorded encounters were by seamen such as Joshua Slocum, who was visited by the ghost of a long-dead mariner. The entity took the helm during a storm when Slocum was below deck with fever. So the story goes.

Perhaps the most famous, though, is the tale from the unflappable polar explorer and British navy captain, Ernest Shackleton. In 1915 on South Georgia Island, Antarctica, Shackleton and seamen Worsley and Crean were making a desperate march across unmapped mountains and glaciers toward a whaling station. Their ship, the *Endurance,* had been crushed to splinters in winter pack ice. Shackleton's crew was out of provisions after a long journey by lifeboat across Antarctic seas; their survival depended on Shackleton reaching the whaling station.

The ragged trio, half lost, exhausted, starved and frozen, marched nonstop for thirty-six hours. After they reached the settlement, Worsley told Shackleton, "Boss, I had a curious feeling that there was another person with us." Shackleton and Crean confessed to the same utterly convincing sensation that a fourth presence was with them during the ordeal.

Shackleton regarded this as a religious experience. So profound was its effect that it was difficult for him to speak about it, even to his biographer. His tale, and the questions it posed, were not lost on T. S. Eliot, who wrote in his poem "The Wasteland":

> *Who is the third who walks beside you?*
> *When I count, there are only you and I together,*
> *But when I look ahead up the white road*
> *There is always another one walking beside you,*
> *Gliding wrapt in a brown mantle, hooded,*
> *I do not know whether a man or a woman*
> *—But who is that on the other side of you?"*

While it is easy to get carried away by the romantic dimensions of such tales, there are medical interpretations. Dr. Peter Hackett, who for fifteen years has studied the effects of altitude on the brain and lungs, spent seven seasons on the slopes of Mount McKinley at the Denali Medical Research Clinic studying and aiding altitude-stricken climbers. He thinks that fever-induced delirium could have conjured up Slocum's visitor and that both Slocum and Shackleton's team may have been suffering from scurvy. In Hackett's opinion, the presence known to mountaineers is directly linked to hypoxia, or the lack of oxygen. That puts the phenomenon almost exclusively in the realm of the mountains, in the rarefied air of high altitude.

"I had an experience descending from Everest's summit in 1981," says Hackett. "I was sharing a tent with Chris Pizzo. During the night my oxygen bottle ran out. I hallucinated that John West [a team member] entered the tent with an oxygen bottle and opened the valve, filling the tent with oxygen. When I thanked John out loud for coming up the mountain to deliver the oxygen, I woke Chris Pizzo, who told me I was crazy. I had run out of oxygen and became hypoxic."

Science has barely scratched the surface of high-altitude physiology and psychology. Certainly, no research or testing of "mystical" altitude experiences has been done. But clearly, humans are not designed for the harsh environment of mountains as high as the Himalaya, where oxygen starvation, dehydration and fatigue can conspire to short-circuit the metabolism.

As you gasp in the thin air of high altitude, desperately trying to take in enough oxygen, you exhale an excessive amount of carbon dioxide. A host of metabolic changes occur, triggering increased urination. High in the mountains, however, it's impossible to consume enough water to stave off the dehydration that results from the urinating and hard breathing in dry air. Vital cellular functions suffer. This, in turn, may lead into the dream world of altitude sickness and disorientation. In breaking-point situations, adrenaline surges may complicate all of this.

A more direct link between oxygen deprivation and distorted perceptions may also exist. Some brain researchers believe perceptions of reality can be altered when oxygen-starved, information-carrying neurotransmitters travel from one brain cell to another.

Your brain is like Pandora's box: open the lid and you cannot control what emerges. On Smythe's Everest attempt, he watched dark, elliptical clouds assume the shape of winged balloons, throbbing to his heartbeat like living things. Similarly, German climber Toni Kinshofer staggered deranged down Nanga Parbat under the impression that he was wandering through a tobacco plantation.

However, those who have experienced the other presence make a distinction between it and hallucinations, which often disorient and misguide. The presence, on the other hand, seems much more real, and it assists climbers by either guiding them toward survival or allaying their fears with companionship.

On Broad Peak, Pete and I were exhausted, hypoxic and lost above 25,000 feet at night. We were freezing in high winds and had been without food or water for hours. Since we needed help so badly, perhaps I imagined we had a helper, an imaginary ally to reinforce that most basic of psychological needs: companionship. The play of my headlamp against slopes and snowsqualls could easily have created the illusion of a figure just out of eyeshot—couldn't it?

But if our unseen companions are really just wishes taking shape, they guide us well. Consider the experience of the late British-Canadian climber Roger Marshall on Kangchenjunga in 1984. As Marshall stumbled down steepening slopes after soloing to the 28,000-foot summit, he felt his strength slipping. He soon found himself on perilously steep terrain, close to falling. Suddenly he heard a Japanese voice, though there were no Japanese on the mountain. He moved toward the voice, found a line of ropes left by a previous Japanese expedition and descended to safety.

Dr. Steve Risse, a Himalayan climber and chief of psychiatry at Veterans' Hospital in Tacoma, Washington, studies victims of combat-induced post-traumatic stress. In his opinion, the other presence can be explained as "delirium caused by global disturbance of brain metabolism—by altitude, dehydration, sensory deprivation, fatigue."

Rather than dismiss the other presence as something imagined by a troubled mind, however, Risse reads much about human needs into accounts of the other presence: "Freud said dreams are wish fulfillment. Perhaps we should consider the psychology of the individuals experiencing the other presence. Are they looking for some extraordinary, mystical experience by pushing themselves to the limit, just as medicine men and gurus have long done through fasting, meditation and ritual?

"Probably what happens up there is similar to the experiences of people who clinically die and come back with tales of out-of-body experiences—like floating up above their bodies and watching themselves being revived on the operating table. Perhaps in the mountains, under enough psychological stress, the conscious and the unconscious split, and our unconscious self takes control."

Austrian Peter Habeler, nearing the top of Everest without oxygen, described being outside his body, watching someone else climb—just as I had felt on Broad Peak. Another Austrian, Robert Schauer, was sitting on a ledge of the west face on Gasherbrum IV, near K2, when he felt himself leave his body and enter that of a raven. Through the bird's eyes, he pitied himself as a poor, flightless human wreck on a vast mountainside.

And what of the shape of this presence? Is it human or beast? Most encounters report feelings, voices or a figure just out of sight. Few describe a tangible presence, but there are exceptions.

It was 1978, on the Breach Wall of Mount Kilimanjaro; American Rob Taylor sat alone at the foot of the African mountain, his ankle smashed after a fall. Days passed as his partner marched through misty primeval forests to summon help. Taylor, hunkered in his sleeping bag, smelled his leg turning gangrenous and fell into despair. Seeing a figure perched on a nearby rock, he called out in hope, but the figure sat serenely surveying him. In fear, Taylor accepted the presence, speaking with it, offering it water, seeing it so well he could write: "So taut are the general lines of his body, he appears devoid of clothing, like a dancer in a leotard. Chin in hand, elbow on knee, this drab grey being certainly looks human, but somehow is not."

True, Taylor was riven with fever, and was comparatively low—16,000 feet—compared to altitudes of similar sightings. Yet he was coherent enough to boil water on a stove and tend his injuries.

Reinhold Messner is even more exact when describing his experiences. Messner, who achieved fame when he climbed all fourteen of the world's 8000-meter peaks, is a master of survival, having made a career of pushing himself beyond the limits of endurance. On his two ascents of Pakistan's Nanga Parbat (26,656 feet), he experienced emotional and physical extremes few can comprehend.

In 1970 Messner and his brother, Günther, climbed a new route on the difficult Rupal Face. After a bivouac near the summit, Günther was too weak to descend the route they had come up. Instead, the pair went down the unknown but easier-angled Diamir Face. They spent several nights in the open without shelter, food, water or a rope to aid their descent. At a barrier of ice cliffs they teetered down, kicking their crampons into solid ice. Moving down the ice wall, Reinhold felt the striking presence of a third person just outside his field of vision.

After four days they reached the foot of the mountain. While Reinhold awaited Günther, he found a trickle of water and had his first drink in days. Voices and visions of grazing cattle and people on horseback appeared before him. As he focused his eyes, the cattle became blocks of snow. When he reached out and touched a horse, it became a rock. As Günther followed Reinhold down, an avalanche buried him beneath tons of ice. Frantic with grief, snowblind and frostbitten, Reinhold walked out of the empty valley alone.

In 1978 Messner returned to the Diamir Face of Nanga Parbat to attempt the first complete solo of an 8000-meter peak. Twice the route crossed his 1970 descent route. Early on, at difficult spots, he felt another presence. On several occasions it instructed him to move left or right around a crevasse or ice cliff. After three days, Messner reached the foot of the summit pyramid at 25,000 feet.

As he watched the horizon for signs of storm, he noticed "the feeling that someone was sitting next to me. I couldn't see who it was, but glancing out of the corner of my eye, I got the impression that it was a girl." They talked, and she assured him that the weather would hold and that he would reach the summit the next day, which he did.

Messner's experiences on Nanga Parbat pushed him to

incredible limits. He later wrote of the 1970 experience: "On my way from the peak back down into the valley, I must have passed through all the stages of death." Returning to the mountain to reconfront danger, exhaustion, inner doubt, biochemical turmoil and the emotional agony of reliving his last moments with Günther was a profound catharsis for Messner. With such pressures on his mind amid an atmosphere of loneliness and danger, it is easy to interpret Messner's encounter as the manifestation of his innate need for companionship. To solo a huge mountain, like sailing around the world alone, is to break from the human support system that thousands of years of society has nurtured.

In parts of Asia there exists a belief in a shadow world of spirits. Many mountain tribes believe that *djinns*—demons— inhabit the mountains. In Nepal, Sherpas frequently report seeing ghosts, particularly in the mountains where people have died. On Messner's solo ascent of Everest, he again felt unseen companions—spirits, he believes, of the long-dead English mountaineers George Mallory and Andrew Irvine.

The possibility that high altitude, even hypoxia itself, is an intersection between this world and the shadow world of spirits is an idea that Peter Hackett, who has spent long periods with the Sherpas of Nepal's Khumbu region, does not dismiss. "Nobody knows anything about the physiology or biochemistry of spiritual experiences," says Hackett. "My own philosophy is that there is another layer to this world and that occasionally we get glimpses into it. On our Everest trip in 1981, when Chris Kopczynski reached the point at 27,770 feet where his friend Ray Genet had died in 1979, he had a strong feeling that Ray was nearby. In life, Ray had a particular smell, and Chris smelled it."

Dr. Thomas Hornbein, who reached Everest's summit with the late Willi Unsoeld in 1963, keeps an open mind to spiritual interpretations of the other presence. "The feeling that someone is just behind you is a feeling I've been troubled by when walking down a dark city street at night," he says lightheartedly.

"But I've also reached a stage in my life of knowing there is a space for not knowing, for not understanding. Willi classified this world we cannot understand as the 'mysterium tremendums.'"

Many climbers accept the other presence as a phenomenon likely to occur in serious situations. Jim Wickwire, an attorney from Seattle known for his 1978 ascent of K2, regards the phenomenon as almost commonplace during extreme ordeals.

The encounter he relates came in 1981 at the base of Mount McKinley's remote Wickersham Wall. His partner, Chris Kerrebrock, had just perished in a crevasse, and Jim, who'd broken his shoulder while also being pulled into the crevasse, was in the middle of a two-week solo march to safety. With very little food and only a bivouac sack for shelter, he endured a four-day storm, almost fell into two crevasses and was narrowly missed by an avalanche. By the time a searching Cessna spotted him, he had lost twenty-five pounds.

"What kept me sane through all this was my journal, which I carried with me," he says, citing the following passage in particular: "At times the past week I've almost turned to talk to someone—a sense that a second person is here. From what I understand, that is part of my personality disengaging or separating itself—a fairly common phenomenon."

Wickwire's on-the-spot analysis of the other presence rings truest of any explanation. Perhaps, in times of great trial, we are like a person crawling through the desert, dying of thirst, who sees the mirage of an oasis: we see what we need to see so as not to give up hope.

Whether rooted in hypoxia, in mental chemistry gone haywire, in personal psychology or in the spirit world, the solution to the mystery of the other presence may be inexplicable. Since scientists cannot duplicate the full spectrum of stimuli that produce the phenomenon, we can only speculate. Perhaps, though, this "mysterium tremendums" is better left unsolved. High on a mountain, we need all the help we can get.

Meeting with a Stranger

A mountain called Makalu had caught our eye, and in the monsoon of 1988 we had walked many a crooked mile through the hills of Nepal to reach it, and perhaps climb it. On the last stretch of the two-week walk, on the rocky Barun Glacier, just downhill from our intended base camp beneath the west face of the mountain, I sat resting with my English teammates Sean Smith, Mark Miller and Doug Scott.

Porters filed past, carrying loads nearly as big as themselves. These slight hill people with their warm smiles, sinewy limbs and calloused bare feet are masterful load transporters. I'd studied their style of walking throughout the monsoon-soaked trek, hoping to learn something I could apply to climbing Makalu, which was, essentially, an exercise in carrying a heavy rucksack toward a sublayer of the stratosphere.

The porters moved in short bursts, at a canter, and they paused frequently to rest. At flat spots they'd edge their loads against a boulder to ease the weight from their backs. Huddled together, they'd chatter for a few minutes before trotting off down the path. They slung our duffels over their backs with a tumpline, a padded sling that bore the weight against their foreheads. Consequently their necks were as strong as the boles of trees. When I experimented with carrying a load porter-style, my scrawny neck creaked like a matchstick about to snap.

Although my English friends and I sat on a flat and comfortable knoll speckled with boulders, the porters didn't pause here to rest, but hurried past, unsmiling, eager to leave this patch of glacier. Something about the place scared them. Then I saw it, in a little hollow in the undulating glacier: a drab form 200 feet away, like a bundle of rags.

"That's a body over there," I said after studying the object for a minute.

Sean squinted at it. Even through sunglasses, the glare from the ice walls around us was incandescently bright.

"No. It's just some old clothing a Sherpa has tossed away," he said.

So we crossed the rubble to see. Long before we got there, we knew I'd guessed right. It was the skeleton of a man. He lay on a pile of white granite slabs, propped up in a restful position, his head tilted back as if he were gazing at the sky. In the arid atmosphere—nearly 17,000 feet where we stood—his body had dried like a piece of driftwood, floating down with the glacier at the rate of two feet per year. Parchmentlike skin wrapped his cheeks and hands. Tawny wisps of beard and hair clung to his chin and head. His tall stature, the striped thermal underwear he wore and the red scarf knotted around his neck marked him as a Western mountaineer, as did the shiny white teeth in his jaw. Maybe he'd been dead a year, maybe ten; we couldn't tell. It appeared from the large stones surrounding him that someone had buried him, but sun had melted the ice around the stones, causing them to topple over, exposing him. I wondered if other travelers had encountered him, reburying him when they did, and I imagined his progress down the glacier over the coming decades, alternately being buried and reappearing to generations of climbers, the way the remains of Maurice Wilson, George Leigh Mallory and Andrew Irvine—British climbers who disappeared on Everest in the 1920s and 1930s—emerge from the snows and appear periodically on Everest.

"I wonder who he is?" asked Sean, standing over the skeleton.

"A trekker probably," suggested Mark. "Probably died of altitude sickness, is my guess."

We searched for a marker, a chiseled inscription on a stone, something to identify him. If his companions had left anything, it had been consumed in the chaos of the glacier. We tried to recall if any expedition reports we'd studied before coming here had mentioned a death and burial on the Barun Glacier. None had, though several climbers lie high on Makalu, where altitude or exhaustion had taken them. Doug, who was ahead with the porters, had found such a fellow on Makalu's south ridge in 1984. Doug had been on his way up and was nearly at the summit when he and his partners encountered a body sitting among some rocks. It looked as if the guy had decided to take a rest and hadn't bothered to get back up. They later determined he was a Slovak who'd disappeared a year before, but right then the shock of the meeting put the wind up them all. Shortly after, for no definite reason, the trio retreated out of the so-called death zone to the land of the living, abandoning the summit.

The corpse before us appeared peaceful too, and we sat around him, looking into hollow sockets where eyes once shone. This was a man. Someone I might have talked to, shook hands with. Curiosity got the better of me. I ran my fingers over his hand. There was no revulsion, no sense of touching something unclean. He was a part of the mountain now, like a boulder.

We left after a few minutes, to walk the last few miles to base camp, agreeing to return in a few days to rebury him. There seemed no hurry to do it now; whoever he was, he wasn't going anywhere.

Days passed. We rushed around on the mountain, making the most of clear spells in the postmonsoon weather, climbing to the notch called Makalu La, between the big chunk of granite and ice—27,824 feet of it—that is Makalu and its satellite peak, Kangchungtse.

The skeleton occupied our thoughts. I, for one, trod more

cautiously on the mountain. Meeting the stranger had pricked my sense of mortality. When I awoke one night at 22,000 feet with a throbbing head and all the signs of severe altitude malaise that could quickly turn into cerebral edema, I mustered my dizzy mind and ran down the mountain. I wasn't going to end up buried on Makalu, if I could help it. All the way down I thought of the speed with which death strikes in the mountains. I recalled hauling the lifeless body of a young girl out of a crevasse in the French Alps. She'd been crossing a snowbridge with a large group. Heavier people than her had already crossed the snowbridge, but her footsteps were the ones that broke the bonds of snow. It was a terrible shock to haul such a lovely girl from that icy gash. She was at that perfect stage of youth and innocence when one is uncorrupted by the moral and physical decay of maturity. There seemed no justification for her death; yet mountains don't need a reason. On each of her fingers she wore a gold ring, a sight I'd never forget. Nor would I forget the events on Broad Peak in 1983, when my friend Pete Thexton died from pulmonary edema.

Climbing big mountains had forced me to look at and think about death more than was healthy. Inwardly, I had become morbid.

On a cloudy day when the mountain wasn't accepting visitors, I accompanied Sean, Mark and one of the expedition doctors, Christine, on a walk down the glacier to bury the stranger. Again we sat quietly around the skeleton. Staring at it wasn't horrible at all. It was like admiring a flower that had blossomed unexpectedly out of the glacier. There was undeniable beauty in the way the joints and teeth fitted together so perfectly, and in the smooth whiteness of the bones. Yet, there was also sadness here, for though we knew nothing of this man's history, each life is a story, and this stranger's story had ended, abruptly.

We cradled him in our arms—rigid like a tree limb, he was,

yet fragile—and placed him into a hollow in the ice. We then stacked slabs of granite around him into a high, broad mound, like a Buddhist stupa. As we arranged the rocks, Sean found a piton, no doubt a memento left by the stranger's friends, something symbolic to aid him in the journey ahead. We slipped the piton into a chink in the rocks. It tinkled through the cracks, back to its place beside its owner.

As we worked, Christine examined our expressions. She noted the way we lifted the body carefully, as if it were a sick child. Our reverence for this bag of anonymous bones puzzled her. Christine was a doctor, not a climber. She had a rational, forensic approach to events such as finding corpses.

"What do you think of when you see this sort of thing in the mountains?" she asked us.

There was a round of shrugs. Who could express the thoughts tied up inside us? Here we were, touching the texture of death, the thing we feared most. The skeleton was like a huge warning sign—"Tread carefully," it said. Stating our obvious fear—that as mountaineers we, too, might end up like this before the end of the expedition—seemed banal. Given the talent climbers have for denying risk, for believing that accidents befall the next guy but not ourselves, we probably didn't believe Makalu or the next peak would kill us, anyway. But I hazarded an answer to Christine's question.

"I think of the sadness for his family. I think of him cut down in his prime. I think of the moment the clock stopped for him, and I wonder what he was thinking. I think of this"—I pointed to the skeleton—"as the ultimate sadness of mountaineering."

The others nodded. "Yeah. It's just sad," said Sean.

"Well, I don't see what all the fuss is about," Christine said bluntly.

"Doesn't this strike you as tragic?" asked Sean, amazed at her detachment.

"I'll tell you what I call tragic," she said. "I'll tell you the worst thing I've seen, as a doctor. I was called to a cottage in a country town in Scotland to treat a woman. She was terribly retarded. Her family had kept her in an attic all her life because they were ashamed of her. When her parents died she'd sat locked in that attic, alone for weeks, starving in her own filth and madness till someone found her. It was awful. That's a tragedy, to me."

The vision of the disturbed woman was a demon haunting Christine's thoughts. To her, the way we treated the skeleton seemed overly precious, melodramatic. Get emotional about the living, forget the dead, she seemed to be saying. Yet she hadn't invested a third of her life in the mountains, hadn't known the tearing feeling when a friend dies climbing. The meaning of finding this stranger on the glacier cut close to the bone for us. For her, it was like disposing of a pile of soiled bandages.

I thought back to the year before, in 1987. I'd been a thousand miles from Makalu, at K2 base camp. There, at the memorial and graveyard to climbers who have died on K2 and the surrounding peaks, crosses and plaques and mounds of stones mark the dead. I stood there with fellow Australian Tim Macartney-Snape, Voytek Kurtyka of Poland and Jean Troillet of Switzerland. Shifting rocks had uncovered a grave, so we spent a few minutes restacking stones over it. Glossy ravens, nesting in the cliffs above, made beautiful, mysterious noises to us.

"Our societies place so much importance on death, yet we always avoid contact with the dead," said Voytek. "I think we should accept it more. Touch it even, if we wish. After all, it's only natural."

As we walked away from the memorial a sudden breeze brought a fetid smell with it.

"You smell it?" asked Voytek.

"Yes. It must be the graveyard," I replied seriously.

"I'm sorry to disappoint you," said Jean, "but you have only smelled my fart."

We had a good laugh over that. We needed it.

All rituals concerning death, no matter how creative or steeped in tradition, just seem like ways of facing the unfaceable. Tibetan monks had a practice of celestial burial, in which the dead were dismembered so the blood could soak into the earth and the body could be eaten by birds and animals in order that body as well as spirit might diffuse into the cosmos. Hindus, on the other hand, cremate their dead. In Kathmandu I'd watched funeral pyres blaze and seen human ashes shoveled into the river. According to the British explorer Wilfred Thesiger, natives of the Kenyan highlands threw their dead down cliffs and pelted them with stones till they were covered. And, some Asian societies bury their dead head down, so the spirit cannot rise out of the grave to bother the living.

Death, as portrayed a hundred times a night on television, fascinates and excites. "Death," said Peter Pan, "will be a big adventure." But addressing death from a personal perspective—that is, being honest about one's experiences with it—is often offensive, unsavory. We hide it away, whisper about it, pretend it doesn't happen. But in the end, there it is.

Two years after that trip to Makalu, in Denver, Colorado, I gave a slide lecture about K2. At the end, a fellow in the audience began chatting about expeditions with me. He told me he'd tried to climb Kangchungtse, but there'd been a tragedy. One of his companions had gotten pulmonary edema. They'd been helping him down the Barun Glacier when....

I finished the story for him. He fell silent, clearly shocked. When I told him we'd reburied his friend he thanked me, and I thanked him for slotting the final piece of the puzzle together by giving the stranger on the glacier a name. A few weeks later I received an envelope in the mail. A news clipping from 1985 described the accident. Accompanying it was a photo of the man we'd buried, taken shortly before he'd died. I recognized the tawny beard, the bright teeth, the striped thermal underwear, the red scarf. He smiled at the camera. Some things you never forget. Births. Marriages. Deaths. Burials. People are like that.

GLOSSARY OF CLIMBING TERMS

aid climbing: climbing rock walls by hanging from one piece of equipment to another.

alpenglow: vibrant evening light in the mountains.

alpine style: in mountaineering, to climb a peak in one continuous ascent, without using fixed rope.

anchor: the point at which the rope is tied off, at the end of a pitch.

angle: a type of piton.

arch: a leaning corner.

ascender: see jumar.

belay: the act of one climber paying the rope in or out, usually through a locking device, to safeguard the other climber in case of a fall.

big-wall climbing: climbing long, vertical cliffs.

bivouac, bivy: a night spent on a mountain or climb.

bolt: a steel stud drilled into the rock.

camming device, cam: devices used in cracks for protection.

carabiner, 'biner: an alloy snaplink, used for connecting the rope to protection and anchors.

ceiling: a rooflike rock feature.

cerebral edema: fluid buildup in the brain caused by exposure to high altitude. Potentially deadly.

copperhead: a metal device hammered into cracks.

cornice: a wind-carved formation of snow found on ridges.

couloir: a snow- or ice-filled gully.

crampons: metal spikes strapped to the boots, for ice and snow climbing.

crevasse: a deep fissure in glacial ice.

cwm: a deep, steep-walled basin on a mountain.

death zone: the region above 8000 meters, so called due to its dangerously thin air.

dihedral: a corner.

etrier: a step ladder of slings, for aid climbing.

expanding flake: a loose flake.

exposure: either a feeling of airiness on a cliff, or a feeling of intense cold.

face: a wall; the side of a cliff or mountain.

fixed rope: rope laid over a mountain to aid the ascent, ideally removed after the climb.

free climbing: opposite of aid climbing, where a rock wall is climbed by edging fingers and feet on natural formations on the wall and moving with a gymnastic flow.

Friend: tradename for a spring-loaded camming device used in cracks for protection.

glacier: a long passage of ice which erodes through mountains.

grade VI: the grade that denotes a multiday big-wall climb.

hand jam, jam: to cram hands or other parts of the body into a crack.

harness: the waist-belt worn by climbers.

hypothermia: a feeling of intense, life-threatening cold.

hypoxia: shortness of breath and disorientation from high altitude and oxygen starvation.

ice axe: metal ice climbing tool, with a spikelike pick and a spadelike end called an adze.

icefall: a broken section of a glacier.

ice hammer: ice climbing tool like an ice axe, but having a hammer and pick.

ice screw: a threaded metal tube screwed into ice. Used as protection.

incipient crack: a tiny crack.

jumar: a rope-ascending device.

knife blade, blade-piton: a thin piton.

lenticular cloud: cloud shaped like a flying saucer.

nailing, nail up: aid climbing using pitons.

nut: a metal device wedged into a crack, for protection.

objective danger: features of a mountain that present hazards, like seracs, avalanche slopes, crevasses.

off-width: a wide crack.

parapente: a parachute canopy that performs like a hang glider.

pendulum: a rope maneuver involving swinging back and forth, like the pendule of a clock.

pitch: a section of a climb the length of a rope (about 150 feet).

piton, pin, peg: steel spikes of various sizes and designs hammered into cracks in a cliff.

placement: a piece of climbing gear placed in a crack.

porta-ledge: a metal-framed hanging tent used for camping in on big-wall climbs.

protection: equipment placed in cracks for anchors and safety during a climb.

pulmonary edema: fluid buildup in the lungs caused by exposure to high altitude. Potentially deadly.

rappel: a method of descending a rope using a friction device.

ridge: a feature of a mountain, like a fin.

rivet: a small metal rod drilled into the rock for aid climbing.

RURP: a tiny piton.

scree: fine rubble.

serac: an ice cliff, often the cause of avalanches.

skyhook, bathook, hook: steel claws the climber hangs from in aid climbing.

slab: a low-angle rock face.

sling: a nylon loop.

solo, soloing: climbing without a partner; free soloing is climbing without partner or rope, with a fall having serious consequences. Roped soloing uses a self-belay method.

spindrift: very fine wind-driven snow.

spire: a slender rock tower.

sport climbing: the modern school of rock climbing, which uses many bolts for protection and which concentrates on extreme gymnastic difficulty.

stopper: a type of nut, tapered like a wedge.

talus: coarse rubble.

About the author:

Greg Child began climbing as a teenager in his native Australia, where he established numerous rock routes before moving to the United States to accomplish similar feats. Among these were two big-wall first ascents—Lost in America and Aurora—on El Capitan in Yosemite. Child has also climbed extensively in the Himalaya, with ascents of many new routes and significant repeats at high altitude, including those of Shivling, Losbang Spire, Broad Beak, Gasherbrum IV, K2, and Trango Tower. A writer and photographer whose work has appeared in adventure magazines around the world, Child won the American Alpine Club's Literary Award in 1987. He is the author of *Thin Air: Encounters in the Himalaya.*

THE MOUNTAINEERS, founded in 1906, is a nonprofit outdoor activity and conservation club, whose mission is "to explore, study, preserve, and enjoy the natural beauty of the outdoors...." Based in Seattle, Washington, the club is now the third-largest such organization in the United States, with 12,000 members and four branches throughout Washington State.

The Mountaineers sponsors both classes and year-round outdoor activities in the Pacific Northwest, which include hiking, mountain climbing, ski-touring, snowshoeing, bicycling, camping, kayaking and canoeing, nature study, sailing, and adventure travel. The club's conservation division supports environmental causes through educational activities, sponsoring legislation, and presenting informational programs. All club activities are led by skilled, experienced volunteers, who are dedicated to promoting safe and responsible enjoyment and preservation of the outdoors.

The Mountaineers Books, an active, nonprofit publishing program of the club, produces guidebooks, instructional texts, historical works, natural history guides, and works on environmental conservation. All books produced by The Mountaineers are aimed at fulfilling the club's mission.

If you would like to participate in these organized outdoor activities or the club's programs, consider a membership in The Mountaineers. For information and an application, write or call The Mountaineers, Club Headquarters, 300 Third Avenue West, Seattle, Washington 98119; (206) 284-6310.

Other titles you may enjoy from The Mountaineers:

Stories Off the Wall, John Roskelley. America's preeminent climber John Roskelley explores the watershed events in his life that helped define him both as a man and a climber. A fascinating compilation from one of climbing's most accomplished characters.

Beyond Risk: Conversations With Climbers, Nicholas O'Connell. Famous climbers reflect on their accomplishments, the future of the sport, controversial issues and the drive to climb. Includes Messner, Cesen, Robbins, Scott, Diemberger, Hill, Destivelle, Croft, and many others.

Mount McKinley: Icy Crown of North America, Fred Beckey. Portrait of a great climbing challenge traces its natural history and influence on natives, prospectors, and the men who have been drawn to its summit.

The Ascent of Everest, John Hunt. Expedition leader Hunt's detailed account of the first ascent of Mount Everest's summit in 1953 by Sir Edmund Hillary and Sherpa Tenzing Norgay.

K2: The 1939 Tragedy, Andrew J. Kauffman & William L. Putnam. Contemporary evidence sheds new light on the story of the 1939 American K2 expedition, which was marred by mystery and death.

The Endless Knot: Mountain of Dreams and Destiny, Kurt Diemberger. Compelling account of the author's growing obsession with K2, and the tragic events on its slopes in the summer of 1986.

Antarctica: Both Heaven and Hell, Reinhold Messner. Detailed account of the author's and Arved Fuchs' 1,800-mile, 92-day journey on foot across Antarctica. Text includes unabridged diary of the expedition.

Reinhold Messner, Free Spirit: A Climber's Life, Reinhold Messner. Definitive autobiography chronicles author's remarkable career as one of the most innovative and disciplined climbers of our time.

To the Top of the World, Reinhold Messner. World-renowned climber recalls some of his most spectacular and unique mountaineering achievements during his early days in the Himalaya and Karakorum.

Summits and Secrets, Kurt Diemberger. Autobiography details the eventful, 30-year career of this preeminent climber, conveying the author's personal philosophy, joy, and inspiration as a mountaineer.

My Vertical World, Jerzy Kukuczka. Autobiography of the late Polish climber whose quiet determination and singular achievements ranked him among the world's most accomplished mountaineers.

Available from your local book or outdoor store, or from The Mountaineers Books, 1011 SW Klickitat Way, Suite 107, Seattle, WA 98134. Or call for a catalog of over 200 outdoor books: 1-800-553-4453.